McGRAW-HILL European Series in Education

Other titles

Unwin: Media and methods
Instructional Technology in Higher Education

Jones: Explorations
A Practical Study of Children writing Poetry

Gregory: A shorter text book of human development

Educational aspects of simulation

edited by

P. J. Tansey
Senior Lecturer in Education,
Berkshire College of Education

McGRAW-HILL · LONDON

New York · St Louis · San Francisco · Düsseldorf · Toronto · Sydney
Mexico · Johannesburg · Panama · Kuala Lumpur · Montreal · New
Delhi · Rio de Janeiro · Singapore

Published by
McGRAW-HILL Publishing Company Limited
MAIDENHEAD · BERKSHIRE · ENGLAND

07 094150 5

PRINTED AND BOUND IN GREAT BRITAIN

To Jane Helen Tansey
and her mother
Maisie Rita Tansey
for whom I am grateful

Preface

This book is intended primarily as a reference work in a field so new that its complete content is known to very few, and its educational applications have been seen for no more than ten years. The editor, who has been working single-mindedly in the field for over three years, has been concerned about the slow dissemination of information and the distinctiveness and separateness of the different approaches of isolated groups of people. An attempt has been made to draw these various strands together and to find a continuum along which they proceed. One large field has been left out, that so ably lead by James S. Coleman of Johns Hopkins University. This area has been well documented in the past by Boocock and Schild, by Clarice S. Stoll, Michael Inbar and by Coleman himself. The references are well documented in the present text, and repetition here might have been considered tautologous.

Because the subject matter is so new, and because the range of applicability is so wide, it has been necessary to cater for a wide area of interests. There can be little doubt that simulation is a growth point in education. In America, in its most sophisticated and expensive form, it has become almost universally known because of its applications in the NASA space programme. In Great Britain, its value is being seen in areas of education such as moral education, the raising of the school leaving age, as well as in the narrower confines of subject areas.

The intention is that the book should be a starting place from which interest can develop. From this starting place it will be possible for interested readers, by means of the textual references, to develop their interests quickly and informatively in a way that was less easy before its publication. It is hoped that teachers in a wide variety of interests and at a great number of levels from junior schools to post-graduate level may find something in it which will kindle their interest and which will give them an alternative teaching tool. It is improbable that any reader will find all of it of immediate applicability to his needs, but, it is hoped, most will find something which will fire them to further reading. This, surely, is the prime function of a reference work.

The general overview is intended to be of assistance to those who have no knowledge of simulation at all, but who want to know its areas of application. It attempts to describe what simulation is, constructs a paradigm, and describes methods of presentation and advantages of the technique within the general field of education. From here, it proceeds through a philosophical rationale of education to the place of certain *autotellic* games within that philosophy. These games are in no sense simulations but are their kin. They represent one extreme of a continuum which has as its other extreme sociodrama. Along this continuum lie all the other simulations described in the book, if they be considered in a linear sense rather than the areal sense of the paradigm. The authors of these two chapters, Goodman and Allen, are associates whose work and status are internationally known and respected. Their contributions complement each other and should be read together.

Describing non-simulation games, they claim certain advantages for them. Allen says that they are not concerned with models but give experience within the system itself. Thus the participant learns the actual processes of mathematics and logic, and not what the simulator considers he should learn. Walford's chapter is also concerned with games, but simulation games based on a model. Beyond games he is concerned, as Goodman was, with the processes of education. Tracing the beginnings of regional geography from its early development by Herbertson and Mackinder through its *determinist* and *behaviourist* phases, he arrives at systems analysis and the functions of a model in geography. This is seen as a preliminary to simulation which in its turn is seen as '. . . not only a shift in subject matter, but a radical change in class organization'. He is aware of the similarity between the laboratory in the physical sciences and the simulations of the natural sciences: that is, as an amalgam between theory and practice as individual and complementary parts of an entity, not as alternatives. The examples of simulations with which he concludes the chapter are all taken from the topic of *urban geography*. They clearly show the value and applications of simulation and point the way to its uses in other areas of study.

With increasing complexity in models, and with the need for a variety of calculations to be done quickly in many simulations, the computer plays an increasingly important part in this field, as it is doing in life generally. Atherton has described a simulation which explains the functioning of computers in a way that makes them understandable to a wide range of people. His game is simple enough to be played in junior schools; the photograph on page 93 shows it being used in this way. The game is clearly explained in the text and examples are given. In this game, no previous knowledge of computing science is needed. It will enable very young children to gain a familiarity with the processes of computing.

The classic model in the simulation of international relations is due to Guetzkow. Smoker has developed and extended this into a second generation, man–machine simulation. His chapter gives a first rate indication of the technique of operating international relations simulations in general as well as a description of his own International Processes Simulation. This is a complex simulation used by political science students at Northwestern University. Boardman and Mitchell have developed several simpler, manual simulations along the same lines and have used them with children of sixteen to eighteen years in British schools. The problems seem to differ between the two kinds of game, control having a much greater responsibility in the Boardman and Mitchell type of game. One such game, not described in this chapter, was played over three days at St John's College, Oxford. The control team was kept extremely busy, involvement was intense, and tempers tended to fray. Its subsequent presentation on BBC 2 television introduced it to a wide audience.

Garvey, in his chapter, discusses the uses of simulation, and its advantages. This chapter will be of use to the person just introduced to the techniques of simulation and gaming, as it will allow him to see its applications as a teaching aid are wide indeed. One of the problems of simulation is the difficulty of evaluating its effectiveness. Garvey discusses this and refers to some of the research in this area.

The SRA Teaching Problems Laboratory makes teacher training a problem based technique rather than a narrative one. This was designed by Cruickshank and associates, and his chapter looks at the applications of simulation to pre-service teacher training. It would seem that few people are satisfied with the methods of teacher training in any part of the Western world. This chapter makes a case for the inclusion of simulation techniques that is very strong indeed. Twelker also has an interest in the use of simulation in the training of teachers. On the other hand, he is a pioneer in the whole field of simulation, and his interests and knowledge in the field of education are wider than those of most workers in simulation. In this chapter one gets an impression of the vastness and variety of its present uses and of its future potential. Unwin's chapter is a practically useful one. He has taken a selection of simulations and games now being marketed and tried to make it representational of as large a part of education as was possible. No claims are made about it being complete, nor is it up to date due to the slow process of book publishing.

The readily available literature on simulation is very sparse. It is hoped that this book will come to be regarded as a standard reference in the way that those of Guetzkow, Boocock and Schild, Giffin, and Tansey and Unwin have been. The editor hopes that it will be useful

Contents

1

A primer of simulation: its methods, models, and application in educational processes

P. J. Tansey

Pat Tansey was born in Christchurch, New Zealand, in 1921. After service in the Royal New Zealand Air Force from 1941–46 as a Flight Engineer, he gained his B.Sc. from Otago University, followed by a Diploma in Teaching Studies. He taught for several years in primary, rural, and city secondary schools, and then came to England in 1957. After periods of teaching in Leeds and Bournemouth secondary modern schools, he went to Oxford University, where he was one of the first two candidates to pass the new Advanced certificate of Education. He is at present Senior Lecturer in Education at Berkshire College of Education in Reading.

One reason why simulation is not as well known, or as widely used in education as it well might be, is that formal publication in books and journals is a slow process. As a result of this, a system whereby cyclostyled and mimeographed papers are circulated amongst interested workers, particularly in America, has developed. This method has overcome publishing delays and has made sure that workers in particular areas are aware of both the findings and of the blind alleys of others with the same interests. There are obvious advantages in this method of information diffusion. How many of the present crop of teachers using simulation have avoided mistakes, and modified materials, because of pre-publication papers by such people as Twelker,[1] Cruickshank,[2] Garvey,[3] Smoker,[4] Coleman,[5] Boocock,[6] Abt,[7] Western Behavioral Sciences Institute,[8] in America, and later in this country pre-publications by Aldrich,[9] Garnett,[10] Tansey and Unwin,[11] workers at University College, London,[12] Boyce,[13] and many others? On the other hand, there are disadvantages also. Because the communications are designed to be read by people with interest in and knowledge of the contents, the language tends to become stylized and private, new words are developed to save time and lengthy repetition. This is a common occurrence, and the point may be better understood if it is considered in the context of either sociology or of statistics.

1

As long as this private language is read by, and is used by, only those who are aware of its significance it is extremely effective. In one sense it becomes a barrier to the spread of information, and tends to isolate the workers from the rest. In the first stages of development this is a good thing because it allows progress to be consolidated and errors modified rather than spread before the time is right. But at some time it becomes necessary to go into the highways and byways, for if one has faith, his gospel must be spread. Now the private language becomes a handicap. It is now that the expert is accused of using jargon as a device for the exclusion of those on the outside. In general this is not true, it is merely used as a significant and meaningful shorthand.

It is true that simulation has developed its own language. The word itself covers a wide range of meaning, and it might be as well to begin to explain it by showing something of its boundaries.

The parameters of simulation

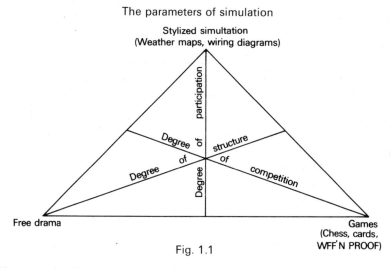

Fig. 1.1

These can be shown by considering the triangular form of Fig. 1.1. The upper apex of this triangle is concerned with stylized kinds of simulation. These are probably the most widely used, and have been since man communicated by means of written characters. There are many examples of stylization in everyday use. The weather map does not accurately represent the physical entity of cloud, sun, wind, and rain, nor does the red line on the map physically represent the equator. If I ask two different men the way, one will direct me by means of pubs, while the other may direct me by way of churches. Neither will describe every house on the way. What each has done is to abstract from the actual situation those parts that are essentially important for him in order that he may temporarily perform the role of instructor. This is also the function of road maps, weather maps, graphs, Egyptian hieroglyphics, and trade marks. They make no claim to being accurate representations of the real thing, but each contains those elements of the real thing that are essential for them to perform the task of instructing. They *simulate* real things or real situations without containing any of the physical ingredients of these things. There is nothing that is *dynamic* about such simulations, they are functional without being representational.

The lower, right-hand apex of the triangle represents games. These are essentially competitive, and are governed to some extent by rules which may, on occasion, be modified or even changed radically. A whole theory called *game theory* has been developed and described by writers such as von Neumann and Morgenstern,[14] Rapaport,[15] and Shubick[16, 17] in an attempt to explain the theories and strategies involved in gaming. Simulation frequently has a built in competitive element, and occasionally academic gaming and simulation are used synonymously. Simulation approaches gaming at one end of a continuum. This is clearly shown by games of the type devised by Layman E. Allen and by Fred J. Goodman. The games that are represented at this apex are the kinds that have rigid, formal rules and which are non representational. Examples include card games, chess, MONOPOLY, and WFF 'N PROOF.

The final apex of the triangle represents drama. There is a large element of drama in any simulation, and both have in common the large element of involvement that they create in those who take part in them. The essential element of difference lies in the fact that in the formal, stage presented drama of the play-writers, both the dialogue and the outcome are predetermined. In simulation, on the other hand, the 'plot' and some background information is supplied so that the outcomes are predetermined in essential details although the action and dialogue are free. Thus it can be seen that at one end of the continuum on which simulation lies there is something in common with free drama. This is the kind of simulation that might well be used in the classroom for such purposes as moral education. This kind of simulation does not try to teach facts but rather to focus attention upon attitudes. Because it is spontaneous and involving it does not reproduce well with the same group. Like televised broadcasts of educational dance, it tends to look stilted, stiff and formal if it is rehearsed before it is produced.

Educational aspects of simulation lie somewhere inside the triangle, touching the sides and the apices but rarely, and yet containing some elements of each of the three components in most of the examples in use at the moment. Should it be ever thought necessary, it would be possible to devise a system of co-ordinates which would locate any particular simulation within the bounds of this triangle. The altitudes of the triangle can be said to represent distinct elements. They are the elements of *structure, competition*, and *participation*. Now, if some scale of values could be devised to show the amount of each of these elements there was in a given simulation, then it would be possible to plot its position as an area, a line, or a point within the triangle. This may possibly have a research use; if, for example, it could be shown that those simulations which could be representable by lines were the most effective vehicles for learning in particular areas. Such a scale of values would not, indeed could not, be absolute but would merely have to be agreed. With the limited amount of knowledge available at the moment, this research use of the paradigm is not feasible, but may well have a future potential.

The method in simulation

Simulation takes those who take part out of the role of spectator and moves them into the role of player. It need not be concerned with the here and now, but can transport the participant to the past or the future. It can make time fly so that the action which, in the simulation, takes an hour can represent a week, a month, a year in real time. It can make time slow down or pass normally. It can change the player from what he is to what he might be. It can make him examine his attitudes and those of others. It transforms the concept of learning because this learning takes place because it is necessary *at that time*, not as an end in itself to be stored away with the squirrel's nut against a future chill winter of necessity. But how is this done?

Simulation uses one or more of three basic methods of presentation. Case studies represent the first of these. They are used to describe the background of a person, organization or situation, and represent an essential element of any simulation. Formerly they have been defined in a rather restrictive way,[18] but reflection indicates that, while there may be many situations in which their use is a sterile approach, there are more occasions when their use is valuable. If, for instance, we give a case study to a person taking part in a simulation and say 'What would you do if you were that person?' then the probability is that it will be sterile because there is little involvement. The person is not involved but is looking at the character portrayed in the case study from outside of himself. On the other hand, if we extend the meaning of case study to include descriptions of organizations, situations and backgrounds then their use is invaluable. Indeed the background information of a simulation, which is often called the *scenario*, is an essential part of it. It is the method of conveying mood and information and is an invaluable use of the case study.

But, if it is true that the case study is static when applied to a personal role, then *role playing* is its dynamic. This is the second technique used in simulation. A student taking part in a simulation may find himself playing the role of a high priest in ancient Sumeria,[19] a banker,[20] a diplomat,[21] a young teacher called Pat Taylor,[22] or Mr Land,[23] an Oxford landlady,[24] or the mayor of Mt Buren.[25] A simulation should involve people; those taking part, playing roles and becoming other people. It is hoped that they will become so immersed in the role that they will become the person that they are playing for the duration of the simulation, and will view the action from the eyes of the person whose role they have assumed.

This leads to spontaneous action. No longer does the player have to say 'In his place I would do this or that.' He is the other person, and takes his decisions. To do this he is frequently transported in time. In one game,[26] MANCHESTER, he is involved in the beginning of the Industrial Revolution in Britain. In another,[27] he is a colonist on a new planet. This game sets its action in the future, although the *scenario* is based on the Articles of Confederation crisis period (1781–1799) of American history. This game shows how time can be manipulated. Action and happenings of the past have been placed in the future, and their historic origins disguised by using false names. It does seem, in this case, that the disguise is exceedingly thin, but this may have been done deliberately. This kind of role playing can be put to good use in the classroom, especially with children of less than average ability.

The most frequently asked question by children such as these is 'What is the use of what we are learning?' In other words, what such children want is immediate relevance in what they are being taught. The Newsom Report[28] stressed this very point, but surely there are things that we need to teach youngsters in their final years at school that are not immediately relevant. We need to prepare them for citizenship, we need to shape attitudes, we should put them into situations that they will be in several years hence.

The role playing aspect of simulation is ideal for this. Very shortly in Great Britain the school leaving age will be raised to sixteen years. A high proportion of our youth already stays on at school beyond this age, but the leaving age has been raised in an effort towards equating educational opportunity for those children who now leave school at the first available opportunity after their fifteenth birthday. Such children are almost certainly bound to come from socially or economically underprivileged homes. They are also, in general, from the ranks of those whose academic ability is below average. By the time they have reached their fifteenth birthday, indeed a long time before it, many have come to terms with

5

their lack of success at school, and most have compensated for it by disliking and rejecting school. If such children are going to be taught formally in the classroom for another year it could well be that it will be a year wasted. It could well be that a very great disciplinary problem will be created. The current rash of student complaints and dissatisfactions could be reflected in the schools.

But the role playing forms of simulation might give such children an opportunity to benefit from a further year of education. This comes about from a variety of causes. We have already mentioned both relevance and involvement, but there is another point that must be mentioned. In the normal classroom the teacher has a dual role. He is expected to be both judge and counsellor. In the former role he has to judge performance and to control behaviour. For pupils whose behaviour and performance are consistently judged to be good this does not lead to any friction with the teacher. For the rest, the teacher, as the representative of a system in which they have failed, is often viewed with hostility. His role in simulation changes. Because the pupils are interested and involved, the teacher does not have to worry about control problems, and he ceases to be a focal point. His class relationship can be much more that of *primus inter pares*. So a much more friendly atmosphere develops in the classroom, learning becomes important and necessary in order to take part in the simulation, and as a consequence the learning is effective.

The third technique used in simulation is that of the *in-basket*. Initially, in the world of business the in-basket was used to represent the items that might come to the attention of an executive during the course of his working day. Latterly it has had a much wider application and is now used to indicate the method of introducing problems into a simulated situation.

In-basket presentations can be written, or media assisted. Kersh[29] used moving film and multiple projection methods almost exclusively in the training of teachers, Cruickshank, Broadbent, and Bubb[30] used 16mm film, written problems, and role plays for the same purpose. The in-basket has an important controlling function in simulation. It permits flexibility, and allows information to be fed into the participants as the controller wishes it. It ensures that not all of the information need be given at the start. It also allows particular participants to be given separate, and sometimes confidential, information.

It is necessary to keep participants involved in their roles in simulation. A bored player has time to get outside of it, to become aware of surroundings, and possibly to become a distraction to others. More will be said later about simulation design which helps to prevent this. One way of keeping people involved is by the use of ongoing exercises. Aldrich,[31] who trains youth leaders, has his groups design a programme for their youth club. His in-baskets are interruptions of this ongoing task and tend to distract his trainees from getting on with it. Thus they are cleverly forced to make decisions against the pressure of time. His in-baskets use written messages and people very convincingly playing the roles of various village people concerned either with youth work or with young people. Twelker[32] has used film to show a day in a classroom, and the participant's ongoing task is the watching of the film in order to notice when things are going wrong and a crisis situation is developing. The ongoing situation is a most important part of a simulation, and those that are successful have all managed to find stimulating ones.

The model in simulation

Simulation is a technique that is used for a number of reasons. Amongst them is the fact that the real life situation, whether it be one used for concept or for skill training, is too complex or difficult or dangerous. When this is the case a model of the situation is designed, and this forms the basis of a simulation.

The study of international relations is one of great complexity, and it is natural that this field was among the first to make use of simulation. It was in this field that the first educational simulations were carried out, although they were not as carefully modelled in the first examples as they have been subsequent to Guetzkow's[33] early theoretical contributions. The first simulations modelled such international organizations as the League of Nations and the United Nations Security Council. They were, in the main, devised by able teachers for current affairs classes and made few pretensions about being reproductions of the actual organizations on which they were based. The models had to become more representational, and the *scenarios* more accurate when they began to be used in higher education for the purposes of studying such things as foreign policy, national interest and relationships between nations.

The task of constructing a model for the study of international relations is a complex one. If a student is to benefit from such a simulation, it should show him, in as clear a way as possible, those interacting processes that are essential features of the system that is being studied. The designer of the model must then make certain value judgements. He must decide what are the essential processes and what processes are secondary. In other words he must obviously decide what has to be left out. His aim, at this stage, is to reduce the complexity of a real life situation, to simplify it in order that its essence may be studied beneficially. His dilemma is that if he puts too much of the actual situation in he may so complicate the simulation as to make it a poor vehicle for instruction. On the other hand, if he leaves too much out he may produce a model that does not accurately represent the system he wishes to present. He must also be aware of the danger of personal interest and the tendency towards bias and distortion.

To test the model, researchers such as Herman and Herman[34] have used the criterion of historical validity. They simulated the outbreak of the First World War, and compared a sample of simulation events with actual events. Their article indicates the difficulties of this approach, and Smoker (q.v.) has indicated that it might be reasonable to expect validation only in a limited area of the simulation. Indeed, warning about the predictive use of such simulations, Bloomfield and Paddleford[35] say that they do distort reality. They also remind us that there is no guarantee that a group of students in one culture can think like politicians of another culture who were subjected to different pressures.

The design of international simulations varies a great deal. One person will take an actual situation, use real nations and real time. Another might use the same situation but disguise the nations. A third might take a situation such as the present Middle East situation and set a simulation in the future. In some simulations, the action takes place in a crisis such as the German occupation of the Rhur,[36] in others against a general background of trouble such as the Vietnam War,[37, 38, 39] or the Middle East crisis.[40,41]

The fixing of a mathematical model has been attempted by Guetzkow, and is available in commercial form as the Inter-Nation Simulation.[42] This model sets the parameters for simulations and permits participants to measure their performance. It permits them to view the political, economic and military situations of their nations and to determine whether they have improved their national status during each games period. The model is a fairly complex one, in the writer's view difficult for participants to follow, and requiring a large amount of calculation. Smoker[43] has developed a second generation simulation based on this but more complex. The calculations are carried out by machine.

Simulations of international events tend to occupy several days at a time, and have not been used in British schools below sixth form level. While they are motivating, they frequently raise the frustration level of participants to a dangerously high extent. Having taken part in several of these extended games, the author is of the opinion that a great deal of work needs to be done on small group theory in order to increase their effectiveness, and to reduce participant frustration level. It is probable that their greatest value might be at the level of insight rather than of prediction. It is given to few of us to be heads of state and diplomats. On the other hand many can participate in an international simulation. After participation one is aware of the difficulties of decision making and of the complexity of dilemmas that face leaders. Such an awareness in a thinking person must bring in its wake, tolerance, and that can be no bad thing.

Simulators

Simulators are mechanical models. They occur over a wide range of skills training and research projects. There has long been a cultural dichotomy between practice and theory with the skilled practical man holding himself to be superior to the purveyor of theory. Rapid technological advances in the immediate past have made this position no longer tenable. Technology has evolved situations and skills for which no 'on the job' practice is possible, situations where skills are imperative but where the skills cannot be practised without developing new techniques. This is the age of the computer and the high cost project, the era of the importance of natural prestige. The *Concorde* has flown, and man is on the moon. In each case someone did it first, and failure did not happen. Each of these first men knew in advance what was going to happen, and this was made possible by simulators, each of which was a considerable cost factor in the project budget. That they made success possible also made them good value for money.

Both of these operations required skills that could not be learned 'end on' in the live situation. In each of them there was a high element of risk, and in each the cost of failure would have been immeasurably high. These difficult, dangerous, and complex skills are best practised by simulation so that skills can be rehearsed until known, and where the price of failure is no higher than personal embarrassment. The computer has made them possible, and though it is too costly a process to play an important part in formal education at the present time, even in America, there can be no doubt that the computer, and simulators, will be increasingly used for skill training in the future.

Uses of simulation in education

There is a markedly conservative element in education in the Western world. There is a belief that what we have is the best that we can have. This has possibly been due to the fact that historically the church has been the main educating influence. This conservatism has taken a variety of forms. In Britain it has given us an élitist society in which the members of élites choose those who are to become the élite in their turn. The leaders, then, have decided on the body of knowledge and the values they believe to be true, the parents have accepted them, and the schools have taught them. In America, things have been seen in a different light. There, the myth is that all men are created equal and each can find his own level in fair competition with his peers. But in each society what is important has been pre-determined, and in each culture *things* are of paramount importance. In other words there has been an over emphasis on content.

There can be no doubt that these attitudes are changing, and that old beliefs and intolerances are being swept away. There is an increasing awareness that education is not instruction, and that feeling, sensitivity, and awareness are not intuitive aspects of human nature, but can be inculcated by education. It is as well for simulation that this change has come about.

As a means of teaching content, simulation does not have a lot to be said for it. There are probably many ways that it can be better done. What it does do is change the classroom relationship between teacher and pupil, and by so doing, offer a chance of a different method of education. This is often a kind of finding out which is not possible under more rigid conditions. It gives the person who is being taught a chance to formulate and voice opinions in a punishment free environment, and to find out instead of being told. Even Allen's games which are highly stylized, and do set out to teach content, do so in such a way that they can be played for enjoyment. In them the content learning is disguised by the fun of participating.

Classroom simulations One of the greatest benefits of simulation is the ease with which particular simulations can be put together. This, together with the fact that they are most effective in conceptual situations, makes them very effective teaching situations in a wide variety of different classrooms. In the field of moral education, the teacher can take what is current news and with about four hours' work turn it into a simulation that will be useful over a wide range of abilities and ages. Most educational innovations in recent years have tended to restrict the teacher's choice of what and how to teach. Examples that come readily to mind are programmed learning (because it takes so long to write each programme), the new mathematics (because the content and purpose of the study is not clear to many people), and the systems of unit study with their packages (because the material is so carefully prepared and comprehensive that the initiative for providing materials and considering methods has been taken out of the teacher's hands). On the other hand, if the teacher is aware of simulation she can see an item in this morning's newspaper and have a simulation prepared for her class by tomorrow.

She can concern her class in acts of vandalism, intolerance and injustice as they are happening in the world.

This is excellent teaching for the teacher need not present any value judgements at all. These will all come from the children. The method of presentation permits insight into the problem. It has been suggested that it could also be a method for reinforcing prejudice. In a community where intolerance is a way of life, is it possible that a mere classroom technique could have any influence? Would a simulation on desegregation amongst the community of Little Rock, or one on racial prejudice against non Aryans in Hitler's Germany, have had any chance of success? Even in the most intolerant, the most ignorant, the most biassed communities there are thinking, sensitive people. Now simulation, because of the element of role playing involved, provides a vehicle where such people can speak up and try to convince others. Remember that they speak, not with their own voices, but in the role that they are assigned. Thus the situation is punishment free for the timid, who can later claim, if that is what they have to do, that the sentiments they uttered were those of the person they were playing and not their own. Once prejudice has been openly declared and recognized it will subsequently bloom in less profusion. It may not be a universal panacea, but it is a step in the right direction, and is much more effective than talk.

There is an essential difference between the way that classroom simulation has developed in America and in Britain. The American way is typified by games that have been developed at Johns Hopkins University, Western Behavioral Sciences Institute, and Abt Associates, a commercial games making firm. The common factor in these games is the element of competition that seems to be in all of them. There seems to be a need to declare a winner. That does not imply that the competition is on a one to one basis, though it frequently is. Nor does it mean that there is no room for co-operation, because there frequently is. What it does mean is that the person who constructs the game has to fit in another elaboration, that is a scoring system. This makes the game a little more complex and harder to construct. It also causes a withdrawal for those few who do not wish to see their world in competitive terms. Let nobody say that that is how the world is: competitive. True it is how we make it, but a co-operative environment might be a more effective one.

In Britain, with the exception of geography, the classroom uses of simulation have tended to leave out the competitive element, and the score sheet does not figure largely in simulation here. There is greater emphasis placed on co-operation, and this has an interesting side effect concerning accrued benefit from the exercise. A game is a contest, and a contest can be won or lost, but it is the winning or losing that matters. The world tends to look at people who discuss and analyse games afterwards as boorish. This can be seen when 'post mortems' are held after hands of cards, or when chess games are analysed. This is what experts do; the average person wants no part of it. In simulation there is this same feeling of relief and relaxation at the conclusion of the game. The sense of involvement goes, and that generally most effective part of the simulation, the post play analysis, loses some of its edge. Another aspect of competition is that there are two ways to play games. They can be played to win, but when hope of winning has passed they must be played to minimize losses. This is an obvious aspect of spectator games in Britain that does not seem to have a parallel in America. The two great spectator games in this country are soccer and cricket. Both of these lend themselves to the attitude of win, draw, but do not lose. The great, non participating public of this country views its team's failure as a diminution of its manhood. In terms of simulation, this attitude of not loosing results in conservative behaviour, and to a certain extent inhibits action and attitude in participants of the game. It may well not be by chance that these two different ways of presenting classroom simulations have arisen on the different sides of the Atlantic. Possibly we are all conditioned subconsciously by our national ethos, and we occasionally, unknowingly choose the right path.

Simulation in teacher training   In the area of training in education simulation makes use of a variety of media and techniques. This is especially true of teacher training. Here a great deal of use has been made of visual impact in an effort to bring reality to the exercises. Much has been written on the transfer of training, and on 'realism' in the training of teachers by such writers as Kersh,[44] Kimble and Wulff,[45] Kittell,[46] and Twelker.[47] Where visual imagery is used the sense of reality is enhanced, and the simulation may well be more effective, especially if the production of the visual material is well done.

In the professional (as opposed to academic) training of teachers, the function of simulation is to move the student into a situation that he will have to encounter in the future, that of a teacher who has just finished training and has a class of her own for the first time. The use that is made of it here is the same as that made of it in careers guidance in the upper secondary school. It is a sort of projective function that allows the participant to view his own performance of the future, and to assess it coolly and in an atmosphere free from blame. Simulation lets us overcome one great difficulty in teacher training. Tutors very frequently have students come to see them with problems of classroom control. It is very hard to advise students about the effective methods of handling classroom difficulties unless one is there and can see the trouble brewing. As a result, we tend to talk to students in generalities and abstractions. Consequently, they face the initial stages of their teaching practices with a great deal of apprehension. Also they frequently seem to have an ivory tower attitude to teaching made up of these abstractions; an ability to talk about education but not about individual children. Often the difference between the real world of the classroom and their conception of it causes young teachers to become afraid of making mistakes. This fear causes conservatism in the teaching methods and sometimes tensions between the teacher and the pupils.

It is difficult for a young teacher to recognize the beginning of a classroom problem. One of the advantages of visual presentation of problems in simulation is that the build ups to such problems can be seen. Cruickshank. Broadbent, and Bubb[48] and Twelker[49] have made this clear by their insistence on the student first identifying the problem and then suggesting ways of dealing with it in their simulated classrooms. It would seem that there is no other method of allowing young teachers to recognize the building up of problems which can compare with simulation on a cost effectiveness basis. The other advantage to simulations is that they allow problems to develop as the instructor wants them. If we wished to show a student a classroom problem in a real situation we might have to wait for a long time before we saw it, depending on the ability of the class teacher and on the friendliness of the children. With simulation we can have the action acted out on film or on video tape and can then reproduce it when we wish.

Simulation is also used in the academic and main subject areas of pre-service teacher training, but here they differ very little from the methods of using them in the schools on the one hand, and the university departments on the other. There is a novel use that has been made of the method at the Berkshire College of Education. Women, and a few men, who are mature and who have had another career are accepted into colleges of education. Many of these people are in their later forties. Many of them have not had dealings with young children for a considerable time. One of the results is that they are intolerant of, and often impatient with, the children's ideas. In moral education seminars, an effort has been made to use simulation to induce tolerance.

A number of case studies of children have been prepared. These are difficult cases concerning people whose backgrounds and ways of life are different from the students'. Each student is asked to assume one of these roles and to argue as that person would on a discussion of a moral nature during the seminar. It is felt that by putting the mature student into the position of the at least different but possibly under privileged simulated student she will begin to feel more tolerant, more able to see the other point of view, less liable to have personality clashes with her pupils. Of course it is hard to assess the value of such seminars. It is hard to devise an objective measure of intolerance, intractability or prejudice, so that we can apply pre and post tests of attitude. It is also not much use asking students because when their attitudes have changed they are reluctant to recognize that they had the other, less sociably desirable ones.

Prognostic uses of simulation There is a further use for simulation in fitness for the job studies. If case studies are made dynamic by role playing, then aptitude tests, vocational guidance, and personnel selection could also be given a dynamic quality if simulation was used. In one form or another it frequently is used now, but the element of similarity between the test and the actuality is often extremely obscure. It would appear that these tests have evolved from eclecticism which has been given a consequent theoretical justification. One is frequently moved to think that correlation could have been used but that validity might not have been given sufficient emphasis. Thus it might have been noticed that numbers of women who assemble small electronic components have a skill at assembling jig-saw puzzles, and a vocational test to indicate suitability for the job might be constructed on the construction of jig-saws. But is it a valid test? Frequently this might not have been sufficiently investigated.

The prognostic simulation can be based on different criteria. In teaching, for instance, the job itself can be analysed and problem areas identified. If a simulation is built around these problem areas the next procedure is to determine how skilled encumbents of the positions deal with them. This can be done by having such people take part in the simulation in sufficient numbers to determine modal performance peaks, and personal deviations from these modal scores. If then an applicant for the job is asked to take part in the simulation, his score might be one indication of his probability of satisfactory performance in the job. In any case it must be worth investigating and could not be more subjective than the interview method that is almost universally used in Britain.

There is also a diagnostic use for simulation. If simulation is used in pre-job training, mistakes occur in a punishment free atmosphere as part of the whole system. When they are noticed they can be isolated, and remedial action can be taken in order to correct them. To this end, micro teaching methods would be a valuable adjunct to the diagnostic use of simulation. It should not be thought that each of the suggested uses of simulation is a separate one. There may be many uses for any given simulation, and a carefully constructed simulation may serve a number of purposes.

Devising a simulation

Simulation is a method of presentation of certain kinds of material, but is not a whole teaching system. Rather it is the central part of such a system and we must be aware of the beginnings and the ending if it is to be effective. Before we can present a simulation it has to be physically prepared. This important work enables us to determine our educational aims. The simulation process enables us to programme them, and the post simulation stages makes sure that they are reinforced.

Different kinds of simulations require different kinds of organization. If a teacher wished to use one of the large, complex, commercial simulations of international relations, the article by Burgess, Peterson, and Frantz[50] in *Social Education* would make a good starting point, especially as it is unlikely that a person who was inexperienced in the technique of simulation would be able to organize one from the handbooks of the INS kit. On the other hand, if one wished to design a game of the kind that can be played in the classroom, and which has to operate against constrictions of time (the duration of a lesson) and space (the amount of room in a classroom), then Abt Associates[51] or Gordon[52] are good starting places.

When devising a simulation, the first thing to attempt to make absolutely clear is the educational objective of the exercise. It is also important that rudimentary cost efficiency considerations are undertaken at this stage. This merely consists of asking can this educational objective be better achieved by some other method. The active elements in simulation that are present in other elements in less abundance are motivation, involvement and flexibility. If these are considered to be of paramount importance then it is probable that simulation will be of use. If the learning of fact is the most important educational aim, there is no assurance from research that it can be done more efficiently through simulation than through any of the more conventional methods of factual presentation. What it might do, of course, is help the tutor towards an orderly grouping and presentation of those facts, but the effort may be greater than the reward.

The method of presentation must now be considered. There are a number of elements in this, and a preliminary one must be the degree of competition involved. In other words will the simulation produce a winner and loosers? If the desire is to reinforce desirable behaviour, then competition is a way of achieving it, for a player can succeed only by conforming within the rules of the game. On the other hand, there is a danger that he will see it only as a game, and will not transfer those rules into the educational area that is desired. The presumption of transfer of training is a major justification of simulation, and if it does not occur then the exercise can only be judged to be a failure. Not only do rule bound simulations tend to control responses, but also they tend to inhibit the experimental behaviour patterns that should be encouraged in the punishment free atmosphere of simulation. It seems that there is a place for competitive games but that there is also an important area of education that is best served by co-operative simulations.

Simulation implies involvement, but occasionally there are pupils who do not involve themselves. As often as not this is because they are bored with the exercise because they have not got enough to do. When this happens they try to distract the other participants and either cause frustration or make the simulation less effective. The simulation designer can frequently prevent this from happening by making sure that each player's part is an important and involving one. Not all parts have to be played, minor ones can be abstractions, described on paper only. If any action is required from such minor roles it can be written in by the simulation controller. The aim then is to have each participant's part in the simulation of about equal importance. It is also important to involve all members of the class. This does not imply that only simulations that have thirty odd parts are of any use; what it means is that where there are fewer, some special technique must be used. Roles can be so organized that they are developed by a group of pupils, or the class may be divided into sets each one of which plays the simulation separately, or part of the class can be made into a jury.

The length of run of the simulation is also of importance. Patently it should be just long enough to fit into a timetable period. It is impossible to design games or simulations which do fit this requirement. What is necessary is that the designer play his game, see how long it takes and then modify it. Sometimes it is possible to break a game up into parts so that it can be ongoing while at the same time fitting into a timetable pattern. Many of the competitive American simulations have a built in time scale. The result of this is that participants often ignore it or else become frustrated by it. Unless this is part of the deliberate design of the game it is better to let the game run several times, modifying it after each run until it fits into the timetable naturally.

The simulation itself begins with a good idea. This good idea will form the basis of the *scenario* which sets the stage for the whole simulation.

Take, for example, the simulation that aims to initiate discussion of racial intolerance. The good idea came with the board and residence column of the evening paper. The coloured student applied by post for accommodation with the landlady, was offered a room, but forgot to say that he was not white. This formed the basis for the simulation. The *scenario* develops easily from this, once the next step of deciding the role set has been completed. Such simulations are easy to prepare, take very little of a teacher's time. This one was completed in four hours, and it can be used frequently with different age ranges and abilities of children. The *scenario*, just as it was prepared, is offered as Appendix 1.1. No pre-play instructions or suggestions for post-play developments are included because any competent teacher can decide on these for himself. This is a simulation that might be conducted by a part of the class so that there are several of them going at the one time. In this case each group would report its findings to the whole class where they would be discussed. Alternatively it could be performed by the whole class in either of two ways. Groups could be assigned to each role in order to develop it, or those members of the class who were not assigned a role could be the members of the Race Relations Board (an actual body in this country).

Simulations of this kind can be developed by the pupils themselves. One such is described (pages 140–145) in Tansey and Unwin.[53]

This chapter has been a very much do it yourself type of writing. That is because the writer found that when he first became interested in simulation it was difficult to make a start. It was not that people were unwilling to help, but it seemed very difficult to find anywhere in the literature an explanation of what simulation was about and what it involved. In one sense, most of the chapters in this book contain this element of explanation, although most of them expect the reader to be informed about simulation to some extent before he begins to read them. As this chapter is the first in the book, if it has been read before going on, this expectation will have been realized. The references will be useful to enlarge aspects that have not been dealt with in great enough detail.

REFERENCES

1. Twelker, Paul A.: 'Simulation, an Overview'. Monmouth, Teaching Research Division, Oregon State System of Higher Education, July 1968, mimeo.
2. Cruickshank, Donald R.: 'The Use of Simulation in Teacher Education, a Developing Phenomenon'. Knoxville, University of Tennessee, College of Education, undated, mimeo.
3. Garvey, Dale M.: 'A Preliminary Evaluation of Simulation'. Paper presented

at the 46th Annual Meeting of the National Council for Social Studies, Cleveland, Ohio, 23–26 November 1966.

4. Smoker, Paul: 'Simulation for Social Anticipation and Creation'. Evanston, Illinois, Northwestern University, 1969, mimeo.

5. Coleman, James S.: 'The Social System of a School, and the Game of Adolescence'. Paper read at the Conference of Simulated Environments, IBM, Yorktown Heights, 28–29 June 1962.

6. Boocock, Sarane S.: 'Simulation of a Learning Environment for Career Planning and Vocational Choice'. Baltimore, Maryland, Johns Hopkins University, undated, mimeo.

7. Abt, Clark C.: 'Games for Learning'. Occasional Paper No. 7, The Social Studies Curriculum Program, Educational Development Center, Cambridge, Mass., 1966.

8. Western Behavioral Sciences Institute: 'Occasional Newsletters about Uses of Simulations and Games for Education and Training'. Project SIMILE, La Jola, California.

9. Aldrich, Andrew A.: 'Nonsuch Youth Club'. Wiltshire Training Agency, Wiltshire County Council, Trowbridge, Wiltshire, England, 1967.

10. Garnett, J., Bolam, R., et al: 'Vietnam Crisis Simulation Workshop'. Bingley College of Education, Yorkshire, England, September 1967, mimeo.

11. Tansey, P. J., and Unwin, Derick: 'Academic Gaming and Simulation, a Bibliography and Notes'. Bulmershe College of Education, Reading, England, 1968, mimeo.

12. Banks, M., Groom, J., and Oppenheim, A.: 'International Crisis'. London School of Economics and University College, London, 1967, mimeo.

13. Boyce, Thomas: 'Business Games and Exercises'. University of Wales, Institute of Science and Technology, Cardiff, undated, mimeo.

14. von Neumann, John, and Morgenstern, Oskar: Theory of Games and Economic Behavior. Princeton, Princeton University Press, 1944.

15. Rapaport, Anatol: Fights, Games and Debates. Ann Arbor, University of Michigan Press, 1960.

16. Shubik, Martin: Game Theory and Related Approaches: Selection. N.Y., John Wiley & Sons Inc., 1964.

17. Shubik, Martin: Readings in Game Theory and Political Behavior. N.Y., Doubleday & Co., 1954.

18. Tansey, P. J., and Unwin, Derick: 'Simulation in Education'. Technical Education and Industrial Training, 10 August 1968, pp. 316–17.

19. Wing, Richard L.: 'Two Computer Based Economic Games for Sixth Graders'. American Behavioral Scientist, 10 November 1966, pp. 31–4.

20. Rausch, Erwin: Economic Decision Games. Chicago, Science Research Associates, 1968. A series of eight games, one of which is entitled BANKING.

21. Cherryholmes, Cleo H.: Inter-Nation Simulation. Chicago, Science Research Associates, 1968.

22. Cruickshank, Donald R., Broadbent, Frank W., and Bubb, Roy: Teaching Problems Laboratory. Chicago, Science Research Associates, 1968.

23. Kersh, Bert Y.: 'Classroom Simulation: Further Studies on Dimensions of Realism'. Teaching Research, Monmouth, Oregon State System of Higher Education, Title VII, Project No. 5-0848.

24. Tansey, M. R.: 'Racial Problems'. Langtree Comprehensive School, Woodcote, Oxfordshire, England, 1968, mimeo.

25. Gearon, John D.: 'Simulation and Stimulation: Teaching Politics and Government in High School Social Studies'. *Social Education*, XXXII (3), March 1968, pp. 273–8 and 281.
26. MANCHESTER, designed by Abt Associates for Educational Services Inc. (now Educational Development Center), Cambridge, Mass.
27. Yount, David, and De Kock, Paul. 'Disunia: American Studies Simulation'. El Capitan High School, Lakeside, California, undated.
28. *Half Our Future*. Report of the Minister of Education's Central Advisory Council, Chairman John H. Newsom, 1963.
29. Kersh, Bert Y.: 'The Classroom Simulator: an Audiovisual Environment for Practice Teaching'. *Audiovisual Instruction*, 6 November 1961, pp. 447–8.
30. Cruickshank, Donald R., and Broadbent, Frank W.: 'The Simulation and Analysis of Problems of Beginning Teachers'. U.S. Department of Health, Education and Welfare, Final Report, Project No. 5-0798, October 1968.
31. Aldrich, Andrew A., op. cit.
32. Twelker, Paul A.: 'Classroom Simulation and Teacher Preparation'. *School Review*, 75, summer 1967, pp. 197–204.
33. Guetzkow, Harold: 'A Use of Simulation in the Study of International Relations'. *Behavioral Science*, 4, July 1959, pp. 183–91.
34. Herman, C. F., and Herman, M. G.: 'An Attempt to Simulate the Outbreak of World War I'. *American Political Science Review*, 61, June 1967, pp. 400–16.
35. Bloomfield, L. P., and Paddleford, N. J.: 'Three Experiments in Political Gaming'. *American Political Science Review*, 52, December 1959, pp. 1105–15.
36. Tansey, P. J.: 'World Diplomacy'. Bulmershe College of Education, Reading, England, 1968, mimeo.
37. Boardman, Robert, Podmore, W., and Lewis, B.: *Manex: a Vietnam Crisis Game*. Manchester, 1968.
38. Bolam, R., Garnett, J., *et al*: 'Adventure in Learning: Vietnam Simulation Exercise'. Bingley College of Education, Yorkshire, England, September 1967.
39. Laulicht, Jerome, Smoker, Paul, Jenkins, Robin, McRae, John, and Fabri, David: 'A Vietnam Simulation'. Peace Research Centre, England and Canada, *Journal of Peace Research*, No. 1, 1967.
40. Groom, A. J. R., and Banks, Michael H.: 'Conex I: a Simulation of a Middle Eastern Conflict Situation'. Conflict Research Society, Nottingham, England, 25–27 March 1966.
41. Nicholson, Michael: *The War That Might Have Been*. BBC Radio Three, 31 July 1968.
42. Cherryholmes, Cleo H., and Guetzkow, Harold: *Inter-Nation Simulation*, Chicago, Science Research Associates, 1968.
43. Smoker, Paul: 'International Processes Simulation: a Man–Computer Model'. Northwestern University, Evanston, Illinois, 1968, mimeo.
44. Kersh, Bert Y.: 'Classroom Simulation, a New Dimension in Teacher Education'. Training Research, Monmouth, Oregon System of Higher Education, Title VII NDEA Project No. 886, 1963.
45. Kimble, G. A., and Wulff, J. J.: 'Response Guidance, as a Factor in the Value of Student Participation in Film Instruction'. In *Student Response in Programmed Instruction*, A. A. Lumsdaine (ed.), National Academy of Sciences, National Research Council, Washington D.C., 1961.
46. Kittell, J. E.: 'An Experimental Study of the Effects of External Direction

During Learning on Transfer and Retention of Principles'. *Journal of Educational Psychology*, 48, 1957, pp. 391–405.

47. Twelker, Paul A.: 'The Effects of Prompts on Transfer of Training'. Paper read at the Western Psychological Association, Portland, Oregon, April 1964.
48. Cruickshank, Broadbent, and Bubb: *Teaching Problems Laboratory*, q.v.
49. Twelker, Paul A.: 'Interaction Analysis and Classroom Simulation as Adjunct Instruction in Teacher Education'. Training Research, Monmouth, Oregon System of Higher Education, Final Report, Project No. 5-1117, February 1968.
50. Burgess, Philip M., Peterson, Lawrence E., and Frantz, Carl D.: 'Organizing Simulated Environments'. *Social Education*, XXXIII (2), February 1969, pp. 185–92 and 204.
51. Abt Associates Inc.: 'Training Games'. Cambridge, Mass., undated, mimeo.
52. Gordon, Alice Kaplan: 'Home Made Games'. Unit Eight, Educational Games Extension Service, Chicago, Science Research Associates, 15 May 1968.
53. Tansey, P. J., and Unwin, Derick: *Simulation and Gaming in Education*. London, Methuen, 1969.

Appendix 1.1

The *scenario* included below was designed by Mrs M. R. Tansey, Senior Mistress, Langtree Comprehensive School, Oxfordshire. It is included to show a simple, easily designed simulation which can be used in the field of moral education. It is more concerned with idea training than with the teaching of content.

Racial problems

Situation: Hearing of Race Relations Tribunal
          —consisting of 3 members (could be more)
Case before the Tribunal: It has been reported to the Race Relations Board that *Mrs Elizabeth Morris*, landlady at 4 Norton Street, Oxford, refused to have Mr John Brown, an African negro, as a lodger on the grounds that he is coloured.

Background information regarding the report: Mrs Morris usually takes 4 students each with a room. They eat breakfast and dinner with the family. Two of the students are in their second year at the University, (1) Miss Margaret Clarke aged 19, (2) Mr Richard Harris aged 20. One is a mature student, Mr Robert Shaw, aged 36.

In September there was a vacancy because a third year student left last year. In that month Mr John Brown wrote to Mrs Morris from London asking if she could have him for the year; he did not say in his letter that he was from Zambia. She replied that she had a vacancy. On 20 September Mr Brown arrived at 4 Norton Street. Mrs Morris was shocked when she saw him, called her husband, Patrick Morris, who told him that he could not stay, giving as his reason the fact that his daughter, Fiona, aged 17, was expecting a friend at the weekend and they would therefore need the room.

Copy of correspondence between Mrs Morris and Mr Brown.

46, Alder Road,
Hampstead,
London N.W.8.
2nd September 1968

Dear Mrs Morris,

In reply to your advertisement in the Evening Post, Sept. 1st I should like to enquire about the vacancy in your home for a student. I am 38 years old and will be attending an Advanced Course in Education at the University. The course lasts for a year. If you are able to accommodate me I should like to come on Sept. 20th.

Yours faithfully,
John Brown

4, Norton Street,
Oxford.
7th Sept. 1968

Dear Mr Brown,

We should be pleased to give you a room for the next year. I provide breakfast and dinner during the week and all meals at the weekend. The cost is £6 a week. There are three other students living here at the moment.

We shall look forward to seeing you on Sept. 20th.

Yours sincerely,
Elizabeth Morris.

Background of the people involved:

Mrs Elizabeth Morris aged 38

Quiet and rather nervous. Has had students in her house for the last 8 years. She enjoys having them because she likes cooking and cleaning and the extra money comes in handy. She has no decided views, but is influenced mostly by her husband. She is a good, competent landlady and the students who stay with her are always comfortable and satisfied.

Mr Patrick Morris aged 47

Occupation: Post Office Engineer.

An ex-soldier, sergeant in last war. *Very prejudiced* views against all foreigners and particularly coloured people. He is very dominating and rules his house, wife and daughter with a rod of iron. He likes an ordered, organized existence, is not particularly keen on the students in his house but he accepts them because he likes the extra money.

P. J. Tansey

Fiona Morris aged 17
Quiet like her mother. She is intelligent and is in the sixth form at the grammar school. She studies hard and very rarely goes out unless it is with another girl friend. She has never had much freedom anyway. She is much more tolerant than her father and certainly has no colour prejudice though she would never tell her father this.

Margaret Clarke aged 19
Second year student, studying languages. She has been with the Morris family since she started at Oxford. Her father is a doctor in Canterbury, Kent, and her up-bringing and education have been conventional and sound. She went to a girls' boarding school. Her views on coloured people are that she accepts them in the surroundings of the University on equal terms but she has never been faced with living with coloured students before. She is a kind, popular girl who is usually fairly tolerant.

Richard Harris aged 20
Second year student, studying science. He comes from Birmingham, his parents never had much money, his father is a postman and it has been a struggle to keep Richard at school and then at University. Richard has seen in Birmingham large areas overrun with coloured immigrants and this has always irritated him. He is certainly prejudiced against coloured immigrants and tends towards the views of Mr Morris.

Robert Shaw aged 36
At the university for one year where he is studying for the Advanced Certificate in Education. He is headmaster of a Primary School in Wolverhampton. His views are liberal and tolerant and he has found himself getting angry with Mr Morris and his unreasoned prejudices. He has had personal experience of the colour problem in his school and knows that it cannot be solved by prejudice. He hears the conversation when Mr Brown arrives at the house and is extremely angry. He has since left 4 Norton Street and is living elsewhere in Oxford.

Mr John Brown aged 38
A college lecturer from Zambia, in Oxford to do the same course as Mr Shaw. Arrived in London on 5 August and saw the advertisement for this accommodation in September. Believing Oxford to be liberal and tolerant of coloured students, it did not occur to him to mention in his letter to Mrs Morris that he was coloured. He was therefore extremely upset and hurt by his reception. He has since found accommodation in Oxford but the occasion under discussion has left its mark on him.

22

Peter Johnson aged 46

Lives at 2 Norton Street. Solicitor's clerk. Next door neighbour of the Morris family. Has lived there for 10 years. Has never been happy about students living next door though there has never really been anything to complain about except for occasional noise. Would be most annoyed if coloured students were to live next door since this would, in his opinion, lower the tone of the neighbourhood and devalue his property.

Bryan Nicholls aged 38

Landlord of the 'Red Dragon' public house near to Morris house. Knows the Morris family since Mr Morris usually plays darts at the weekend. Also knows the students from the house. He knows the views of Mr Morris but does not agree with them. He is quite accustomed to coloured students in his pub and has never had any trouble with them. He knows Mr Brown because on the day he was refused at the Morris house Mr Brown came to him for help in finding a room. He found Mr Brown quiet and reasonable though naturally upset and he was able to find him a room at a friend's house. Since then he has not seen Mr Brown.

Mary Arkell aged 45

Takes students at 23 Norham Gardens. Mr Nicholls sent Mr Brown to her on 20 September. She is a widow and for the last 3 years has had students, mostly coloured men and women. This seems quite natural to her and she was pleased to have Mr Brown who she finds is a perfect lodger, considerate and co-operative. She finds him quiet and withdrawn and does not feel that he is very happy.

James Bandez aged 30

A student from Ghana, coloured. Staying at Mrs Arkell's. He is friendly with Mr Brown. He has occasionally found hostility to him in the town but this does not worry him because he has always been accepted in the students' lodgings. He knows that John Brown has never forgotten the time he was refused at the Morris's. It was a long time before John mentioned this to him and he can never persuade John to go anywhere with him if white people are likely to be there. Once he wanted him to go to a party at a friend's house but the friend is white and the party would be mixed. John would not go. James does not think that this attitude will ever change.

Dr Charles Bradford
Tutor to John Brown. Knows John to be a very hard worker, most conscientious. Feels that he is too withdrawn and afraid to make his feelings known in group discussions. He has in his group 7 students, all coloured, and John is the only one who does not mix with white students on the same course (though in different tutor groups).

Appendix 1.2

In this appendix an effort is made to diagrammatically show something of the range of simulation.

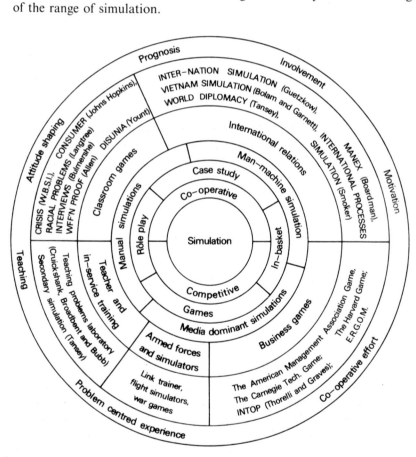

Fig. 1.2   A visual image of some aspects of simulation

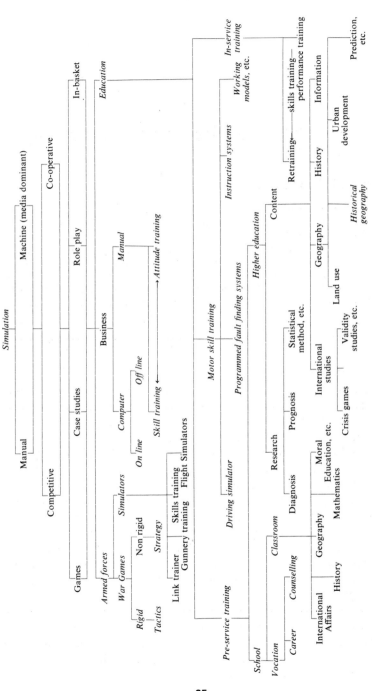

Fig. 1.3 A pattern of simulation use

2

An introduction to the virtues of gaming

Frederick L. Goodman

Frederick L. Goodman is a Professor of Education at the University of Michigan in the United States. Educated at Harvard and at the University of Michigan, he is the designer of several social science simulations. He edits the Games Review column for *Simulations and Games* and is preparing the review of research on gaming and simulation for the second edition of the *Handbook of Research on Learning and Teaching* for the American Educational Research Association. Active also in the area of information retrieval, he has been a consultant to the Educational Resources Information Center (ERIC) of the U.S. Office of Education.

A philosophy of teaching

Among educators, responses to academic games are of two kinds: some reject them as inadequate to the task at hand, and others have recourse to them. Quite often, rejection is of the derisive sort: games are simply not to be taken seriously, and they cannot therefore be brought into a meaningful relationship with the serious business of education. Among those who accept games into the classroom, too many do so out of a feeling of frustration: they feel that, since things are so poor in the classroom anyway, they might as well try games which will, at least, occupy their pupils. Others feel that they are useful as auxiliary experiences, as devices which can be welcomed for their 'enrichment value'. It is my contention that games can be taken seriously. I also believe that their choice as an alternative educational tool can be both rational and considered. This essay proposes to demonstrate the reasonableness of these views.

I have often found it convenient to use a rather simple model of alternative kinds of educational methods as a way of placing academic gaming into a more comprehensive context. This model uses two distinctions and their combinations as its fundamental structure. The first distinction is between those methods which favour direct, and those which favour indirect procedures. Direct procedures are those in which the student is in a relatively passive role: he *is given* an education which he *absorbs* more or less adequately. Indirect procedures are those in which the student is in a relatively active role: he *acquires* an education through a process of *discovering* for himself.

The second distinction is between educational methods which are essentialist and those which are not. By essentialism I mean, of course, the conviction that there is a more or less discrete and complete body of facts and concepts, the absorption or discovery of which constitutes an adequate education. In contrast to this view, and the educational methods which it entails, would be the view that there are no facts or concepts which are essential in this way. Consequently non-essentialist methods would tend to stress general intellectual operations, habits of mind, as their central focus.

On the basis of these two distinctions one can develop a graphic presentation. It would look like this:

ESSENTIALISM			
INDIRECT		DIRECT	
D	C	B	A

Fig. 2.1   A classification of educational methods

The four classes of methods thus generated (A, B, C, D) can now be related to a general development in this history of education. Although all four classes of methods have always been available to educators and, indeed, all of them have been used at all times, it is equally clear that certain classes have been especially favoured at particular times.

Class A, those methods which are both direct and non-essentialistic, were favoured prior to about 1850 both in Europe and in the United States. Perhaps the archetypal pattern of this class of methods is the pounding of Latin into the heads of despairing pupils. Based essentially on the need to educate a small and highly selected group of students, and to educate them for a limited range of upper-class social roles, this approach could afford to be difficult, often to the point of obscurity. The student's experience was analogous to that of an extreme ordeal through which, it was assumed, only the fittest could survive.

By about 1900, the second class (Class B) of educational methods, still direct but now essentialistic in outlook, was in the ascendancy, particularly in the United States. Working from the dual imperatives of

27

education for everyone and *education need not be tough*, the direct essentialists sought for defined curricula of necessary facts and concepts, the teaching of which would give 'the man in the street' an easy but 'adequate' education for his role as citizen in a populist democracy.

The advantages of such methods as these derive from the perceived ease and efficiency with which essentials may generally be learned and taught. The familiar formula, *If you learn these facts, you will know this subject*, is appealing to many students. And, especially with the textbook to rely on, extrapolating the 'essential' concepts, rules, and facts, along with an illustrative example or two, is no extraordinarily demanding feat for the educator.

Such direct essentialism, however, may not capture students' imaginations especially well. By the middle of this century, educators both in America and in England had come to prefer more exciting methods which are labelled variously, but which generally include the term 'discovery'. In application, these methods frequently belong to the class that I have labelled indirect essentialism (Class C). Rather than giving the generalization followed by an illustrative example or two, these methods advocate more inductive and experimental activities for their students. In the context of *direct* essentialism, for example, the student would be told that a magnet attracts ferrous substances, and would then be shown two or three instances. In the context of *indirect* essentialism, on the other hand, the student takes a magnet and a set of substances, some ferrous and others not. He 'experiments' with this environment to 'discover' the rule for himself. This latter instance, which is typical of the discovery approach as it is generally employed, is clearly essentialistic. After all, in either case, the teacher is very likely to have selected the essential rule which the student is to learn.

An interesting aspect of arguments supporting some discovery methods of teaching is the pretence that such methods are non-authoritative, that they free students from having teachers decide what is essential or 'relevant' to their educations. Clearly this can often be a mistaken assertion, and, in addition, it has some rather dangerous implications. By providing students with the illusion of exploration, this class of methods saves the educator from the often embarrassing position of having to justify the necessities he is imposing on their learning experiences. In so far as we value the scepticism of our students, we must deplore the possibility of its being falsely allayed. In so far as we value the continual testing and re-affirmation of our own considered opinions, we must equally deplore the intellectual fearfulness that would seek to mask these opinions and protect them from open scrutiny. From the pharmacist's point of view, the difficulty with sugar-coated pills is the temptation to concentrate on their palatibility and to pay insufficient attention to their therapeutic value. From the point of view of the patient, the difficulty with sugar-coated pills is not so much that they are sugar-coated as that he, placated by sugar, may forget that they are still pills and not perhaps his best medicine.

The fourth class of methods (Class D) is more a theoretical possibility than a wide-spread current practice. It must be remembered here that I am discussing teaching, or at least formal learning, and not simply any learning in general. Indeed, the fourth class of methods has always been of tremendous interest to teachers, for it models so closely the way learning occurs outside of schools. This class of methods includes some of the fondest hopes of the discovery method theoreticians. To find systematic rather than spasmodic or chance examples of indirect non-essentialistic teaching, we have to move to the upper reaches of schooling, to the experiences offered the very bright, or the experiences offered those who have been in school for a very long time. There, a student proceeds very much on his own to learn about matters, the import of which is his own determination. At the outer limits of such learning there is no help available from a teacher, even within a so-called formal schooling environment. The student is on his own: his discoveries are left completely to his own devices. But between that outer limit and the indirect essentialism of Class C, there lies a range of guided discovery that is non-essentialistic (or essentialistic in a very different way from what is normally understood as such). Members of a research team teach each other in this way; dissertation chairmen guide their students in this way; and some of the most interesting kinds of academic games guide their players in this way.

The difference between no guidance and guided discovery is an important one, and rests upon a critical distinction between liberty and freedom. Liberty may be defined as the absence of any constraints. Freedom, to me, means the capacity to make choices among a given set of alternatives. In contrast to liberty, freedom includes the presence of limitations. Together with liberty, however, freedom stands opposite to a complete determinism from which choice is absolutely excluded.

It is my view that freedom is a state much to be valued in an educational setting, whereas liberty is ultimately destructive to such a setting. This is because complete liberty is an anomalitic state for the individual, and results in paralysis rather than activity. Anyone who has made the error of assigning a 'free' essay—that is, an assignment to write in any way on any subject—knows that complete liberty is most often educationally destructive. The most mature students excepted, most others find such liberty impossible to cope with: it is somehow inhuman, they feel. And the reason that the most mature students are excepted from such paralysis is that they very quickly create a set of constraints for themselves. In this way they compare with the image of the lone researcher who does not flounder aimlessly only because he provides his own guidance.

My point, then, is relatively simple. If, at least as part of a total educational programme, we value a discovery approach and are genuine in our commitment to avoid essentialism, however indirect its operation, we have two alternatives available. We can either disband the classroom, forfeiting our claim to be teachers, and leave students to their own devices; or we must think very clearly about the meaning of the term 'guided discovery', and understand more clearly the role of the educator as guide.

One type of guide, indeed, a very familiar type, operates in a Class B sense, leading a person as directly as possible to what is deemed essential. Another familiar type of guide is the Class C type, the one who knows the territory well and who gently, indirectly, provides the advice necessary to bring his charge to all the essential areas of interest. But there is also the Class D type of guide. A surprisingly rigid type of person in many instances, he insists that his charges proceed according to a limited set of rules, at least for a given period of time, but he does not participate at a given moment in the actual decisions made within this rigid framework he has provided. The best example of such a guide might be a coach who has supplied his players not just with a thorough understanding of a game's formal rules, but even with a thorough understanding of the rules of a particular set of moves and a particular strategy. What an individual player discovers as a result of a given choice within this rule framework is, however, more directly a function of his own skill and that of his competitors' than a function of what his coach has said or done. Each rule he has received through the coach is something to be tested and evaluated (even a formal game rule); it is not to be accepted as an ultimate simply because the coach favours it, or even insists on it.

As already noted, at one extreme of this range, the extreme of the gifted lonely researcher, the individual, without the aid of a teacher, operates with a wide-ranging imagination, continually stipulating structures to contain and explain the facts and ideas he is discovering. These structures also guide him to further discovery by providing tentative limitations by means of which he, actively choosing, learns. At the other extreme, the learner is actually learning to value the discovery that his teacher is arranging for him to value. Between these extremes, the teacher guides the student's discoveries by stipulating his rule for him, but then leaving him to discover the consequences of these tentative limitations for himself. By virtue of the illustration of a coach, one can readily see the relationship of this type of teaching to games. It is precisely because games have rules, because they provide stipulative limiting structures, that players are guided to discoveries which we cannot assume they would make if they were interacting at random with a set of people or even with a set of objects. This is precisely the distinction between random play and games. One might happen to learn something by playing at random; it is difficult to argue that one can be *taught* anything during such a period, unless that play was in fact structured, and not random. It is also difficult to argue that a player learns directly just what his coach teaches him; he learns by noting the consequences of his own actions, within the structure provided by the game. But, before I continue developing this line of thought further, it might be helpful to describe some of the games which display the qualities under consideration especially well. I have chosen examples of two types. The first, developed by Layman E. Allen (of WFF 'N PROOF fame), is called EQUATIONS. The second, called the POLICY NEGOTIATIONS GAME, was developed by the author.

Equations The object of EQUATIONS is to shape valid mathematical equations from a set of limited symbolic resources generated at random. These resources include numbers from 0 to 9, and mathematical operations. They are printed on different faces of dice and the dice are organized in groups of different colours, with symbols of varying degrees of difficulty imprinted on dice of varying colours. Thus, elementary mathematics students might choose to use only the first coloured set of dice, which includes the numerical symbols $\boxed{0}$, $\boxed{1}$, $\boxed{2}$, $\boxed{3}$, and the operational symbols $\boxed{+}$ and $\boxed{-}$. Advanced students might use all the different colours, thus adding the numbers $\boxed{4}$, $\boxed{5}$, $\boxed{6}$, $\boxed{7}$, $\boxed{8}$, $\boxed{9}$, and the operations $\boxed{\times}$, $\boxed{\div}$, $\boxed{\sqrt{}}$, and $\boxed{*}$ (the symbol of an exponential operation in this game, whereby, for example, 4^2 is symbolically represented as $\boxed{4}\,\boxed{*}\,\boxed{2}$).

After deciding which colours to use, the players toss the dice, generating a limited, constrained, set of numerical and operational symbols (one sixth of the total possible resources). The players take turns using these symbols. They 'use' them by manipulating them in order to keep the possibility of making a valid equation open without actually making one. The first player sets the goal of the equation—that is, the right-hand member. Subsequent to that initial move, the players alternate moves by placing one of the available symbol resources in one of three boxes. These boxes are labelled 'required', 'permitted', and 'forbidden'. A

31

symbol placed in the 'required' box *must be used* as part of the equation, those in the 'forbidden' box *may not be used*, and those which are 'permitted' may *or* may not be used. Guiding the players in their choice of moves is the principle, already mentioned, that they must keep the possibility of making a valid equation open while not actually making one. If a player moves in such a way as to enable an equation to be made in the next move or to eliminate the possibility of making one on any subsequent move, and if he is challenged by another player, he loses the game. But the challenger must explain the error. Let us say, for example, that the situation of a game in progress, after five moves, is as follows:

REQUIRED	PERMITTED	FORBIDDEN
move four $\boxed{2}$		move five $\boxed{2}$ move three $\boxed{4}$ $\boxed{+}$ move two

EQUATION	move one	UNALLOCATED RESOURCES
$= \boxed{3}$		? $\boxed{5}, \boxed{-}, \boxed{-}$ move six

Fig. 2.2   The game of EQUATIONS (after Layman E. Allen: 'EQUATIONS'. Autotelic Instruction Materials Publishers, 1963)

This condition means that, using the 'required' $\boxed{2}$ and some of the resources as yet unallocated, it is possible to make a valid equation, the right hand member of which equals $\boxed{3}$. Obviously, the potential equation is $\boxed{5}\,\boxed{-}\,\boxed{2} = \boxed{3}$. Now, if the next player moves either the $\boxed{5}$ or the $\boxed{-}$ into the 'forbidden' box, he can be challenged, since he has eliminated the possibility of making a valid equation using the available resources. If he moves either the $\boxed{5}$ or the $\boxed{-}$ into either the 'required' or the 'permitted' box, he can also be challenged, since he has made it possible for the equation $\boxed{5}\,\boxed{-}\,\boxed{2} = \boxed{3}$ to be formed by the next player. If a player makes an error, is challenged, and the challenger successfully explains the error, the game is over, and the players can begin again by generating a new set of resources and setting a new goal. A perfectly played game will end in a draw. (See Allen, Chapter 4, for further examples.)

The Policy Negotiations Game The POLICY NEGOTIATIONS GAME is rather more complex than EQUATIONS. The structural components of the game include provisions for all of the central elements in any policy negotiations situation. A group of players, each representing a particular constituency, interest group, or employer, negotiate a set of issues or policies. The policies are considered in a particular order, referred to as the agenda, which the players determine. Each policy has a particular historical propensity to pass or fail, a propensity which may change during the playing of the game, and which contributes to the passage or failure of that issue when it is directly negotiated.

The central resource of the game is units of influence, and it is considered a limited resource. A specified amount of influence is held by each player, and is the currency, so to speak, of his moves. He allocates his influence in one of four ways. First, he may allocate all or part of it directly to the passage or failure of an issue which is being directly considered. Second, he can use his influence, or a part of it, to influence the placement of issues on the agenda, helping to put them higher or lower in the order of consideration. Third, he can allocate all or part of his influence towards increasing his prestige with the constituency, interest group, or employer that he is representing. Finally, he can allocate his influence, or a portion of it, to external social agencies. Subsequently, he may activate this stored influence to influence more powerfully the passage or failure of other issues. This last alternative is analogous to a kind of 'savings bank' for influence units.

A round of the POLICY NEGOTIATIONS GAME is defined as the period of time during which players allocate their influence, with respect to one issue, in any of the four ways available to them. Their allocation, with respect to the issue under consideration, is either directly from the units of influence in their immediate possession, or indirectly, by bringing 'saved' influence, previously 'stored' in the external social agencies, to bear.

At the end of a round, the leader computes all influence units which have been allocated for or against the particular issue, adds to that the amount of influence for or against passage which is inherent in the historical propensity of the issue, and announces passage or failure. In addition, the agenda and prestige levels are readjusted, if any of the players chose to allocate all or some of their influence towards these ends. Finally, the leader announces the results of the round in terms of the effect which passage or failure of the considered issue may have had on the other elements in the game. This 'feedback' may affect each element in a positive or negative way, or not at all. It is stipulated in a notebook and is to be viewed as part of the game's rules. These effects include the increase, decrease, or stability of historical propensities, agenda positions, influence levels, prestige levels, and external social agency capacities for exerting influence. After all necessary adjustments have been made, the highest issue on the agenda is announced, a new set of influence pegs is given to each player in accordance with his revised level of influence, and a new round thereby begins.

Gaming as a learning device

The most interesting feature of the POLICY NEGOTIATIONS GAME, however, has not yet been mentioned. This game is not so much a game as a three-phase gaming process. The first phase is the play of what is called a priming game: that is, a game in which each of the structural elements is pre-defined. One of the current priming games, for example, involves a policy negotiation between teachers and members of the school board. The issues include salary plans, class sizes, and similar policies; the players have particular constituencies, ranging from a suburban member of the school board to a new-to-the-system teacher. Following the priming phase, the primary purpose of which is to familiarize the participants with the structural elements and their interrelations, is a design phase. In the design phase, the participants themselves specify the definitions of the elements to accord with the perceived nature of a policy negotiating situation they are interested in studying. This could be their own situation or the situation of a group they are simply interested in understanding. That group could be contemporary, or from the past, or in the future. The last phase of this process involves playing the game which has been designed and discovering more about the dynamics of the actual negotiations by simulating them. Thus, players are to learn by exploring the consequences of detailed rules which they have, themselves, stipulated, within a very general framework of rules provided by the game designer who, in effect, is the teacher guiding the players' discovery.

Although EQUATIONS and the POLICY NEGOTIATIONS GAME are widely disparate in their subject matter, in their relative complexity, and in almost every way, they nevertheless share some qualities in common. It is these qualities which are characteristic of the type of academic games that are of particular interest in this context. Of course, other kinds of games such as guessing games and drill games have long been employed in other contexts. These are examples of Class C and Class B respectively. It is my view that the two games I have just described belong properly to Class D.

Both EQUATIONS and the POLICY NEGOTIATIONS GAME, along with all games, have sets of rules governing their play. These rules form a set of significant limitations on the players who, in a sense, discover how to play in a way which they deem successful while remaining within them. This discovery involves, in large part, maximizing possibilities through making sound choices among available alternatives. While the players are not tyrannized by the rules, and while the rules do not completely determine their every move, the rules do guide the movements of the players. In other words, although these games do not place the players in a choking determinism, they also do not place them in a meaningless liberty. Instead, the games give the players precisely that kind of freedom which we identified as particularly valuable in Class D kinds of educational methods. By following the rules, by being disciplined by them, the players are guided in their discovery, whether of mathematical concepts or of the nature of elemental relationships in a conflict situation.

As already suggested with respect to the POLICY NEGOTIATIONS GAME, a further aspect of this freedom giving quality of such academic games is that they include, in their structure, certain rules which enable the players (by guiding them) to formulate further rules on their own. Thus, for example, the players generate their own resources and their own goal in EQUATIONS. In an advanced variation of the game, players even generate new rules or symbols (such as, let the left member of any equation be equal to the number set as a goal *plus or minus two*', or 'let the symbol $\boxed{*}$ stand for factorial') which they want to explore, tentatively, in their play of the game. In the POLICY NEGOTIATIONS GAME, players generate, in the design phase, the very definitions of the elements of the game, in accordance with their perceptions of the situation they are interested in understanding. In this way, the games provide mechanisms which are analogous to the mental habits of the lone researcher, who stipulates structures to guide his further discovery, thus moving ever closer to the far extreme of the Class D range of possibilities.

In addition to providing freedom for the players, these games also provide necessary guidance. The players are not left to their own devices; the activities are not chosen at random by students trying desperately to cope with a complete and inhuman liberty. Such games do not, as has been emphasized, impose predetermined conclusions on the players; they are in no way essentialistic in the sense previously discussed. The end of the game is not in sight as it begins; the players discover it (often quite variously) as they play. Thus the games provide necessary guidance through the limitations of rules, while not in any way imposing the discovery of preconceived essentials on the players, either directly or indirectly. This is characteristic, not of all games, but of some kinds.

Such kinds of games may succeed remarkably in allowing for pure, and yet guided, discovery.

In addition, both of the games used as illustrations involve an experience which is dramatic without being decisive. The players, in addition to having freedom to discover ends not predetermined, also have the freedom which comes from the tentativeness of the gaming situation. Although a game is exciting, involving, enraging even, it is never 'for real'. Similar to the traditional conception of the essay, games, too, are tentative attempts which pretend neither to absolute truth nor to final outcomes. They are, rather, an exploration, and consequently winning and success may be relatively unimportant in the long run. Thus, for example, the 'loser' of EQUATIONS may, through an error, have come to discover an additional property of a certain mathematical operation which he had not realized before. And who is prepared to define in what 'winning' consists when considering the POLICY NEGOTIATIONS GAME? Does one win if his influence level is highest, or if his favoured issues have passed, or if every player has had one of his issues passed and one failed, or if all present agree on the excellence and accuracy of a newly designed game? In this game, it seems particularly clear that winning has more to do with successful learning than with any scorekeeping principle. It is as if every engaged player wins, perhaps not blue chips or a new contract, but some further insight, some glimpses, however tentative, of further discovery.

In emphasizing these aspects of academic games, their tentative and exploratory character, I do not, however, mean to minimize their dramatic qualities. On the contrary, the sense of engagement in an important activity, the conviction that there are stakes to play for, is also a marked quality of successful academic games. If the combination of engagement and tentativeness seems paradoxical, it is the same paradox that has, throughout the years, made the drama an important human activity. Those who are concerned with the 'validity' of academic games are very much like those who are concerned with the absolute realism of drama. Both have made the error of confusing the way things would be if they were to occur with the likelihood that this or that will occur, demanding the latter when it is the former which is of central importance. Although not 'for real' in the sense of an absolute correspondence to life, both drama and gaming draw much of their force because they both show, in their abstraction from life, a high degree of correspondence to the way things might work out if they were 'for real'.

Thus, although we take the results of these activities, both drama and academic games, seriously, these results do not impinge directly and immediately and irrevocably on our actual lives. And, to develop the correspondence just one step further, although we engage in these activities as ends in themselves, we also discover, because they deal in human probabilities, much knowledge about the 'way things are'. Another way of saying this is to note that both games and playing have both intrinsic consummatory value and extrinsic instrumental value. It is because of this combination that we value the experience of dramatic literature as part of our lives. I propose, for this and for the other reasons I have mentioned, that certain types of academic games are to be especially valued not simply as attractive ways of packaging essentials, but as one of a very few ways of furthering the ends of educators committed to guided discovery. In fact, because they require no special sensitivity to verbal modes of communication, academic games may well prove capable of engaging students for whom the experience of dramatic literature is too demanding an activity. To move greater numbers of students beyond a concept of learning which involves the mastery of essentials, to get more students engaged in explorations of the type which are normally the prerogative of the very gifted or the very mature would be no small accomplishment.

Lest I appear to be naïvely modernistic in my assertions, however, let it be noted that values such as I propose have long been a part of our educational heritage. It is no accident that Plato commends athletic games, or that English public schools find games so important a part of their traditional curriculum. It might be objected that these commendations are based exclusively on a recognition of the importance of physical training. To this, we must respond by recommending careful observation of the variety of educational methods employed by the effective coach. It is clearly not only to muscular agility that a coach addresses his concern. He is as concerned about the agility of the whole athlete, and that athlete's wholeness includes his emotions and desires and his possession of an agile and inquiring mind, a mind that chooses confidently, though tentatively, among a limited range of alternatives. It is not at all unusual for an athlete to perform finally far better than his coach could, but most athletes know that they owe this self-realization, in large measure, to the structured guidance provided by the coach.

3
The role of simulations and games in the development of geography teaching

Rex Walford

Rex Walford gained degrees at the London School of Economics, and King's College, London, before teaching in a London secondary modern school. He gained a scholarship to do postgraduate work at Northwestern University, Evanston, Illinois, in 1961, and has since taught both there and at the University of British Columbia.

He is at present the Senior Tutor, and a Principal Lecturer in Geography at Maria Grey College of Education, Twickenham, London, and has spent several years experimenting with simulation material of various kinds in schools. His *Games in Geography* (Longmans, 1969) was an early contribution to the English literature on the subject.

The 'capes and bays' rote learning of the nineteenth century has been replaced by more outwardly sophisticated approaches, yet the end product of many geographical educations can still be a random assortment of interesting but irrelevant facts. No one would dispute the need for facts as a framework on which to base other understandings; but some certainly feel that the balance may have tipped too far. The average school leaver, when asked to remember what he has learnt in geography, will usually offer a list of towns or products or resources; the minutiae of the subject seem to dominate its wider horizons.

The emphasis on factual learning stems, at least in part, from the demands of examinations. Questions are easier to devise and evaluate when related to specifically factual material. (A 1966 study showed that 85 per cent of questions in British physics examinations could be answered by recall of learnt facts, and geography examinations show a similar high figure.) But besides facts, many would argue that a complete geographic education should give:

(a) understanding of process and system; (b) ability to recognize and abstract principles and then apply them to problems; (c) skill to synthesize and interpret data; (d) insight to analyse and evaluate new problems in the light of information already known.

These other aspects are more difficult to identify and test in any subject, but in geography particularly they should be playing an increasing part in the development of the subject, since the currency of facts becomes devalued day by day. 'Globes make my head spin. By the time I locate the place, they've changed the boundaries.'[1] World geography, in the human sphere, is altering so quickly in the present decades that any perceived pattern is transitory; new settlements, enterprises, political developments, methods of communication make atlases out of date overnight.

Concern about the value of excessive fact-gathering, and of the related lack of depth in geographical studies, has led to the suggestion of alternative schemes of approach in recent years. Within these, simulations and games may have an important part to play in helping to recast ideas about teaching school geography.

To understand the situation more usefully, however, it is desirable to look more closely at the development of geography as a modern academic subject. In doing this it is possible to see how changes in thought and approach have had their inevitable linked influence on what is taught in many school classrooms.

The development of regional geography

Geography became a regularly accepted school subject (in other than rudimentary form) by the turn of the nineteenth century in Britain. Among those prominent in the founding and development of the Geographical Association, the body which caters especially for the teaching of the subject, were A. J. Herbertson (1865–1915) and H. J. Mackinder (1861–1947), both scholars and leaders of great influence.

They were active at a time when 'classical' geography had begun to expose its shortcomings. The writings of men such as Alexander von Humboldt (1769–1859) and Carl Ritter (1779–1859) had done much to bring a methodology to what was previously little more than 'travellers' tales'. They had sought to give coherence to gathered material by delving into cause and effect and by postulating 'laws of general application'. But the weakness of the method was its use of the analogies of physical science in problems of social study; and it gave some of the conclusions reached an unreal and almost metaphysical stamp against which there was eventual reaction.

Such reaction took place in several ways. One of these was notably influenced by a famous paper of Herbertson's on 'The Major Natural

Regions of the World'[2] which formed the framework for many later textbooks. In this, the canvas was world-wide, but the aim of the paper was to seek criteria for spatial differences; Herbertson used climate as a dominant factor in his delimitation of natural regions, but also drew on vegetational and structural differences. Mackinder also urged the 'treatment by regions [as] a more thorough test of the logic of the geographic argument' and his 'Britain and the British Seas'[3] was an important example of this approach. Other powerful exponents of the world natural region were to be J. F. Unstead and E. G. R. Taylor, both significantly influential as writers of school texts in the following years.[4]

In France, roughly coincident with this, the work of Paul Vidal de la Blache[5] (1845–1918) was being widely read. Vidal saw people and environment linked inseparably and sought to study confined areas of his own country as a complete unit. To him landscape was both physical and cultural and made best sense when studied closely in small areas. Each of these areas, said Vidal, had a life-style of its own, adapted to its distinctive local setting.

This regional emphasis in macro-scale and micro-scale structured almost all the chapters of school textbooks in human geography in the first part of the twentieth century. Syllabuses were devised in regional rather than systematic style; description given in regional survey; the art of regional synthesis seen as a culminating end-product to most geographical work.

Some trenchant criticisms of this approach were made by G. H. Kimble in 1951[6] and following this others have expressed reservations also. One recent critic, E. H. Wrigley, wrote, concerning the regional approach, that

> What we have seen is a concept overtaken by the course of historical change. 'Regional' geography in the great mould has been as much a victim of the Industrial Revolution as the peasant, landed society, the horse, and the village community, and for the same reason.[7]

Wrigley refers to the fact that, as Vidal himself recognized, distinctive regions were disappearing before his eyes as he wrote. As personal and economic mobility increased, local independence and distinctiveness began to disappear.

Today, for example, the Weald becomes increasingly unrealistic as a regional unity divorced from London, with places such as Ashford an hour's train journey from the centre of the metropolis. Wooldridge's distinctive physical region will be replaced by Peter Hall's prophetic concept of 'London 2000' with commuters living on the Sussex coast.[8] (And can even London be seen only in this regional view? Channel

Tunnel and Common Market may make Ashford a suburb of *Paris* by 1990.) The more useful world view today is not the one of idiographic regions but of the 'global village'. Though the region will no doubt remain a means of classification in geographical method, it is clearly true that regional synthesis and description is becoming less fruitful as an end. A return to systematic emphases in human geography, and to a search for similarities and generalities can now be made with sharper tools than those of the 'classical' school. The rigorous investigational procedures of the newer social sciences, particularly sociology and psychology, have given geographers fresh approaches to the investigation of spatial phenomena.

School geography, however, as yet remains heavily under the regional influence. Following reaction against formal regional study in some universities there are signs of change, but this current academic tide is by no means the only reason to hope for a shift in emphasis.

Another reason relates to the way in which regional study has become uninspiring in schools. When the masters of the art developed regional syntheses, they were usually sensitive and artistic pieces of writing in which the eye of the geographer and the skill of the elegant prose stylist fitted together. Some school textbooks echoed this skill.

Pupils required to learn the material at secondhand, however, frequently lost the distilled flavour of the original in a homemade brew of staccato notes penned hopefully and exclusively for the sake of examinations. They took from the books, not the qualities of reasoning and deduction that had gone into the original, but only a catalogue of memorized facts. They lost the imaginative 'feel' and spirit of an area which Vidal and his contemporaries importantly retained and saw the material only in gazeteer terms. The well written regional essay is a difficult art to any but the specialist; tried secondhand in many twentieth-century classrooms it has been frequently reduced to uninspired and dimly understood cliché.

The legacy of determinism

Darwin's *Origin of Species* was one of the most important works of the nineteenth century and much influenced geographers of the later 'classical' period. If animals were seen to adapt and evolve through a close relationship with their environment it seemed fruitful to pursue a similar line of inquiry in relation to human activity and organization. Thus arose a focus of interest which eventually led to what is usually known as 'determinism'—the idea that the earth conditioned man's ends and that his activity was consciously or otherwise always in debt to the environment in which he lived. This idea was most persuasively extended through the writings of Ellen Semple (1863–1932) and Ellsworth Huntington (1876–1947) and the school textbooks of Griffith Taylor (1880–1963) also had great influence in developing these ideas.[9] This view of the world became difficult to reconcile with man's increasing power over his physical surroundings through the advance of technology; and it later transmuted into 'possibilism', a more refined view of the man-land relationship in which, as the name indicates, various alternatives of action for man were considered possible, although environmental influence still postulated as final.

The 'determinist/possibilist' approach was an accepted one in geography for the early part of this century, and still has its defendants and its disciples.[10] But it has been lately challenged on two counts. Some geographers [and notably Peter Haggett in a remarkable book called *Locational Analysis in Human Geography*[11]] see geography in terms of a purer form of spatial analysis in which the man–land relationship is often important but not prime. The geometrical base of the subject is emphasized and mathematical styles of analysis used with intensity. Much of the current debate about quantification in geography has sprung up because of the vigorous and unusual work done by workers following this approach.

A second challenge comes from those who can, perhaps, be called 'behaviourists'. They would argue that man indeed responds to an environment but it is the environment which he *perceives*, one which can be radically different from that which actually *exists*. They would also suggest that man does not necessarily behave rationally, choosing the 'best' sites or routeways, for instance, but more often finds one satisfactory solution out of several and is content with it. In Simon's terms,[12] he is a '*satisficer*' rather than an '*optimizer*'. To know more about human geography, therefore, we basically need to know more about human behaviour and then to observe the spatial consequences of it.

Current work which emphasizes the transformation of orthodox maps[13] is in line with this kind of thinking; discussion about whether field work is the ultimate in 'real' geography also stems from increased concern about the nature of relevant perception. Perhaps most fundamentally some of McLuhan's ideas about the multiplicity of environments which surround modern man illustrate the behaviourist view. (The Battle of Waterloo being won on the playing fields of Eton is a spatial metaphor which we have long accepted; the battles of Vietnam being fought in American living-rooms through television updates the metaphor and reveals its power in actually *affecting* subsequent political decisions.)

A simple example may help to emphasize the fact that mental maps of the environment (even mistaken ones) are possibly crucial to spatial activity and distribution. A man sets out to drive from Birmingham to Brighton. Based on his previous knowledge he decides to take a route through London via Waterloo Bridge. By looking at a map it might be possible to prove that this is not the *shortest* route; by the experience of others it might be possible to demonstrate that a *quicker* route time would be made by avoiding London altogether. Such information is irrelevant if the driver is happy with his own perception of the situation. He drives down the M1 into London instead and phlegmatically becomes another statistic in an Oxford Street traffic jam.

Determinism's legacy to the classroom is still apparent in the test questions that seek for specifically 'geographical' factors to explain factory location or growth of crops. The tradition has also led to a tendency to over-simplify causal relationships where they do exist. Thus statements such as 'rubber grows in tropical forest regions *because of* high temperature and humidity' appear in textbooks and gently distort the complexity of the truth. They inevitably lead pupils into superficial comments about the environment. Explanations at this level of reasoning have led other sciences to look askance at the discipline of the geographer; a subsequent result has been an uncomfortable academic isolation and a related withdrawal in some cases from practical environmental issues.[14]

The shortcomings of old style determinism are generally recognized today. Its simplicity may be a helpful introduction to the environment for the very young child, but it is essential to go beyond it at a later stage of education. The alternative is not simply to hedge every explanation; but perhaps to find other approaches to the methodology of the subject. And here, both the geometrical and behaviourist interpretations of the subject may yet be seen to have significance to a wide constituency, beyond their present strengths in research fields.

New developments in geography teaching

The ebb tide of regional synthesis and determinism leaves behind some interesting clues for the geographical beachcomber. One of these is the possible introduction of the ideas of *general systems theory* and *analysis* into the subject. This sees the environment as a web of inter-related systems in which change in any one part automatically causes repercussions in the others. It would need considerable space to try to explain the principles of systems analysis here, but it is a language already well-used and understood in other adjacent disciplines to geography, and it therefore has integrating possibilities, some of which are immediately appropriate ones.

Systems analysis investigates organically rather than mechanistically, and therefore frequently makes use of models (theoretical and practical) to simulate the systems under scrutiny. In the geographical sphere it would be possible to do this to such diverse topics as the world economy, the weather, an individual business enterprise, a national transport network or (more familiarly) the erosion cycle.[15]

To see the world in these terms is usually a step away from the closed description of the regional 'package'. There have been theoretical models in geography before this (notably the Davisian one of landscape formation) but the idea of serious and extended study of them—particularly in human geography—is fresh to many classrooms. Chorley and Haggett, in a key volume recently developing the view in an extensive range of areas,[16] noted the importance of models for the subject. They identified the characteristics of models as *selective* (in terms of essential information identified for study), *structured* (in the sense that aspects of the web of reality are exploited in terms of their connections), and *suggestive* (in throwing up ideas for further study).

Models are based on the hypotheses that the model-builders themselves make about the environment; but the observation of their working may encourage the alteration or extension of such hypotheses. They are, in fact, linked to the 'behaviourist' outlook in this way. Curry emphasized this point in another book of similar contributions which are mostly American:

> Methods of representing various phenomena of nature, and speculation about their inter-relationships are closely tied together. It is too often forgotten that geographic studies are not studies of the real world, but rather, perceptions passed through the double-filter of the author's mind and his available tools of argument and representation. We cannot know reality; we can only have an abstract picture of aspects of it. All our descriptions of relation or process are theories—or, when formalized, better called models. Thus explicit model building . . . is no innovation, but rather a frank recognition of human frailty.[17]

Chorley and Haggett went on to enumerate the functions of models in geography and suggested that they were . . .

(a) psychologically helpful 'in enabling some group of phenomena to be visualized and comprehended which could otherwise not be because of its magnitude or complexity';

(b) acquisitively helpful in providing a 'framework wherein information may be defined, collected and ordered';

(c) organizational in respect of data, with a fertility which allowed the maximum amount of information to be squeezed out of them;

(d) logical in helping to explain how particular phenomena happened;
(e) systematic in viewing reality in terms of 'interlocking systems';
(f) constructionally helpful in forming stepping stones to the building of theories and laws;
(g) cognitive in promoting the communication of scientific ideas.[18]

Even if only a proportion of these claims is justified, it would seem that models have considerable significance in promoting the kind of geographic understanding mentioned in the second paragraph of this chapter. Translated to the classroom, models are usually best studied by observation 'from within'. That is to say, rather than have them explained by the teacher or the lecturer, it is helpful for classes to operate models themselves in order to discover interactions; to 'pull the strings' to see how things work and to experience some part of the process, if that is at all possible. Within this context, model theories are often called simulations or games, and these terms will be used with this intention in the rest of this chapter.

The introduction of simulations to the classroom is, in some cases, not only a shift in subject matter, but also a radical change in class organization. Classes nourished on the informational bias of geography may be well accustomed to the relatively passive role of note-taking and fact-learning. Even when aural and visual variety has been provided, with slides, films, and tapes, there is not necessarily frequent opportunity for active class involvement in lessons. The use of simulations, however, not only encourages but requires individual and group participation in many cases; and the examples which follow in the second part of this chapter indicate this. In most cases the teacher's role is that of manager and coach, rather than of judge or fountain-head; here simulations are in accord with more general educational ideas which suggest that roles and relationships in 'old style' classrooms are in need of change. (Indeed, in the current fast-changing world, the geography teacher who poses as 'expert' is indeed brave, in any case.)

In primary schools, there is already a body of experience and literature to testify to the success of such changes. Where children have been encouraged to leave their desks for work in purposeful group activity, to have discussion with their fellows during lessons, and to work at individual projects as their own interests and endeavour have led them, there have been many rewards. Writing of one such research project in 1966, D. E. M. Gardner[19] pointed out that

the greater opportunities in 'experimental' schools for children to exchange ideas and participate in discussion appears to have had a very favourable effect on their power over language . . . and in such tests as concentration, listening and remembering, neatness and care, the 'experimental' children have not been found inferior—indeed on the whole they have done better.

Some of the same developments are apparent in higher and further education. The April 1968 conference on 'Innovation and Experiment in University Teaching Methods' was significant in this respect, and here the use of simulation exercises was prominently reported. Within secondary schools there has also been experiment, despite the conflicting pressures of examination work, though here the pace has been slower.

Geographers, in particular, may find the value of simulation approaches a timely piece of assistance. The information available for factual learning is now in such profusion that it is almost an embarrassment; and, unless data banks can be instituted and made readily accessible, it threatens to overwhelm those who seek to remain abreast of it. On the other hand, one finds increasing dissatisfaction from discerning pupils who find that even post-determinist geography does not explain to any real depth some of the vital missing unknowns in any man–land equation. To meet both these needs, the development of models and simulations in the classroom may be a way forward. In offering a revitalization and a reorientation to the academic core of geography in schools, it also relates more generally to fundamental changes taking place in the modern classroom.

A sample set of existing simulations

It would be an unrewarding, if not an impossible task even to note the wide variety of geographical simulations known to exist, let alone to describe them. No brief list could be comprehensive, and no description would convey an adequate flavour of the original. Many teachers will have created, adapted and borrowed for their own individual purposes. They will still be evaluating and redesigning their own work, but since literature on the subject is not at present extensive, many of these ideas will be little known. There is a certain amount of knowledge available, however, about some simulations tested with success, and these, whilst not being perfect or complete models in any sense, have provided useful comparisons and guides for others who wish to work with similar ideas. It may be most useful to choose a normal geographic topic—urban geography—and briefly write of a group of simulations connected with the topic in order to demonstrate the wide variations of style and level which the method encompasses. The six sets of simulations described below have varying origins but are part of the same methodological approach. They include:

(a) A simple exercise in which individuals simulate decisions made about TOWN SITING
(b) Some more elaborate projects in which groups co-operatively simulate decisions concerning the process of TOWN GROWTH
(c) A complex project in which groups simulate decisions concerning the PATTERNS OF LAND USE in a town
(d) Some straightforward operational games in which participants simulate decisions relating to aspects of URBAN ROUTES AND TRANSPORTATION
(e) A model introducing ideas of probability in simulating PATTERNS OF SETTLEMENT DEVELOPMENT
(f) A role playing exercise for a large group in which participants simulate the attitudes of people involved in PROBLEMS OF PLANNING.

A simulation concerning the siting of towns Trying to discover the reasons for settlement sites is an important aspect of human geography. Textbooks often give brief and apparently definitive statements about this, usually in relation to the physical landscape, i.e., town X is a gap-town, village Y is a spring-line settlement, and so on.

The American High School Geography Project[20] (set up in 1961 to improve the content of United States school geography courses and to devise instructional material for new courses) approached urban geography in a systematic way through two 'Units', and in one of these, written by Arthur and Judith Getis,[21] the first activity suggested was an elementary simulation approach to town siting.

The exercise in Fig. 3.1 puts pupils in the position of deciding about town sites at certain stages in time. It can be done individually in exercise books, or discussed as a class problem. Given a United States context in 1800, would it be wise to venture as far inland as site D? Does not site A control the likely routeways most effectively? Would not site C be the most suitable from the defensive point of view? Such simplified reasoning might well draw out some of the physical factors whose presence influenced the selection of town sites at this period, without finding a 'best' one. The physical features may influence but not exclusively determine choice of sites; the 'behavioural element' of the pupil's own decision is built into the problem and may emerge in the discussion. The most-favoured site may not be the most obviously logical. The exercise further points to the differences that time makes in such a decision. The advent of railways and highways alter the factors and can transform site possibilities. In the final square the pupil is invited to draw in his own background before reaching a decision.

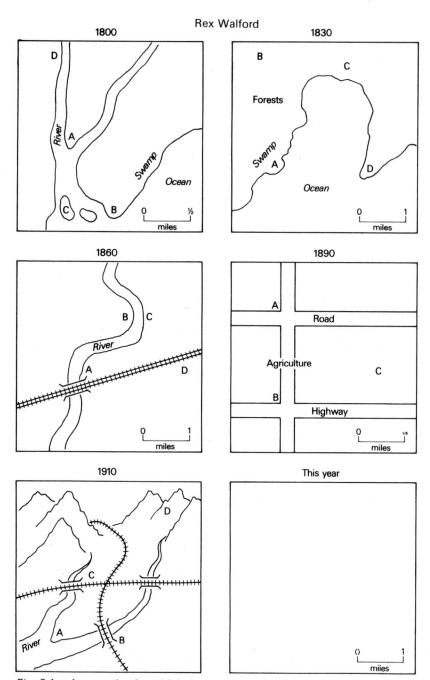

Fig. 3.1   An exercise from Unit 1 of the American High School Geography Project. Pupils are asked to select the letter representing the site at which a settlement is most likely to develop in the year indicated

48

In this urban unit, a consideration of whether the Jamestown settlers made a wise choice of site follows; pupils are asked to enumerate the advantages and disadvantages of the site. Thus, from such exercises it is hoped that pupils emerge not with knowledge about why a particular town was sited but with a clearer grasp of the principles underlying the decision to put it there. This may seem an almost elementary step forward, but it is one not always apparent from some older textbooks. The possibilities of this kind of exercise have been fruitfully explored in J. A. Everson and B. P. FitzGerald's *Settlement Geography* (chapter 2); the book also uses many other simulation ideas in setting out practical classroom work.[22]

A simulation concerning town growth   The American High School Project also stimulated a simulation idea on town growth, known as the 'Portsville' model. In this, pupils were given a kind of constructional kit (resembling 'Lego' bricks) and invited to work in co-operation with each other in planning and building a city from a given physical base and an identified core settlement. Pupils discussed issues and the consequences of decisions among themselves as they became town builders. Portsville was designed with the grid-iron rectangular block pattern of American cities in mind, and an adaptation of it for British use was first made by Dr M. A. Morgan at Bristol University. His 'Micropolis' model was later simplified for classroom use by Everson and FitzGerald and has now been used, with variations, in a good number of secondary school classrooms.

These town building simulations are based on boards measuring each about 24 in. × 24 in. A number of them can be provided so that groups of five or six pupils can work at each board in a large classroom. Each group is provided with sets of cheap adhesive plastic material which can be cut out easily and stuck to the hardboard in any shape. Different colours of the material are used for housing, factories, shops, etc., and strips of white, blue and black for roads, rivers and canals, and railways respectively. Pupils are also provided with data sheets which give guidance about the amount of development that might be expected in a typical English market and industrial town in the periods 1800–1850, 1850–1900, 1900–1960, including the rise in population and the birth of new industries. The space that such development would need is also indicated. For instance, on one data sheet of this kind of simulation, the following information is provided:

Map board scale = 12 in. to 1 mile. 1 sq. in. = 4·5 acres. 1 sq. cm. = 0·75 acres.

Victorian terrace housing = 0·5 cm. deep, 10 houses per 1 cm.
Victorian villas = 0·75 cm. deep, 4 houses per 1 cm.
Victorian local school = 1 cm. × 1 cm.
Gas works = 8 cm. × 5 cm.
(This is a sample, and is not the complete information that would be available.)

Armed with this guide to size, pupils simulate, for instance, the growth of the population from 2,500 to 6,000 in the period 1800–1850. They have lists of factories likely to develop, together with estimates of numbers of employees. Some factories cease to be productive later and derelict land results. A railway and a canal are programmed also. The groups work at the boards, placing houses, shops, factories, and roads as they think most realistic, following discussion among themselves. In order to speed the spatial development of the town it is often decided to divide functions among the group, so that one acts as house builder, another as developer of communications and so on. Early decisions cast the die for many later ones. The placing of the first industries may shape the subsequent growth of the industrial area of the town, influence the pattern of railways and roads, and the eventual shape of the total settlement. Certain concentrations of housing may generate bypass roads, new shopping centres and further community provision. The teacher discusses and highlights the needs and problems of each simulated town in consultation with pupils as they work at the boards.

Usually, after five or six periods, the simulation is completed and boards are looked at by the whole class. If five or six have been used it is most unlikely that any two will look the same. They represent alternative possibilities within a range of spatial choices and yield no 'right answer'. Most importantly, they give insight into the processes of growth in contrast to observation of it as a finished event. They also emphasize that it is *people* who take decisions about town growth, taking many perceived and unconscious considerations into account as they do so.

A simulation concerning patterns of land use   Simulations have already become standard tools in some areas of job training and research.[23] One group of people who find them helpful are planners, anxious to see the effects of large-scale projected developments, and thus several advanced simulations concerned with land use patterns have emanated from university town planning departments and from Government research establishments. Three influential examples have been American; POGE (the Planning Operational Gaming Experiment), devised for the North Carolina Chapter of the American Institute of Planners (1960); METROPOLIS, a community development game designed by R. D.

Duke (1964); and CLUG (the Community Land Use Game) developed at Cornell University by Allan Feldt (1965).[24] Each of these simulations includes the representation of developers, local community interests, and planners in a situation where they interact; the context is naturally an American one, however. One simplified version of these approaches to suit English conditions has been made by J. L. Taylor and R. N. Maddison.[25] Their LUGS (Land Use Gaming Simulation) is used in first year undergraduate courses and has also been played with success in school sixth forms.

In this game a board of one hundred two inch squares is used to represent plots of forty acres each. Between each plot is a half inch space to indicate the presence of road, gas, sewerage, and electricity links, and to note any zoning restrictions which may be placed on the plot as the game proceeds. Players (in groups of two to five) represent teams of entrepreneurs, the local authority (which administrates the game) and professional planners. The game is played in about twelve periods, each period of about half an hour representing a two-year cycle of actual time. Transactions within each period are in money terms, and each team of entrepreneurs begins with 'initial assets' (in units of £1,000) and possibly some 'operating assets'. The team of planners prepare a development plan for the board, and this is subject to general community approval with the local authority having a casting vote on proposals. Following this, within each period there are 'community discussions and decisions' about the construction of communication links, public building units, open spaces, and transport facilities; all of these add to the total rates assessment of the model town. Then comes a session in which the local authority determines the cost to teams of chance gales, fires, or floods; it is followed by auctioning publicly or privately owned plots of land. Then follows a session in which teams can construct different types of building on land that they own, and calculate resultant income. A calculation of rates assessment and of net balance conclude the stages to each round. Teams are aiming to run financially successful enterprises and at the same time participate in community decision making.

The simulation bears at least a superficial resemblance to the MONOPOLY board game, although it is much more complex and realistic in its treatment of property development. It includes, of course, a spatial context in the way that MONOPOLY does not, and can also be extended to include roles played by 'the public' and 'elected politicians'. It is designed to bring out some of the tensions between private speculation and community development and its originators report that it is able to arouse and sustain a high degree of interest and enthusiasm. 'During operating sessions no judgement on the students' performance

51

is needed since shortcomings are largely self-evident. The instructor has simply to stand aside and allow the participant to look upon the effects of his own behaviour.' With over 100 hours of 'operating time' behind it, LUGS now commands a regular place in some student planning courses. Its originators stress, however, that it needs careful briefing and de-briefing sessions for its full value as a simulation to be exploited.

Some simulations concerning urban interaction The development of the operational game at a simple level also has many uses in the classroom. Players working either as individuals or in groups can simulate some of the types of urban activity in which competition against others or against a set target is inherent. The author has had experience of several games designed to illuminate urban routing and transport situations and two are briefly outlined below.[26]

In the simulation of SHOPPING, participants are confronted with a board (which can be simply mapped out on paper or card) of a shopping centre. The centre can be an invented one, a local one faithfully reproduced, or a combination of these two. An example is given in Fig. 3.2.

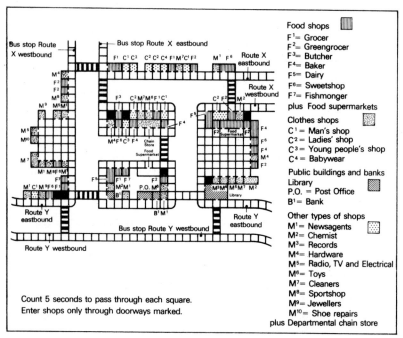

Fig. 3.2   Map for SHOPPING game (from R. Walford: *Games in Geography.* Longmans)

Types of shops are marked on the map, and the surrounding pavement divided into grid squares. The map shows up the 'adjacency propensities' of certain types of shops which thus give rise to certain 'quarters' of the centre in which, perhaps, clothing or antique shops may be important. Groups who are participating in the simulation are then given a 'shopping list' and asked to devise an efficient route around the shopping centre in completing it. They are assumed to take five seconds in passing through each square and to cross roads only by zebra crossings (fifteen seconds). Possible delays can be encountered (simulated by dice throw) in supermarkets or department stores, although these offer the opportunity of buying more than one kind of purchase at a time. Shoppers must begin at a designated bus stop and return to a stop on the same route on the opposite side of the road. Participants usually take some time to discuss and plot their route. If the map has been drawn on a blackboard the simulation can be operated quite satisfactorily in the classroom by each group coming to the board in turn and marking the route, one purchase at a time. At the end of five or six rounds groups should have completed their purchases and their total time can be calculated.

The simulation is an elementary approach to route efficiency concepts, but its relation to *reality* is also an important discussion area. Have groups used the most efficient routes? How much more time could they have saved by better planning? Do housewives shop with the same route efficiency—and if not, why not? Further elaborations towards reality are included in the game description, to be used if required. A final response to the simulation might be to go to the local shopping centre to observe patterns there, already armed with particular notions and expectations about how pedestrians plan their routes. Such hypotheses can then be tested, reinforced or rejected.

A similar kind of board game, which can be played either by whole classes or small groups, is concerned with COMMUTING. Here the board represents a set of alternative routes from a suburban house to an office in the city centre. The routes include various methods of transport, and have possible delay factors written into them. The idea of the simulation is to see the 'journey to work' in terms of a game situation; recognizing that for many commuters the aim is to leave home as late as possible without being late into the office! Participants compete against a target—their own estimate of journey time. Rash commuters may chance delays and leave late; cautious ones leave early. The game progresses in rounds made up of ten-minute stages, and each commuter charts his progress during that time with a marker. Trains may be late, traffic jams may occur, buses may be withdrawn; the possibility of changing routes and trying even to thumb a lift is written in as a desperate last gamble! If the game seems entirely frivolous, one can only point out that it was based exclusively on the real life adventures of one London commuter who spent many weeks experimenting with different routes and timings in an endeavour to 'beat the traffic'. The game may at least open up some of the problems of urban traffic systems in a practical way, and can be easily adapted to simulate an environment in the immediate knowledge of those who play it.

Simulations concerning the distribution of towns Suggesting, in 1951, that 'an element of determinism remains inevitable in geography', Wooldridge and East in their valuable and wide-ranging book *The Spirit and Purpose of Geography* wrote these words. 'If, in a geographical context, we are asked to *describe and account for* the distribution of population in Sweden, our *accounting for* cannot and will not include the myriad individual decisions which entered, unrecorded and un-explained, into the making of the settlement pattern'.[27] Only twelve years later, armed with a probability model, R. L. Morrill coincidentally wrote a now often-quoted paper[28] in which he surveyed the same geographical area with exactly these thoughts in mind. His simulation model could not explain each individual decision, but could make some calculation concerning the probability of its logic, and the factors that it would take into account. He was using a technique known as 'Monte Carlo' simulation, perhaps best explained briefly by recourse to the simple diagram in Fig. 3.3.

Diagram (a) shows a grading of areas on the map into levels of attrac-tiveness. It is postulated that the chances of District I being chosen for settlement are twice those of District II and three times that of District III. Thus in diagram (b) this attractiveness is stated numerically in terms of 'how many chances in a hundred' each grid square has of settlement. In Diagram (c) this is further translated by giving each square a particular value in the 1–99 scale, dependent on its probability value in Diagram B. Diagram (d) shows a simulated distribution, assuming that eight settle-ments are likely to occur in a particular period. The eight locations were selected by looking up a random numbers table and taking the first eight two-figure numbers. Thus each square on the map had a 'chance' of receiving settlement; some had more chances than others. Environ-mental attractiveness and chance decision both played a part in the selection of settlement locations.

This simple illustration can serve only as an introduction to Morrill's sophisticated model, which it would be impossible to describe adequately here. He worked on the assumption of 24,025 possible migration paths for each period of time in which he was working; and he was simulating

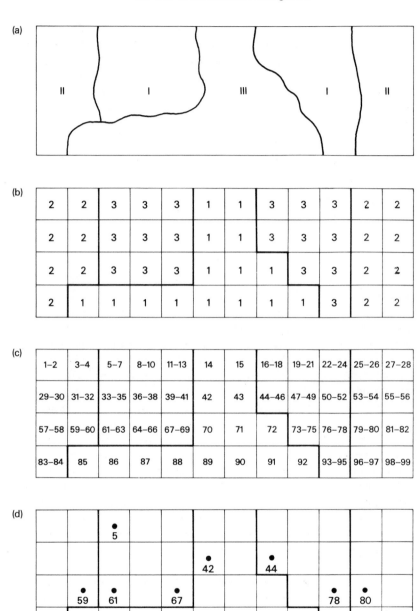

(a)

(b)

(c)

(d)

Fig. 3.3 Hypothetical probability matrix for the allocation of eight settlements in relation to three environmental classes, I, II, III (Chorley and Haggett: *Frontiers in Geographical Teaching*. Methuen)

the development of Swedish settlement in twenty-year periods from 1800 to 1980. His calculations were inevitably done by computer. The complexity of the actual mechanics of the model derived from something similar to the simple illustration in Fig. 3.3, however. His starting point was the population pattern of an area in southern Sweden in 1800. He first assigned the likely development of transport links in a manner like that of the model, using a pattern of probabilities combined with random number choice. He then assigned manufacturing activities with a different set of probabilities which he had worked out, and thirdly central-place (market) activities. Armed then with a much transformed map of the environment, he again assigned probabilities to existing settlements, this time in relation to the likelihood of their receiving migrants. (He took into account the distance between origin and possible destinations, the attractiveness of areas in themselves, and the likelihood of information being known about a place in his calculations here.) Then, having used the random number tables again he assigned migrants to areas according to the number known to have moved during the twenty-year period.

At the end of his work Morrill could report that 'the model can be considered realistic from the point of view of distribution and from the point of view of process'. He later used the technique with significant success in analysing the development of immigrant ghettos in large cities.[29] Others have used it to predict possible developments in the areal growth of cities.[30]

Morrill's original simulation is noted here in order to show the possible complexity of simulation techniques. Other much simpler 'Monte Carlo' simulations have been used at school level, however, to combine environmental factors with the hazards of chance, and have demonstrated evolution and diffusion with considerable success. Such exercises can reasonably be undertaken by individuals or groups, and modified and developed by them in searching for the explanation of patterns in the environment of many kinds. By letting them run on past the time of the present pattern, they can, as in Morrill's work contain a valuable predictive element which modern geography finds useful.

A simulation concerning town planning Some simulations have a minimum of rules and prescribed operations but give extensive chance for the exploration of particular attitudes and ideas. One kind of simulation in this field (worked out with several variations) is that in which pupils in a group are assigned roles to play and asked to take certain decisions in the light of these, at a Town Council meeting, Government Inquiry, or Planning Board. In this case the simulation is based on the provision of factual data and background material and brief biographies of the participants are spelled out. Thus participants (usually more senior pupils) consciously assume roles such as Town Clerk or Chairman of a Preservation Society and act them out, rather than relying on their own hunches.

In higher education, these simulations can be evolved in quite elaborate forms. T. T. Paterson, describing a simulation evolved at the University of Strathclyde concerning the 1966 seamen's strike, sought a group of twenty-four students to represent seamen and employers. The students were given a preliminary exercise to bring out their own presuppositions and attitudes and also were tested on the Eysenck Scale of Values. The combination of these two indicators was taken into account in the initial assignment of roles (e.g., four members of the group who had already assumed union roles in the preliminary exercise were found to have value systems that were both 'radical' and 'tough-minded' on the Eysenck scale; they were assigned to Trotskyite roles. . .).

The Strathclyde example took weeks of preparation and days of actual play; the role play need not be as elaborate as this, however. The author recently participated in one which was satisfactorily completed in an hour, although preparatory printing and reading of documents had been done before this.

The simulation in question was one of a Planning Committee of a Borough Council. Participants were assigned the roles of various Council departments, elected Councillors, and some specialist co-opted members. Others who did not wish to be fully involved were satisfied to observe as 'public gallery'. Each department and Councillor was given a role biography and some data concerning two major decisions to be taken at the meeting. A small group of enthusiasts, assigned to the role of Planning Department, did preliminary work and prepared plans for discussion. The two major topics on the agenda were the possible development of a piece of land adjoining 'Green Belt' countryside, and the proposed renewal of the Borough's historic but over-crowded town centre. One raised the tension between town and countryside in relation to 'in-filling'; the other raised the issues of justifiable finance and preservation/modernization in relation to central areas. The participants argued hotly for the duration of the meeting with a variety of maps and statistical data as ammunition. The Planning Officer displayed visionary sketches of pedestrian precincts, separated traffic systems and multi-storey car-parks. Others spoke eloquently for the preservation of the past. Eventually, votes were taken on the two issues. Some members changed sides not once but two or three times as debate continued. It demonstrated neatly that human persuasions and prejudices were often bound up with 'geographical' factors in the making of similar real life decisions.

57

These six simulations range from the relatively unstructured Planning Meeting to the precise statistical calculations of the Monte Carlo style simulation; from the complexity of LUGS to the simplicity of operational games like SHOPPING, from co-operational practical projects like PORTSVILLE to the individual exercise (done in a textbook) like TOWN SITING. Their common link is the seeking of insights into the decision-making processes that affect the pattern of the landscape. Though urban simulations have been exemplified here, similar families could be found for agricultural, social, industrial or international aspects of geography.

Devising simulations

There are many cases where a simulation can be best devised individually by the teacher who requires it. Existing simulations may have their use, however, when dealing with general topics. There is probably little distinctive in the geographical field concerning the techniques of building and adapting simulations, but it may be worth noting that the building process for geographical simulations seems to fall generally into four major phases:

(a) The identification of the concept or process which it is desired to illuminate—an essential first task.
(b) Considerations about the general nature of the simulation—should it have rules or be unstructured? Should it be a practical 'kit' or a theoretical exercise controlled by the teacher? Etc.
(c) Construction of the rule framework of the game. Participants should be identified, their ultimate objectives specified, and the methods of interaction in each round of play worked out.
(d) Comparison of the finished simulation with the reality which it is desired to illuminate. If this is not satisfactory, the simulation should be re-designed or scrapped.

The process of building is itself a valuable educational tool since it lays bare the principles involved in the system under scrutiny. For some senior pupils in schools, involvement in simulation construction may be more valuable than actual participation. Similarly, the simplification of a complex model may also help to reveal what is basic to a particular process. Here, older pupils may again help in preparing and managing simulations for younger age groups.

The context of simulations

Chorley and Haggett suggest that 'most geographical model builders would judge the value of a model almost entirely in terms of its re-applicability to the real world',[31] but they also acknowledge Black's comment that 'there is no such thing as a perfectly faithful model; only by being unfaithful in some respect can a model represent its original'.[32] This draws attention to the importance of integrating simulation work into more orthodox teaching work in the classroom, rather than leaving it as an exotic excursion divorced from all else.

In order that links can be securely made with the situations and systems which are the subject of simulations, 'briefing' and 'de-briefing' sessions are needed. Such sessions not only help in preparation and explanation, and in examining the structure of the simulation in retrospect; they consider the causes and consequences of decisions taken during the simulation, and also link the work with expository material from textbooks. They generally help to increase interest in the topic from other angles. For example, in the town growth simulation mentioned above (b), the simulation might well have been prefaced by some reading and discussion about town growth in general, and the local town in particular. If work had been done in history on the consequences of the Industrial Revolution this might be recalled and related to the topic. If participants begin with some previous knowledge, their own decision making will be better informed, at least at a basic notional level.

After the completion of the simulation, the patterns on boards would probably be compared and their genesis explained by their creators. Particular key decisions would be pointed out by the teacher, and perhaps the presuppositions of certain groups examined. Then might follow an examination of some actual town maps and an attempt to discover patterns of growth from completed maps. The need for briefing and de-briefing may seem to further emphasize the need for extensive time to be given to simulation work. It also crystallizes, however, the aim of seeing selected systems and concepts in depth.

Simulations and the development of the curriculum

The extended use of simulation techniques is, inevitably, at some variance with the present demands of many geography syllabuses. Where there is a need to cover all the major continents of the world in a five-year course, the chance to linger for five or six lessons on one topic or small area is restricted. Though some teachers have been able to try out simulations of the kind described earlier in this chapter, such experiments are usually only interludes in the regular rapid coverage of regional geography. There have been indications in recent years that the shape of some syllabuses may be changing in response to new tides of educational thought. The opportunity given to teachers by C.S.E. Mode 3 has yet to be fully realized, perhaps because of the daunting thought not only of syllabus preparation, but of syllabus justification before a Regional Board. In geography, the notable example of the Oxford and Cambridge Board 'A' level syllabus is now being paralleled by several other boards who are allowing more scope to candidates in their choice and approach to questions, and are encouraging more thorough coverage of a selective range of topics. More fundamentally, there is thinking abroad on the restructuring of the curriculum in general. J. S. Bruner's concept of the spiral curriculum[33] involving a limited number of fundamental ideas taught with increasing sophistication each year may have considerable relevance to geography. At present there are extant several preliminary attempts to try and identify sets of fundamental processes and ideas.[34]

If geography syllabuses become more concept and process based they may then be able to use changing sample material, taking illustration for fundamentals from matters of current world focus and interest. Thus the subject would have a stable base but a flexible cap, with the latter able to stay relevant and up to date to meet the needs of pupils preparing for citizenship. A new syllabus might abandon formal regional or continental structure and instead work from a defined set of principles and systems.

A more rigorous training in the discipline of geographic thinking might go hand in hand with understanding in some depth of current world problems. (A third element to new syllabuses might well be the inculcation of some kind of active commitment towards the environmental quality of the surroundings for each pupil—but this is not directly relevant to this discussion.) It is possible to imagine, perhaps, migration studied in relation to the development of immigrant enclaves in towns; locational decisions studied in relation to the provision of new factories in the local area; transportation and routing studied in relation to changing patterns of trade caused by new discoveries (e.g., oil in Alaska).

This syllabus pattern might move British school geography away from its regionally based dominance but give it a more immediately relevant and deeper approach to the world. It would also give opportunity for pupils to find deeper motivation to their subject and to experience a variety of newer techniques of teaching. Among these, simulations may be of great importance. They seem to involve and encourage pupils to 'get under the skin' of decisions and events and to see spatial patterns with more perception and understanding. They offer an opportunity for geography to release itself from a somewhat prosaic general image and to move into the mainstream of sensible and progressive change in education.

The role of simulations and games

REFERENCES

1. McLuhan, M., and Fiore Q.: *War and peace in the global village.* Bantam Books, 1969.
2. Herbertson, A. J.: 'The Major Natural Regions of the World'. *Geographical Journal*, 25, 1905, pp. 300–12.
3. Mackinder, H. J.: *Britain and the British Seas*, Heinemann, 1902.
4. See, for instance: Unstead, J. F., and Taylor, E. G.: *General and Regional Geography for Students*, Philip, 6 editions 1910–20. Also note: Unstead, J. F.: 'A System of Regional Geography'. *Geography*, 18, 1933, pp. 175–87.
5. Vidal la Blache, P.: *Tableau de la Géographie de la France*, Paris, 1911, *France de l'Est*, Paris, 1917.
6. Kimble, G. H.: 'The Inadequacy of the Regional Concept'. *London Essays in Geography*, ed. L. D. Stamp and S. W. Wooldridge, chapter 9, Longmans, 1952.
   Kimble's arguments are opposed in R. Minshull, *Regional Geography*, chapter 7, Hutchinson, 1967.
7. Wrigley, E. H.: 'Changes in the Philosophy of Geography'. *Frontiers in Geographical Teaching*, eds. R. J. Chorley and P. Haggett, chapter 1, Methuen, 1965.
8. Hall, P.: *London 2000.* Especially pp. 204–9, Faber, 1963.
9. See, for instance: Semple, E.: *Influences of Geographic Environment*, Holt, 1911; Huntington, E.: *The Character of Races*, Scribner, 1927; Huntington, E.: *The Human Habitat*, Chapman and Holt, 1928; Taylor, G.: *Environment and Nation*, Toronto, 1936; Taylor, G.: *Australia,* Methuen, 7 editions up to 1951; Taylor, G.: *Canada,* Methuen, 3 editions up to 1957.
10. Martin, A. F.: *Transactions of the Institute of British Geographers*, 17, 1951, pp. 1–11.
11. Haggett, P.: *Locational Analysis in Human Geography.* E. Arnold, 1966.
12. Simon, H. A.: *Models of man.* Wiley, 1957.
13. See, for instance: Bunge, W.: *Theoretical Geography*, chapter 2, University of Lund, Sweden, 2nd edition, 1966; Hall, P.: 'Britain's Uneven Shrinkage'. *New Society*, 14 April 1966; 'After Mercator'. *Esso magazine*, Vol. XVII, No. 4, 1968.
14. *The Geographical Magazine*, August 1969, noted that no body of professional geographers had given evidence to either the Maud Commission on the reorganization of local government, or to the Edwards Commission on the future of air transport.
15. One early attempt to develop this is M. E. Eliot Hurst and R. McDaniel, *A Systems Analytic Approach to Economic Geography.* Association of American Geographers, 1968.
16. Chorley, R. J., and Haggett, P. (eds.): *Models in Geography.* Methuen, 1968. (Reproduced with permission.)
17. Curry, L. J.: 'Climatic Change as Random Series'. *Spatial Analysis*, ed. B. J. L. Berry and D. D. Marble, Prentice-Hall, 1968, pp. 184–193. Reproduced by permission from the *Annals* of the Association of American Geographers, Vol. 52, 1962.
18. Chorley, R. J., and Haggett, P.: *Models in Geography*, op. cit., p. 24.
19. Gardner, D. E. M.: *Experiment and Tradition in Primary Schools.* Methuen, 1966.

20. The American High School Geography Project. Materials available in UK from Collier-Macmillan, London, N.19.
21. Getis, A. and J.: *Geography of Cities*. Unit 1 of 'Geography in an Urban Age', A.H.S.G.P., Boulder, Colorado.
22. Everson, J. A., and FitzGerald, B. P.: *Settlement Geography*. Longmans, 1968.
23. For example: BEA use simulation techniques for management training and flight control training; experiments have been made in training police with simulated case studies; many university departments and research units report simulation use, e.g., the Symposium on Simulation Techniques in Higher Education, Birmingham, 1969.
24. POGE—Hendricks, F. H.: 'Planning Operational Gaming Experiment'. A paper presented to the North Carolina Chapter of the American Institute of Planners meeting on 'New Ideas in Planning', November 1960.
    METROPOLIS—Duke, R. D.: 'Gaming-simulation in Urban Research'. Institute for Community Development, Michigan State University, East Lansing, Michigan, 1964.
    CLUG—Feldt, A. G.: 'The Community Land Use Game'. Miscellaneous Paper No. 3, Center for Housing and Environmental Studies, Division of Urban Studies, Cornell University, New York, 1965.
25. Taylor, J. L., and Maddison, R. N.: 'A land Use Gaming Simulation'. *Urban Affairs Quarterly*, Vol. 3, No. 4, June 1968.
26. SHOPPING is fully described with rules set out in Walford, R.: *Games in geography*. Longmans, 1969.
27. East, W. G., and Wooldridge, S. W.: *The Spirit and Purpose of Geography*. Hutchinson, 1952, p. 30.
28. Morrill, R. L.: 'The Development of Spatial Distributions of Towns in Sweden; an Historical-predictive Approach'. *Annals of the Association of American Geographers*, 53, 1963, pp. 1–14.
29. Morrill, R. L.: 'The Negro Ghetto; Problems and Alternatives'. *Geographical Review*, 55, 1965, pp. 339–361.
30. Keeble, D.: 'School Teaching and Urban Geography; Some New Approaches'. *Geography*, 54, January 1969, p. 18.
31. Chorley, R. J., and Haggett, P.: *Models in Geography*, op. cit., p. 24.
32. Black, M.: *Models and Metaphors*. New York, Ithaca, p. 267.
33. Bruner, J. S.: *The process of Education*. New York, Random House, 1960; Bruner J. S.: *Towards a Theory of Instruction*. O.U.P., 1966.
34. See, for instance: Nystuen, J. D.: 'Identification of Some Fundamental Spatial Concepts'. *Spatial Analysis*, op. cit., pp. 35–41; Helburn, N.: 'The Educational Objectives of High School Geography'. *Journal of Geography*, Vol. LXVII, No. 5, May 1968.

4

Some examples of programmed non-simulation games: WFF 'N PROOF, ON-SETS, and EQUATIONS

Layman E. Allen

Educated at Washington and Jefferson College, and the Universities of Princeton, Harvard and Yale, Layman Allen has been an Instructor, Senior Fellow and later Professor at Yale Law School. Since 1966 he has been Professor of Law at the University of Michigan Law School, and Research Social Scientist at the Mental Health Research Institute.

In the instructional games field, Mr Allen is author of WFF 'N PROOF (The Game of Modern Logic), WFF (The Beginner's Game of Logic), EQUATIONS (The Game of Creative Mathematics), ON-SETS (The Game of Set Theory—with co-authors Peter Kugel and Martin Owens), The REAL Numbers Game, and QUERIES 'N THEORIES (The Science and Language Game: a Simulation of Scientific Method and Generative Grammars—with co-authors Peter Kugel and Joan Ross).

The evolution of the WFF 'N PROOF series of games can probably be best characterized as a sequence of happy accidents. A decade ago, if anyone had suggested to me as a young lawyer, just beginning a teaching career at Yale Law School, that I would be seduced into devoting so much time and attention to the use of games as instructional and therapeutic devices, I believe that my reaction would have been a dandy guffaw. But what has happened is another example of just how wrong some human beings can be—and, perhaps, just how unpredictable are others. In response to the often-posed question about how did a lawyer ever get involved in such activity, I am reminded of the apocryphal story of the *summa cum laude* Radcliffe Ph.D. who joined the oldest profession; when asked the similar question she is reported to have remarked, 'Just lucky, I guess.'

The first section will detail a chronological account of the development of the WFF 'N PROOF games. Following that, in the next section will be a more detailed description of the principal games in the WFF 'N PROOF series and suggestions for their classroom use. In the third section the purposes of the WFF 'N PROOF games will be discussed in more detail. Finally, some of the more significant properties of the games in the WFF 'N PROOF series will be considered in the concluding section.[1]

A chronological account of the evolution of the WFF 'N PROOF games

As is so often the case, there were a variety of fortuitous circumstances that kindled my interests in the potentials of games as teaching devices. Among the recollections that stand out are discussions during the 1956–1957 academic year with Richard Helgeson, then a law student at Yale. He, also, had become interested in symbolic logic and its usefulness for lawyers in dealing with certain kinds of communication problems. At the time, Helgeson and his family lived in one of the Yale Bowl Quonset huts just across the way from ours. Frequently in the wee hours of two and three in the morning I would tap on his still-lit kitchen window, and we would wind up chatting about logic problems. Invariably, that is what he would be working at at that time in the morning. I well understood the feeling of exhilaration that accompanied such efforts, being then deeply involved in the study of, and being stimulated by, logic myself. Frequently expressed at those sessions was our surprise that other law students and lawyers had not discovered the joy and usefulness of modern logic. We were even more surprised that so many of the extraordinarily bright students we happened to know, then enrolled at Yale Law School, seemed apprehensive about learning something that 'looked like' mathematics. We were certainly aware that many persons in America do not understand very much about mathematics, are not interested in it, do not like to deal with it, and given free option will avoid studying it whenever possible. I guess, however, we expected that the exceptionally intelligent Yale Law School group would be different. We attributed our impressions to attitude more than aptitude, and, as I recall, it was in this context that we talked about games involving mathematical logic as a possible way of developing more favourable attitudes towards such kinds of symbol-handling activities. We tinkered with a notion of using a big, stuffed, white rabbit with movable ears for signalling messages to nursery-school and kindergarten children about binary logic, and somehow arranging the activity in the form of a game that would be enjoyable and, hopefully, cultivate a favourable attitude toward the subject matter involved. We also considered a card game involving mathematical logic. We went as far as making a preliminary mock-up of such a game, but it really did not seem to be a very interesting one and was never finished.

A year later, I started teaching a seminar at Yale Law School on symbolic logic and law. Having done logic at Yale with exceptional teachers such as Frederic Fitch and Alan Anderson, both of whom succeed in generating a genuine enthusiasm for, as well as an understanding of, the subject, I was concerned that so many of the really astonishingly bright Yale Law School students enrolled in the course seemed to find it hard going. I remember feeling, and apparently saying often enough to well convince myself, that much of the introductory work in modern logic was simple enough for a reasonably bright twelve-year-old to be able to handle it. Fortunately, I had an opportunity to test that intuition, having been prevailed upon to teach a sixth-grade class in the New Haven Unitarian Society that year. That group of sparkling twelve-year-olds and I spent about ten minutes each Sunday morning for a term talking about and working logic problems. The results seemed clear to me: not only could they handle it, they loved it.

While this was under way, I learned from Omar Moore that he had done similar work with twelve-year-olds when he was teaching at Washington University in St Louis and that the results were also highly successful. This was about the time that Moore and Anderson[2] were beginning their now-famous work in teaching pre-nursery school children to read through activities involving an electric typewriter. The almost unbelievable success that they were experiencing in the teaching of reading, when attitude toward the activity was treated as the key variable, led me to wonder whether an approach with a similar emphasis upon attitude could induce young children to learn and like logic.

Two colleagues who were at the time working with me on a study of automatic methods of information retrieval of legal literature, Patricia James, then a graduate student in philosophy, and Robin Brooks, a graduate student in economics, were also interested in trying to teach logic to young children and expressed interest in trying to do something about it. In discussions with Fitch, Anderson, and Harold Lasswell, the three of us were encouraged to pursue these interests, and the outcome was a proposal to the Carnegie Corporation for a research project to develop materials for teaching symbolic logic to elementary school students. Lasswell was particularly helpful in bringing the proposal to the attention of John Gardner, who was then serving as president of the Carnegie Corporation, and the ALL (Accelerated Learning of Logic) Project was funded with a three-year grant from Carnegie.

The major thrust of the ALL Project was to be the development of a programme of self-instructional materials along the lines suggested by

B. F. Skinner in his then recently-published, and now classic, article on teaching machines.[3] A subsidiary objective was to be the development of a series of games to help teach logic and develop more favourable attitudes toward it. Another philosophy graduate student, William Dickoff, joined our group as we embarked on the task of developing a self-instructional programme and the games as two different approaches, hopefully complementary, for teaching logic and generating enthusiasm for it to elementary school students.

We regarded the goal of the games to be the teaching of the symbol-handling skills of logic in a competitive and entertaining atmosphere. They were to be graduated in complexity so that students of widely varying skills and abilities would be able to participate. There were seven characteristics that seemed likely to make the games we had in mind especially useful for facilitating learning:[4]

(a) Practice in logic comes as a by-product of an activity which is enjoyable in itself.

(b) Although young children enjoy these games, the more intricate ones pose a genuine challenge even for adults.

(c) In the play of the games there is no waiting time. Each player proceeds at his own pace throughout the entire time of play. The more adept player is not delayed by those who play more slowly.

(d) Everyone else in these games learns from the best player. His strategies are displayed openly so that all others may learn to adopt them. In effect, the best players act as teachers, although they are not formally assigned this role by the rules of the games.

(e) The games are so ordered that each new game is slightly more intricate than the previous one and each later game uses the skills learned in earlier games.

(f) The games emphasize individual rather than collective decision making. Each player plans and executes his own strategy independently in order to achieve specified goals.

(g) The games are flexible both in the number of persons who may play (two or more) and in the length of time for a game to be played (five minutes or more).

During the first year, the major part of our efforts was devoted to development of the self-instructional programme. We began testing at the Mary L. Tracy School in Orange, Connecticut, both the programme and the games before the initial versions of either were really in finished form. Toward the end of the spring term in 1961 the youngsters moved so fast through the programme that we were sometimes hard put to keep ahead of them. Four half-hour sessions each week were devoted to working through the self-instructional programme by a class of twenty-five sixth-grade students, and on Wednesdays the half-hour session was spent playing the versions of the games then available. In less than four weeks in what ultimately proved to be seventeen weeks of such efforts, there were clear signs that from the viewpoint of the students' attitudes, the games were much more successful than the self-instructional programme. We began to get requests from the students to spend more time on the games and less on the self-instructional programme. Then we began to get requests from the students to borrow the equipment to play the games. When these were declined on the advice of the teacher (because we then had just enough equipment to conduct the sessions in class and she was apprehensive that if it were allowed to be taken home overnight and at weekends, it might not be returned for the class sessions), the youngsters responded by building their own equipment in order to play the games outside of class. We were beginning to get the message.

The opportunity was presented at the Yale-North Haven Summer School to further test the games and programmed materials at the stage of development they had then reached. Robert Allen joined the group for that period to concentrate attention upon further development of the games. A version of the WFF 'N PROOF games emerged from those efforts and was published in 1961. His contributions to the design and ultimate completion of that version of WFF 'N PROOF were especially helpful.

The following year I had the honour and good fortune to be a Fellow at the Center for Advanced Study in the Behavioral Sciences at Stanford, California, and Brooks accompanied me there to continue work on the development of the games. Dickoff and James remained in New Haven to revise and finish the first version of the self-instructional programme, which was ultimately published as a programmed book by McGraw-Hill.[5] The first version of WFF 'N PROOF was a twenty-four game kit which I intended to spend a month or two at the Center revising and polishing. However, so many useful suggestions were made and ideas stimulated by comments and questions from the other Fellows at the Center that not very much of the original version survived. There were many useful questions of the form: 'Why don't you do it this way?' From the beginning my attitude had been that if there was some good reason for doing it some suggested way, and no off-setting disadvantage, the next time the questioner saw the game, we would be doing it that way. Of the original twenty-four games in the initial WFF 'N PROOF kit, only one was carried over to the 1962 version. The Shake-a-WFF game of the first kit was combined with twenty new and different games to comprise what is the current twenty-one game version of WFF 'N PROOF.[6]

Testing of both the games and the self-instructional programme continued as they were further developed. Public and private schools in the New Haven area in Connecticut as well as schools in both northern and southern California participated in these testing and refining efforts. As the research evolved the relative amount of time devoted to the self-instructional programme and the games shifted gradually. It started at the first school with four of the five days each week being devoted to the self-instructional programme, or four-fifths of the time. This went to two-thirds, then to a half, later to a third, and finally, the instructional programme was made entirely optional, to be consulted only whenever a player felt it was useful to him in learning better strategies for playing the games.

During the revision of the WFF 'N PROOF games at the Center in 1961–1962, the way that I viewed games and self-instructional programmes began to change. Rather than continuing to regard them as two separate and distinct approaches, it began to seem more useful to emphasize the similarities between them and regard them as variations of each other. It seemed apparent that good games are fun, and good programmed materials can teach well. Might not an attempt to combine both in a single activity prove interesting? This is the question that bent our efforts in the direction of making the games more like learning programmes, and also for that matter, the learning programmes much more like games.[7] The set of programmed materials that were ultimately incorporated in the WFF 'N PROOF instruction manual significantly differed from the initial version of programmed materials tested in exactly this respect. The new version is more game-like in depending upon the learner himself to participate in the construction of the problems that he is called upon to solve. The learning programme in the WFF 'N PROOF manual, to the best of my knowledge, is still the most extensively 'chained' type learning programme ever constructed. There are examples in that programme where a single stimulus in context is used to set off chains of as many as forty subsequent stimulus-response items.[8]

At this state in the development of the WFF 'N PROOF game it began to be apparent that the type of game that was evolving could be easily adapted to build games out of formal systems; much of logic and mathematics could be incorporated into such a game. But the interesting question is not how much of mathematics or logic is it possible to do in this way, but rather, how much is it worthwhile to do? That remains an interesting empirical question. My own feeling is that once a learner is over the motivation hurdle, once he has a positive attitude about his own capabilities in engaging in this type of symbol-handling activity, there are probably more efficient methods for learning mathematics and logic: reading, discussion, writing, and working problems. However, if a student's attitude is sufficiently negative to make him wish to avoid exposure to new learning situations given half a chance, then it is unlikely that such other methods will ever be brought to bear. It is in giving practice and building confidence in an enjoyable and stimulating setting, that I believe that games have a useful role in mathematics and logic education. This results in developing positive attitudes towards the subject matter, and if used appropriately, it seems likely that games can also contribute significantly to a learner's self-esteem. The most clearcut impressionistic result of the use of such games in the classroom is the building of self-confidence, the emergence of an 'I can do it' attitude. This is also true of the subsequent games that have been developed along the lines of the WFF 'N PROOF game. In general these are all resource-allocation type games. A random set of resources is generated by rolling a set of dice-like cubes out on the table. The resources are the set of symbols imprinted on the turned-up faces of the cubes. The symbols represent ideas in the field that is the subject matter of the game. If the game is about logic the symbols are ones expressing logical ideas; if about arithmetic, then symbols expressing arithmetic ideas; if set theory, then set theoretic symbols. The first player sets a goal from some subset of the resources. In the logic game the goal is the conclusion of a proof, whereas in the arithmetic[9] and set theory[10] games the goal is the right side of an equation. After the goal is set, the task of each of the players is to allocate the remaining resources in such a way that he is the one to make a winning play involving a solution to the goal that has been set. The solution also varies depending upon the game. In the logic game the solution is a set of premisses and the names of a set of rules of inference that form the basis of a logical system within which the conclusion set as a goal can be deduced from the set of premisses specified. In the arithmetic and set theory games the solution is the left side of an equation, and in the advanced version of the set theory game it may also include some statements about sets. The same basic pattern for game construction can be extended to building games for other systems of mathematics and logic, but how far it will be worthwhile going is still an interesting and open question. The group that I am now working with at The University of Michigan is developing such a game for algebra, but how much more is uncertain.

The involvement with games has certainly precipitated a profound shift in my own research interests. It has led from full-time teaching as a law professor at Yale Law School to an affiliation with the Mental Health Research Institute and the Center for Research in Learning and Teaching at The University of Michigan where exploration of the pedagogical and therapeutic implications of instructional games is more appropriate and relevant, and the opportunities for conducting such research more abundant. For the immediate future my legal research interests are being pursued on a part-time basis as a member of the faculty at The University of Michigan Law School. My expectation is, however, that eventually we will learn to construct useful games for use also in legal education. But that is going to take longer to accomplish. The phenomena are much more complex, and will inevitably involve simulation. And it seems to me that the simulation games, if done well, are much more difficult to develop.

The second game that I undertook, one dealing with the judicial decision process, is a simulation game. It is now nearly seven years old, and it still is not, in my judgement, in satisfactory form to warrant publication. One of the central difficulties with simulation games involves the question of whether they are sufficiently representative of the reality that they are meant to simulate to be more helpful than they are misleading. When a great deal is being abstracted out, it is easy to give an over-simplified picture. The criteria for making such judgements are not sufficiently well developed as yet to inspire great confidence. Hopefully, such criteria will evolve as those interested in high-validity simulation games gain more experience in developing such games. It seems to me that we are making progress at this while developing the easier non-simulation type games (such as those in the WFF 'N PROOF series) where the players involved are doing the very thing that you want them to learn how to do, rather than some simulation of it. It seems evident that similar progress is being made by those who are working on simulation games directly; the rest of the articles in this book are evidence of such progress. Because they deal with more complex phenomena, in many cases some aspect of the social process, simulation games are bound to be more challenging and interesting—and probably, more important. It seems to me that the surface has just been scratched in this area of research and that much remains to be investigated that is likely to prove fruitful.

Descriptions of the WFF 'N PROOF games and suggestions for classroom use

General description EQUATIONS, ON-SETS and the proof games of WFF 'N PROOF have essentially the same game rules. Each is a resource-allocation game. A set of resources is randomly generated by shaking out a set of cubes imprinted with the appropriate symbols. The first player sets a **goal** (a number in the case of EQUATIONS and ON-SETS, a WFF in the case of WFF 'N PROOF) and the players then take turns allocating the remaining resources into three categories: forbidden, permitted, and required. The solution is an expression or set of expressions which bears a certain relation to the goal (in EQUATIONS it represents a number equal to the goal; in ON-SETS, the name of a set whose cardinal number is equal to the goal; and in WFF 'N PROOF, a set of premisses and names of rules such that there is a proof of the goal from the premisses using only the rules named). Cubes allocated to forbidden, permitted, or required are (or are not) used in the solution as the names of the categories imply. A player flubs when he

(a) makes a move which makes it impossible for a solution to be built, or
(b) makes a move which allows a solution to be built with one more cube from resources when it was possible to avoid such a move, or
(c) makes a move instead of challenging some previous flub.

A player wins by correctly challenging when another player has flubbed or by being challenged incorrectly when he has not flubbed. The games may be played by any number of players, but three is best for most purposes.

EQUATIONS The symbols imprinted on the cubes are the ten digits and the symbols $+$, $-$, $\times$, $\div$, $*$ (for exponentiation), and $\sqrt{}$ (for root operation, which in the basic game must be preceded by the appropriate index. Square root is denoted by $2\sqrt{}$). Game rules about the form of the goal and the solution necessitate extensive use of the operations. An understanding of the properties of zero and one is particularly vital for effective play. Since a player attempting to build a solution may insert parentheses as he wishes, participants become exceedingly aware of the effect of brackets.

ADVENTUROUS EQUATIONS This is exactly the same game as EQUATIONS except that *each* player is required to invent a new game rule before play begins. This may take the form of a redefinition of one or more of the symbols on the cubes. It may amount to a re-interpretation of the equality relation. A new rule might impose new constraints on the **solution** or the **goal**, or might relax some of the constraints already there. ADVENTUROUS EQUATIONS is limited only by the ingenuity of the players, and it is clear that such a limitation is almost no limitation at all. Of particular interest are the interactions of combinations of new rules. The most important result of ADVENTUROUS EQUATIONS is the propagation of the idea that game rules (and hence games) can be designed (by anyone) to a particular purpose.

ON-SETS The equipment includes a deck of cards. Each card is printed with coloured circles. Some of the cubes are imprinted with circles of the same colours as those on the cards. Before each play of the game, a player turns at least six cards face up. The circles on the cubes are defined to be the names of particular sets of cards (i.e., those cards that have *that* colour circle). Other cubes have the operation signs: ∪ (for set-union), ∩ (for set-intersection), − (for set-difference), and ′ (for complementation).

For ADVANCED ON-SETS, cubes containing the symbols ∨ (for universal set), ∧ (for null set), ⊆ (for set-inclusion), and = (for set-identity) are added. Solutions in this game may consist of a statement (or statements) about sets as well as the name of a set. Such a statement is called a restriction, and it is defined to have the effect of eliminating from the set of upturned cards any card which would make it untrue. In ADVANCED ON-SETS, the number of possible solutions for a given set of resources and goal is usually much larger than in the regular game.

WFF 'N PROOF The cubes are imprinted with the symbols p, q, r, s (variables ranging over WFFs), the symbols C, A, K, E, N (representing the logical operations of material implication, disjunction, conjunction, equivalence, and negation, respectively); and the symbols R, i, o (which are used to form the names of rules of inference). There are several preliminary games (called WFF games) designed to teach the idea of a WFF (or well-formed formula). These games are completely different from the others of the series and can be enjoyed by children of all ages, including those in kindergarten.

When the idea of a WFF is mastered, the ideas of *rule of inference* and *proof* are introduced. Then players may begin to play the PROOF games. There are eleven rules of inference (usually introduced one at a time), and as rules are added, the PROOF games become more difficult. The final PROOF games rival chess in depth and complexity. The game rules of the PROOF games are essentially the same as the rules of EQUATIONS and ON-SETS.

Tournament setting The most important caveat to those who are considering games for classroom use is this: arrange the situation so that each student wins a reasonable percentage of the time. Each will then be more likely to enjoy the game playing experience and begin to perceive himself as capable of mastering the subject matter of the game. Remember, the aim of the games is a sense of competence and confidence on the part of the player. One way to insure that each player has a reasonable opportunity to win is to have the games played in the following kind of tournament: For the initial tournament session, the teacher can make an approximation as to how the students should be arranged. The three brightest players should be assigned to table one, the next three to table two, and so on down to the bottom table. For the next tournament session, a bumping procedure is followed. For example, the winner at table four for session one is bumped up to table three for session two. The loser at table four at session one is bumped down to table five for session two. The other player remains at table four for session two. After several weeks, equilibrium is reached with each player arriving at tables where he is competing with other players on his level. With the players evenly matched in this way, each player engages in a learning experience appropriate to his ability and previous learning. This procedure also makes it possible for ideas to be disseminated throughout a class. For example, a player may lose at table six because his opponent uses something like $2 \div (1 \div 4) = 8$. The next session he is at table seven where this relationship between division operations is as yet unknown and where he can win with it. The ideas get bumped up and down with the players. A tournament like this also gives an opportunity to the student who has been misevaluated by his teacher to achieve recognition by his climb through the hierarchy. After equilibrium is achieved, in a tournament of three-player games, each student will win about one-third of the time. Even when he loses, he should not lose by very much in such a situation. The main aim of the games will be achieved in that each student will gain confidence in his ability to deal with such symbol-handling problems.

Grouping of players into teams It is also desirable to give each student a larger self to identify with. To achieve this, the players may be grouped into teams. The teams do not perform as a group but their scores are aggregated at the end of each playing session. Even if an individual player does not win, his team may win. Furthermore, an individual tends to play harder when a team victory is at stake.

The most important characteristic of a team is that it be heterogeneous. Each team should have at least one first-rate player as well as some average and poorer players. When the top player perceives the importance to the team of the scores of his team-mates, he is often prompted to organize discussions to introduce them to the finer points of the game so that his team can win.

Importance of a tournament newsletter One of the important features of conducting an EQUATIONS, an ON-SETS, or a WFF 'N PROOF tournament as part of the regular mathematics curriculum is the tournament newsletter. The principal purpose of the newsletter that reports the results of each tournament session is to commend the performances of students who have done well. The tournament is structured so that there will be many performances to praise and so that each player and his team will be frequently commended.

Since there are three players in each game, at least one-third of all the players in the tournament will be winners at each session. In case of ties, all those in a game with the high score are winners. Winners are acclaimed by listing their names in the first section of the tournament newsletter. The tournament is arranged so that each player will get his name listed as a winner about one-third of the times played. In the heirarchy of tables at which games are played, since at the end of each session the winners move up a table while the losers move down one and the middle-men remain at the same table for the next round of play, as the tournament progresses this procedure has the effect of moving towards an equilibrium in which the players at each table are evenly matched.

That players be matched in each game with others of comparable understanding is of crucial importance. The game situation supplies a motivation for each player to pose problems in the plays he makes that are just as intricate and difficult as he can conceive of. If the other players are at about the same level of understanding, the next one to move will perceive the problem posed as difficult. He will have to 'sweat' a little to cope with the problem, but still the probability will be relatively high that he can deal with it. The kind of image of himself that a player will be getting in such a situation is that of one who is capable of handling problems that he subjectively perceives as being tough ones. The procedure for bumping winners up a table and losers down not only provides a means for circulating new ideas throughout the class, but also supplies an evaluation mechanism that makes it possible to arrange the learning situation so that it is appropriately paced for each individual player. The attention of each player tends to be focused right at the outer edge of what he now understands of the subject matter being dealt with in the game.

What is true of the individual players will also be true of the teams. The team will tend to win about one-third of the time, lose one-third of the time, and wind up in the middle about one-third of the time. In the tournament a team consists of four or five players, usually one competent player, one who is slow and several in between. As well as he or she can, the teacher should try to make the teams about equal. However, if the teacher miscalculates in the arrangement of teams, there is a built-in correction. To the extent that a team begins to win, its membership drifts upward in the table hierarchy, getting into stiffer and stiffer competition. If a team wins the March tournament, its membership will tend to be playing at a higher level in the April tournament, and it will be more difficult for that team to repeat as the winner for the month.

The importance of teams and the reason why their performance should be reinforced by what is reported in the tournament newsletter is that they furnish incentive for voluntary interaction between the brighter and slower players. Because control of the complexity of problems generated is in the hands of the players, the games at the top tables tend to be more intricate than those at the lower tables, and as a result, take longer to play. The result of this is that the high scorers for the teams tend to be players at the lower tables. It is not long before the leader of a team discovers that the way to help his team do better in the scoring is to teach his team-mates from the lower tables a few of his strategies. When the tournament is operating effectively, a great deal of this peer-group learning occurs voluntarily outside of the formal classroom setting. Teams seem to work better when their membership is kept permanently the same, rather than shifting throughout the year. Also, in the elementary grades it seems to encourage more voluntary interaction if the teams can be all boys or all girls.

The newsletter summarizes each week throughout the month the current and cumulative record of the individual and team performances. In general the criterion for what is included in the newsletter is anything that represents some positive accomplishment of either an individual or a team, with an emphasis upon mentioning as many names as possible.

Problems and puzzles that will help to teach the players new strategies can also be included. One way of encouraging players to submit problems and puzzles for inclusion is to mention whose submission it was. The newsletter is also a convenient place to make announcements about the tournament.

The production of the newsletter can also be a fruitful writing experience for the students, and it should be turned over to them just as rapidly as possible. For the first month or so, however, the teacher should be prepared to provide a good model by doing most of the editing and considerable coaching until they gain experience. A sample newsletter, usually printed on regular $8\frac{1}{2}$ in. $\times$ 11 in. paper, appears as Fig. 4.1.

Layman E. Allen

14 May 1968

GAME WINNERS AND POINTS SCORED Table		CUMULATIVE SCORING LEADERS FOR MAY TOURNAMENT	
1. Joan Laney	10	1. Carlena Carmichael	77
2. John McNaughton	10	2. Wendy Bennett	45
3.· Wendy Bennett	36*	3. Maria Lattimore	45
4. Maria Lattimore	18	4. Nancy Pollack	41
5. Carolyn Bove	8	5. Joan Laney	40
6. William Hastie	8	6. Sheila Douglas	34
7. Sheila Douglas	14	7. James Dowaliby	32
8. Carlena Carmichael	42†	8. Mike Kingsley	32
9. Diana Gates	14	9. William Chambers	27
(*Runner-up †High Scorer)		10. Stuart Trembly	25

THIS WEEK'S CURRENT AND CUMULATIVE POINT SCORES FOR TEAMS

	Current	Cumulative	High Scorer for Teams	
WILLIAMS	83†	103	Wendy Bennett	36
WESLEYAN	33	70	Carlena Carmichael	42
IOWA	40*	69	Maria Lattimore	18
			John McNaughton	10
CORNELL	−17	41	Stuart Trembly	10
			Cleven Coggins	10
DARTMOUTH	−32	32	William Hastie	8
AMHERST	8	−22	Carolyn Bove	8

Williams came through this week with an all-round team effort that has been unmatched in tournament play at any time this spring. Every single member of the Williams team broke into the scoring column. Wendy Bennett paced the Williams scoring with 36 points and was ably assisted by Sheila Douglas, Susan Mitchell, Joan Laney and Nancy Pollack. By virtue of the fine team effort, Williams leap-frogged all the way from fifth place into the league lead. The team's 83-point score has perched Williams at the top of the heap with a cumulative total of 103 points.

Moving up with Williams were both Wesleyan and Iowa. Iowa won runner-up laurels this week with 40 points and moved into third place, just one point behind Wesleyan. Maria Lattimore lead the Hawkeyes' attack with 18 points.

Carlena Carmichael won individual scoring honours this week in pacing the Wesleyan team's drive to take over second place. Her 42-point effort helped boost the team's cumulative total to 70 points.

Carlena has also moved far out in front in the individual cumulative scoring column. Her 77-point total exceeds the 45 points of runners-up Maria Lattimore and Wendy Bennett by a wide margin at this stage of the tournament.

PROBLEMS OF THE WEEK (Complete the EQUATION by moving just one cube from the RESOURCES.)

RESOURCES:	+ ×	*	4	8
FORBIDDEN:				
PERMITTED:	* +	×	7	3
REQUIRED:	3	2		
EQUATION:	——————— = 6561			

RESOURCES:	+ ×	*	1	2	3
FORBIDDEN:				
PERMITTED:	8	6	*	*	*
REQUIRED:	2	−	8	
EQUATION:	——————— = 6305			

SUGGESTED SOLUTIONS: (there may be others)

$$6561 = \mathcal{E} *(\mathcal{Z} * \mathcal{E})$$
$$6305 = (8 * \mathcal{Z}) - (8 * \mathcal{E})$$

More tricky problems involving exponentiation. Do you have a tougher one?

Fig. 4.1 FRONTIER SCHOOL EQUATIONS TOURNAMENT

Parallel with athletic competition James Coleman suggests that instructional games be used to confer recognition for intellectual skill achievement in elementary and secondary school to the same extent that athletic skill is so rewarded: an intellectual competition to parallel athletic competition. This, it seems to me, is a seminal idea that has the potency to significantly improve education as we now know it. He points out the emphasis placed on athletics as a means to success in the high school culture. The excellent athlete had the respect of his school as well as the pleasure of representing his school in inter-scholastic competition. Since the main function of school is usually considered to be educational, it would be appropriate for the excellent scholar, too, to be able to receive recognition from his peers and his community. Such recognition can come from having school teams participate in intellectual games just as they do in physical games.[11]

Some schools systems in Australia, Puerto Rico, and the United States have already started to implement these ideas. Those in the United States include schools in Alabama, Florida, Louisiana, Maine, Michigan, Mississippi, North Carolina, Pennsylvania, and Tennessee. The game-playing year in the American schools comes to a climax in the National Academic Games Olympics that has been held at the Nova School, Fort Lauderdale, Florida, for the past four years. Robert Allen, Director of Academic Games at the Nova Schools, and his staff have pioneered in this development of inter-scholastic instructional games and are primarily responsible for the emergence of this successful programme. This limited experience with the instructional games tournaments has indicated that they work, that the students enjoy them, and that school and community can find gratification in focusing upon the intellectual achievement of some of their members in instructional games. The sense of civic pride is unmistakable in the tributes (reproduced in Figs. 4.2 and 4.3) that were given to students from western Pennsylvania schools for their performance in the 1968 National Academic Games Olympics.

The WFF'N PROOF series of games are particularly appropriate for such tournaments. They are varied enough and deep enough to be played repeatedly. Teams may actually go into intensive training on them. They have (along with some others) been used by all the schools cited above and in the National Academic Games Olympics.

Purposes of the WFF 'N PROOF series of games

Among the purposes of the WFF 'N PROOF series of games are the following:

77

(a) to help develop more favourable attitudes toward mathematics and other rigorous symbol-handling activities;
(b) to help instil in a player a more positive attitude toward himself, to enhance his ego;
(c) to help teach the subject matter of the game; and
(d) to help teach problem solving.

To help develop more favourable attitudes toward mathematics and other rigorous symbol handling activities In our culture we frequently hear people admitting that they dislike mathematics. Even seemingly well-educated persons sometimes proudly proclaim that they want nothing to do with any sort of rigorous abstract activity. This is surprising in view of the fact that increased automation and sophisticated technology place a premium on mathematical ability and capability. Something new is needed to help overcome the fear and dislike that many people have with respect to this subject. Any promising tool should be given a trial. At present, games seem one of the most promising. Man's ability to handle symbols and deal with abstract ideas is the characteristic that most clearly distinguishes him from other forms of life. Even many of those persons who are most apprehensive of mathematics—that quintessence of symbol-handling—readily concede that it represents one of man's crowning intellectual achievements. One of the principal goals of the games in the WFF 'N PROOF series is to expose more people to this kind of symbol handling in a setting that is likely to elicit favourable attitudes toward the subject matter. It would be nice to get many persons enthusiastic about mathematics and logic, but it will be useful even to get a large number feeling comfortable with these subjects. It will be enough to bring many to the place where, shown the need to know, they will have no fear about plunging in and learning. Too many now are paralysed by fear and apprehension arising out of their early exposure to this kind of symbol handling. The day is quickly passing, if it has not already passed, when it is reasonable to allow the persistence of this kind of illiteracy. The WFF 'N PROOF games were designed primarily to help develop more favourable attitudes toward this kind of rigorous symbol handling activity.

To help instil in a player a more positive attitude toward himself, to enhance his ego Game participants are called upon to solve a series of mathematical problems. Game rules place a premium on setting problems at the outer limits of the knowledge of the player. Therefore, if the players are evenly matched, they will have the pleasure of solving a series of problems which they regard as difficult. Thus, they will not

Layman E. Allen

COMMONWEALTH OF PENNSYLVANIA
GOVERNOR'S OFFICE
HARRISBURG

May 13, 1968

GREETINGS:

It is a pleasure to extend heartiest congratulations
and warmest wishes to the Armstrong School District, whose student
representatives to the National Academic Games competition in
Fort Lauderdale, Florida, came home with the majority of the top
prizes.

These students have brought much credit to their
individual schools, their communities, and to our Commonwealth,
through their achievements at these competitions. They also have
demonstrated leadership abilities and serve as fine examples to the
student bodies of their schools.

I hope everyone in the Armstrong School District--
especially the winning teams and their fellow schoolmates--will
keep up their good work! I also hope their future endeavors will
meet with the same success they attained at the National Academic
Games.

RAYMOND P. SHAFER
GOVERNOR

Fig. 4.2

79

Senate of Pennsylvania

HARRISBURG, PA.

OFFICE OF THE SECRETARY

Resolution

In the Senate,
May 13, 1968

Many students from the Armstrong County school system and Fox Chapel excelled at the third annual National Academic Games Olympics, held at Fort Lauderdale, Florida.

The Olympics, sponsored by the Nova Schools, in conjunction with Nova University, seek to perfect programs, games and tests, developed by the Nova Academic Games Project, to help meet the educational requirements of culturally deprived children, "under-achievers," and other students who, for one reason or another, have not fulfilled the academic goals within their reach.

Pennsylvania students from the Fox Chapel area and Armstrong County schools captured five team championships and seven individual championships at the Olympics. A total of nineteen senior high teams and fifteen junior high teams made up the two divisions.

In the senior division, teams from Fox Chapel took first place prizes in Democracy and Propaganda. A team from Armstrong County (Dayton) won the team championship in Wff'n Proof, and a team from Bethel Park won the On-Sets championship. Russell Ayres was individual champion at On-Sets and Wff'n Proof. Carol Mechling of Armstrong County (Elderton) won Democracy, and Georgann Kovacousky, also of Elderton, won Propaganda. A Fox Chapel team was first in the Nation in over-all team standings.

In the junior division, the Kittanning team took first place honors in Equations and On-Sets, and second in the over-all contest. Junior division individual winners from Armstrong County, and their "Game," were: Tom Volek, Kittanning, Equations; Charles Shuster, Kittanning, Democracy, and Dean Yee, Kittanning, On-Sets; therefore be it

RESOLVED, That the Senate of Pennsylvania extend its sincere congratulations to the following students and supervisors of Armstrong School District, Armstrong County, Pennsylvania, who achieved an outstanding record in the National Academic Games Olympics, Fort Lauderdale, Florida, and express its hope that the students will continue to gain further academic recognition in the years ahead:

Dayton - William Hollenbaugh and Walter Woodle, Supervisors - Tim Scaife, Vicky Yeany, Jane Martin, Debbie Rupp, Vicki Kunselman, Jeff Carrick, Darlene Kube, Linda Jordan, Joyce Rumbaugh, Suzanne Travis, Edward Hollenbaugh, Elizabeth Williams, Joanne Good, Marlyn Shay, Mary Calhoun, Steve Ellenberger, Lorraine Buchanan, Brent Calhoun and Ron Shrock.

Ford City - Eugene McBryar, Supervisor - Dennis Shay, Dennis Vojtilla, William Zurney, Shelly Thomaswick and Angelo Rizzardo.

Elderton - Mrs. Leroy Smith, Supervisor - Nancy Van Horn, Richard Murray, Ted Hankey, Georgann Kovacousky, Patricia Dunmire, Kaye Sheasley, Blythe Quinn, Carol Mechling, James Wood, Bernard Kaplin and Rosalie Pugliese.

Shannock Valley - Eugene Brown, Supervisor - Mary Ellen Linko, Edgar Sloan, Mitzi Hall, Diana Schrecengost, Vicki O'Harrow and Alice Terrance.

Kittanning Junior - Miss Dorothea Flemm, Supervisor - Charles Shuster, Tom Volek, Dean Yee, David Toy, Peggy Trulick, Tim Shaffer, Robert Hunia and Robert Rupert.

Kittanning Senior - Melissa Chapman.

East Brady - Barbara Buechele.

Worthington - Paula Adams.

James S. Porter, Assistant Superintendent, Secondary and C. Nicely Hanner, Superintendent; and be it further

RESOLVED, That copies of this resolution be transmitted to the supervisors of each school: William Hollenbaugh and Walter Woodle of Dayton; Eugene McBryar of Ford City; Mrs. Leroy Smith of Elderton; Eugene Brown of Shannock Valley and Miss Dorothea Flemm of Kittanning Junior.

I certify that the foregoing is a true and correct copy of a Senate Resolution introduced by Senators Albert R. Pechan and Robert D. Fleming and adopted by the Senate of Pennsylvania the thirteenth day of May, one thousand nine hundred and sixty-eight.

MARK GRUELL, JR.
Secretary
SENATE OF PENNSYLVANIA

Fig. 4.3

only come to view the subject matter of the game as enjoyable but to view themselves as competent at solving difficult problems. This, it is hoped, will increase their self-confidence and encourage them to go on to further learning—both in the particular subject matter and in general.

To help teach the subject matter of the game The subject matter of EQUATIONS is elementary arithmetic but number facts are presumed known. The player of EQUATIONS (while getting much practice in numerical calculation) is learning about the relations between the operations: addition, substraction, multiplication, division, exponentiation, and root extraction.

In ADVENTUROUS EQUATIONS, where players invent rules, the subject matter is limited only by the mathematical sophistication of the participants. Thus, a large number of the ideas of the secondary mathematics curriculum and many more may enter into the play.

The subject matter of ON-SETS is set theory. The operations of set-union, set-intersection, set-subtraction, and complementation are learned in depth. Experienced ON-SETS players develop the same kind of insight into these operations that ordinary students have for addition and subtraction of whole numbers. The ADVANCED ON-SETS game involves extensive use of the relations of set-inclusion and set-identity.

The subject matter of WFF 'N PROOF is symbolic logic. The basic ideas are those of WFF (well-formed formula), rule of inference, and proof. The WFF 'N PROOF player gains insight into the nature of a WFF, the nature of a proof (and the process of deduction), and the nature of a logical system, as well as the depths of many possible subsystems of the propositional calculus.

To help teach problem solving From the brief description of the game rules, it should be apparent that players may have to solve a rather complex series of problems. Each move purports to solve a given problem at the same time that it creates new problems for the other players. The problems involve several interlocking considerations: mathematical, strategic and psychological. Bluffing and entrapment often enter into the play.

Properties of WFF 'N PROOF type games

Non-simulation When educators discuss games as a teaching device, they usually have in mind 'simulation' games. The distinctive characteristic of such games is that they are designed to give participants an insight into the working of some system or process. They do this by simulating the system or process in question. Usually the game rules are so structured as to be a model for the dynamics of the system.

There is a broad spectrum of simulation games and new ones are being developed all the time. The processes simulated include business decision-making, the democratic legislative process, guidance counselling, international diplomacy, career planning, the economy of ancient Sumer, the relationship of parent to child, the ecology of Isle Royale, policy negotiations between school boards and teacher representatives, the life of a late adolescent and young adult, and the workings of a metropolitan city, as well as many, many others.

Such games are often an outgrowth of some branch of social science. They necessarily reflect the knowledge and insight of their designers and the stage of sophistication of that branch of science. They always involve models of the system that they are intended to portray. The system may be so complicated that play of the game requires a computer. The system encountered by the player is always an abstraction from the real-world system about which he is expected to learn.

A simulation game cannot be expected to give a player all the same insights as the corresponding real life experience. The pupil playing the role of a legislator in the game of DEMOCRACY is at best learning those characteristics of the legislative process considered important by the game designer. Of course if a game designer is not careful, a player may easily be learning unintended ideas. Even if a simulation game is so well done that a player learns only what the game designer wants him to learn, the basic limitation of simulation games still holds: the game can only be as effective as the simulation. These games can in fact be very controversial. One man's view of how the parent-child relationship really works or should work may be an anathema to the next man. None of the foregoing is meant to downgrade simulation games. There is no question that such games can be effective classroom tools. The anecdotal and impressionistic evidence which attests to the enthusiasm of students who have taken part in them is persuasive. There is still some doubt, however, that simulation games are more useful than conventional ways of learning the same material. All the evidence so far is inconclusive.[12]

WFF 'N PROOF and its sister games are *non-simulation* games. The player of EQUATIONS is not setting and solving problems in a system which models elementary arithmetic. He is setting and solving problems in elementary arithmetic itself. The ON-SETS player is not encountering a simulation designed by some set-theoreticians to expose him to the most important ideas of set theory. He is doing set theory—the real thing. There can thus be no controversy about the validity of a non-simulation game. The player of a simulation game is dealing with a model of a system in question. The player of a non-simulation game is dealing with the system itself.

It is not to be expected that the research findings about simulation games will apply to non-simulation games. In fact there is evidence to show that playing WFF 'N PROOF regularly has a significant effect on the I.Q. scores of the participants. In the summer of 1964 a group of forty-three junior high school and high school students enrolled in the summer school at John Burroughs High School, Burbank, California, and played WFF 'N PROOF intensively four hours a day for three weeks. The average increase in non-language I.Q. scores on the California Test of Mental Maturity for this group during the three-week interval was 20·9 points. The mean of the scores of the pre-test was 107·6 while the mean of the post-test scores was 128·4 with a standard deviation of the change in scores of 13·4 and a standard error of the mean change of 2·1. The average increase in scores of a control group of students enrolled in the same summer school for the same period was insignificant. The difference in the increase was significant at the ·01 level.[13]

A further advantage of non-simulation games over simulation games is that many of the latter can be played profitably only once or twice. The important information and insights are extracted in a few exposures, and repeated play is not fruitful. The WFF 'N PROOF series, because the games in it are non-simulation games, and for other reasons arising from the particular game rules, can be profitably played over and over again.[14]

Teaching of students by students   In the WFF 'N PROOF type games, in order to win by building a solution, a player must display his solution to the other players and convince them that it is in fact a solution. If he has used an idea that is not understood by his opponents, he has to explain that idea to them. Where winning and losing is at stake, it is not likely that other participants will be satisfied with an incorrect or incomplete explanation—especially when thorough understanding of the strategy may enable them to win on some future occasion. Hence, the game rules in this type of game positively encourage learning from peers in the course of playing. No participant can keep his understanding and strategies secret for long. If he wishes to win, he must reveal them; and in the course of doing so, teach his brethren. You might say that not only does a winner give the others a lesson in winning but also that in winning, he gives the others a lesson.

Teaching of students by teacher   The game rules in WFF 'N PROOF type games are so structured that a teacher can introduce a new idea by playing with a student (or students). When the teacher makes a deliberate error, if the student does not understand the idea, he does not recognize that the teacher has made a mistake and so he moves a cube instead of challenging. In these circumstances, the teacher should immediately challenge the student for not challenging the previous error and explain what it was (thereby explaining the idea involved). When they play another game, the teacher can continue to make deliberate mistakes stemming from a particular idea that he wants the student to learn. When the student understands the idea, he will have the pleasure of winning the game from the teacher as well as the possibility of using the idea to win games when playing with his classmates (teaching it to them as he does so).

Similarity to programmed instruction The WFF 'N PROOF games can be thought of as a complex sequence of stimuli and responses. Each play presents a new situation to the other players to which they may (or must) respond. Mistakes lead often to challenges. A player who misunderstands is immediately corrected. The feedback is fast and unequivocal. The reward for effective performance is display of competence and winning. Each player has partial control over the situation (for example, a weak player can forbid operations he does not understand). The games are similar to branched programmes in that later events (moves) are functions of previous ones. Thus individual needs are fulfilled, the level of each game being determined by the ability and knowledge of its participants.

When appropriately used, the games strongly resemble a computer-assisted learning programme where the machine is programmed to generate the next stimulus most appropriate to a particular previous series of responses. The main difference is that in the games the computer is replaced by a human being. This may not only be more economical but also adds a human, social element to the learning situation. For those students who prefer a kind of solitaire (either all or some of the time), there are puzzles involving game-type problems. Samples of such puzzles with respect to the EQUATIONS game follow. Plans are also under way to program a computer to play a simplified version of the games and to develop a library of games which can be played by an individual player.

In playing EQUATIONS, when a cube is moved from the Resources to either the Forbidden, the Permitted, or the Required sections of the playing mat, the mover is declaring that the following three claims are true:

C   I Cannot correctly challenge on this turn.

85

A If possible, I am Avoiding by this move allowing a Solution to be built with at most̄ one more cube from Resources.

P It is still Possible for the remaining Resources to be so played that a Solution can be built.

A player can at any time correctly challenge the move of another player that violates any of the above claims.

One-Cube Solution Puzzles
Build a Solution with one cube from Resources.

A.	B.
RESOURCES: $+$ 1 7 5 $\sqrt{}$	RESOURCES: $+ -$ 1 3
FORBIDDEN: 0 * $\sqrt{}$ × 2	FORBIDDEN: 3 5 $- \sqrt{} \sqrt{}$
PERMITTED: 4 8 0 ×	PERMITTED: 1 × * 7 8
REQUIRED: $-$ 3 ÷	REQUIRED: ÷ 2 2
EQUATION: ——————$= 5-7$	EQUATION: ——————$= 9÷4$

Taboo-Move Puzzles
This is a new kind of puzzle. To answer it, you must indicate which moves would violate either the A-claim or the P-claim.

C.	D.
RESOURCES: 0 3 2 $+$ ×	RESOURCES: $\sqrt{}$ * ÷ 3 6
FORBIDDEN: 8 2 3 $- - \sqrt{}$	FORBIDDEN: $\sqrt{} +$ 1 4
PERMITTED: × ÷ $\sqrt{}$ * ÷	PERMITTED: 1 $+$ 0 $-$
REQUIRED: 6 0 *	REQUIRED: 2 3 ×
EQUATION: ——————$= 7$	EQUATION: ——————$= 2\sqrt{27}$

CAP-Claim Puzzles
Tell which claim the indicated move violates and why.

E.	F.
RESOURCES: 3 4 5 $+$ *	RESOURCES: $+ \sqrt{}$ 2
FORBIDDEN: ÷ ÷ $\sqrt{}$ *	FORBIDDEN: 2 ÷ 1 $-$
PERMITTED: 0 $+$ × $-$	PERMITTED: $+ -$ × 0
REQUIRED: 2 $\sqrt{}$	REQUIRED: 3 4 5 6
EQUATION: ——————$= 8$ *(1÷9)	EQUATION: ——————$= 1÷12$

SUGGESTED SOLUTIONS

A. 8 ÷ (3 $-$ 7)
    ↑

B. 2 $+$ (2 ÷ 8)
    ↑

C. Moving the 2 or $+$ to Permitted or Required are Taboo Moves. They violate the A-claim by allowing the one-cube Solution: 6 $+$ (2*0). Similarly, 3 to Permitted or Required is Taboo since it also violates the A-claim (by allowing the one-cube Solution: 6+(3*0)). Moving the $+$ to Forbidden is Taboo because it violates the P-claim. These answers may be abbreviated:

Taboo Moves	Claim Violated	One-Cube Solution
$+$,2,3 → P,R	A	6 $+$ (2 * 0)
		6 $+$ (3 * 0)
$+$ → F	P	——
D. 3,$\sqrt{}$ × P,R	A	3 × (2$\sqrt{}$3)

E. Move violates A-claim by allowing the one-cube Solution: 3$\sqrt{}$2

F. Move violates C-claim. A previous player must have violated the A-claim because the Solution (5 $-$ 6)$\sqrt{}$(4 × 3) can be built with one cube from Resources.

Multiplicity of levels   Each of the WFF 'N PROOF games is in itself a sequence of games rather than a single game. The EQUATIONS kit, for example, contains four different kinds of cubes. The red cubes have on them only the symbols $+$, $-$, 0, 1, 2, and 3. An interesting game can be played with red cubes alone. (The red-cube game is often used for introductory purposes.) The blue cubes have on them the symbols $\times$, $\div$, 0, 1, 2, and 3. At the sixth grade level, blue and red cubes make a good beginning game. There are also green cubes which add the digits 4, 5, and 6 and the operation * (for exponentiation) and black cubes with 7, 8, 9, and $\sqrt{}$. Just the presence of cubes with exotic symbols can serve as a strong stimulus to the understanding of further mathematical ideas. Even when all four kinds of EQUATIONS cubes are regularly used in play, there are many new ideas (stemming from combination of operations) to be discovered. For example, what is the one-half root of three? This is a question that arises naturally from the kind of manipulations involved in an EQUATIONS game.

Basic EQUATIONS is deep and broad enough to be played many, many times before all the mathematical meat is extracted from it. This is particularly true for elementary school students. With ADVENTUROUS EQUATIONS, the possibilities are open-ended. (Since ADVENTUR-OUS EQUATIONS allows redefinition of symbols, the series of EQUATIONS games is literally an infinite one.)

ON-SETS can also be played at several levels. The advanced ON-SETS game is difficult enough for mathematicians to find it challenging. The WFF 'N PROOF game spans a very broad spectrum. The WFF games are a delight to kindergarten children. The final PROOF games seem to be at least as difficult as chess.

Thus, any one of the WFF 'N PROOF, ON-SETS, or EQUATIONS games can be played repeatedly. As soon as the ideas at a given level are thoroughly understood, new ideas can be introduced. The game structure remains, but the game subject matter is expandable.

Encouraging flexibility   The game rules of the WFF 'N PROOF series of games are designed to reward the flexible player. In most of the problems a player faces, there is no single solution. There are instead a set of solutions, and the winner usually is the one most clever at finding alternative solutions, or adapting his solution to fit the constraints. Players that have attained a certain intermediate level of game sophistication often put a premium on the construction of intricate and devious solutions. Such a strategy may succeed for a time, but one sure way to lose is to become so involved in one's own complicated solutions that one overlooks some very simple and obvious solutions. A player *must* learn to consider other alternatives. In these games, *idées fixes* are usually counter-productive.

Continuous attention demand If there are three or more players in a game of WFF 'N PROOF, EQUATIONS, or ON-SETS, the player who had just moved may be challenged by either (or any) of the other players. Since challenging correctly is one way to score, the attention of all the players is always focused upon the problem at hand. Because a player can score not only on his own moves but on the moves of others as well, he must pay close attention to the problem at hand even when it is not his turn to play. This induces an impressive degree of concentration. The first thing an observer notices in a roomful of youngsters playing these games is the extremely strong focus of attention on the playing mat and the cubes.

Mathematical characteristics The mathematical ideas stressed in the games are very much in the spirit of the 'new math'. The basic EQUA-TIONS game, for example, requires much more than merely arithmetical information for winning play. The most important arithmetical ideas to be discovered in the games are the relations between the operations. The understanding of these relations is mathematical knowledge on a considerably higher level than number facts. Furthermore, the kind of exploratory thinking done by an EQUATIONS player is similar to that which the 'new math' was designed to stimulate—creative rather than repetitive.

ADVENTUROUS EQUATIONS is wide open mathematically. It provides motivation for students to seek out new ideas—either in their heads or in books—and then to explore the ideas by using them in the games and teaching them to other players.

Appropriately used, such games can stimulate both mathematical 'research' (at the appropriate level) and the dissemination of 'new' (to the players) mathematical ideas.

Integrity as games Many of the games suggested for classroom use are *only* appropriate as classroom games. It is inconceivable that anyone would play them except when they were being so used. This is not true of the games in the WFF 'N PROOF series. The academic nature of their subject matter makes them appropriate as classroom games but the 'gaminess' of their rules makes them excellent fun for game players everywhere. You do not have to be trying to learn logic to enjoy WFF 'N PROOF. It can stand on its own as one of the more interesting intellectual games, and as such it is as appropriate for recreation as for education.

Conclusion

In concluding, I should mention that one of the interesting developments at The University of Michigan is the emergence of a Tuesday night games workshop. Frederick Goodman of the School of Education has collaborated with me in sponsoring this weekly workshop. It has been open to the general public and has been attended by other university faculty members, graduate and undergraduate students, teachers, from public and parochial schools, educators from Job Corps camps, hospitals, prisons, and other public institutions, as well as elementary, junior and senior high school students. The subject matter dealt with in games that have been considered by the Tuesday night games group during the past two years includes business management, career planning, collective bargaining, communications sciences, conservation, diplomacy, economics, games theory, geometry, guidance counselling, law, legislative process, linguistics, mathematics, music, policy negotiations, political behaviour, propaganda analysis, psychology, resource planning, set theory, sociology, symbolic logic, and therapy.

The sessions are *ad hoc*, determined by the interests of the particular group that happens to turn out on a given Tuesday. Visitors who are interested in learning to play a particular educational game can usually find others at the workshop from whom they can learn. Authors in the midst of designing new games frequently present problems encountered and assistance is often forthcoming in the discussion that ensues.

It seems to me that the emergence of such voluntary groups will prove to be extremely fruitful in contributing to the development of high-validity simulation games. There is already clear evidence of this in some of the games that have been evolving in the discussion of this Michigan Tuesday night group. Persons interested in instructional games are welcome to attend these sessions.[15] Those who are becoming interested in instructional games and wondering how they can become more deeply involved would do well to organize such a voluntary workshop group. Not only will you learn, but it's fun!

REFERENCES

1. I want to acknowledge and thank Joan Ross for assistance in the preparation of this article. Discovering her as a colleague at The University of Michigan has been one of the extraordinary events in further stimulating my interests and efforts in instructional gaming. Her contributions to the games currently being investigated and developed here have been invaluable. She is one of the co-authors of a game that I believe may become a classic among instructional games. Completed in 1970 after four years of development, it is called: QUERIES AND THEORIES: the Game of Science and Linguistics.
2. Anderson, A. R., and Moore, O. K.: 'Autotelic Folk-Models'. Tech. Rep.

No. 8, Interaction Laboratory, Sociology Department, Yale University, New Haven, 1959.

3. Skinner, B. F.: 'Teaching Machines'. *Science*, Vol. 128, 1958, pp. 969–975.

4. Allen, L. E., Brooks, R. B. S., Dickoff, J. W., and James, P. A.: 'The ALL Project (Accelerated Learning of Logic)'. *American Mathematical Monthly*, Vol. 69, 1961, pp. 497–503.

5. Dickoff, J. W., and James, P. A.: *Symbolic Logic and Language: a Programmed Text.* New York, McGraw-Hill, 1965.

6. Allen, L. E.: *WFF 'N PROOF: the Game of Modern Logic.* New Haven, Autotelic Instructional Materials Publishers, 1962.

7. This is described in somewhat more detail in 'Games and Programmed Instruction', pp. 347–372 in *Communications Sciences and Law: Reflections from the Jurimetrics Conference* (edited by L. E. Allen and M. E. Caldwell). Indianapolis, Bobbs-Merrill Co., 1965.

8. For example, see *WFF 'N PROOF: the Game of Modern Logic*, p. 141.

9. *EQUATIONS: the Game of Creative Mathematics*, by L. E. Allen, New Haven, Autotelic Instructional Materials Publishers, 1963.

10. *ON-SETS: the Game of Set Theory*, by L. E. Allen, P. Kugel, and M. F. Owens. New Haven, Autotelic Instructional Materials, 1966.

11. Coleman, J. S.: *The Adolescent Society.* Glencoe Free Press, 1961, pp. 310–322.

12. Cherryholmes, C. H.: 'Some Current Research in Effectiveness of Educational Simulations: Implications for Alternative Strategies'. *American Behavioral Scientist*, Vol. 10, October 1966, pp. 4–7.

13. For more complete details see L. E. Allen, R. W. Allen, and J. Ross, 'The Virtues of Non-Simulation Games: WFF 'N PROOF as an Example' (forthcoming in the *American Behavioral Scientist*).

14. See the discussion on open-endedness, p. 87.

15. The meetings begin at 8 p.m. and continue usually until 10, but sometimes through midnight. The meeting place is the School of Education, University of Michigan, Ann Arbor, Michigan. For information telephone (313) 764-1548.

5
SAM (simulated arithmetic machine): a computer programming and operation simulation

Roy T. Atherton

Born in Manchester, England, in 1933, Roy Atherton left his grammar school at sixteen and during the next ten years worked in a variety of jobs including those of clerk, trainee accountant and research technician. Having qualified for university entrance by attending evening classes, he read honours mathematics at Chelsea College of Science and Technology, London, where he became involved in student affairs and was elected President of the Union. Upon graduating he taught mathematics at Stretford Technical College, Lancashire, and followed an in-service course to gain a teacher's certificate of the University of Manchester. He began his work on computer education at Stretford and after six years moved to the Berkshire College of Education, where he is now Senior Lecturer in Mathematics.

One of the several difficulties experienced by students and pupils in the early stages of learning a computer language is the necessity to grasp the basic operations of the computer as well as the basic principles of programming. This double unfamiliarity sometimes causes bewilderment and loss of motivation, particularly in younger or less able pupils. The simulation of the operation of a digital computer described in this chapter is an attempt to clarify the various machine operations by representing them visually. It has been used successfully with ten-year-old primary school children and with college students.

There are a number of essential operations common to most digital computers, such as 'store', 'load', 'jump' and the four basic arithmetical operations. Since the game simulates these operations it can be adapted easily to conform to any low-level code, but it is clearly desirable to use the same code in the game as the players will eventually use to write their own programs. The programs should then be processed in order to provide what is called, in behaviourist terms, reinforcement. Substantial effort is needed in the logical analysis of a problem and its precise translation into a computer language. Logic and precision are not easy virtues and it is educationally useful that they find their reward in the successful processing of programs.

Fig. 5.1   A game in progress

Two further points need mentioning. Colour is one of SAM's important features. While it is not essential to his logical operation it is a valuable aid, particularly for young children, and it certainly makes him more attractive to work with. A colour scheme for SAM has been very carefully devised, but unfortunately cannot be used directly in this description. Indications of colour are made wherever appropriate in words and the diagrams should be read in conjunction with the colour key provided.

Colour key   Where possible colours are indicated in words but the colours of numbers and mnemonic codes are indicated by lines above or below the characters as shown.

10	red
200	brown
STORE	purple
100	green
ADD	blue
RNT	orange

Secondly, the distinction in SAM between storage locations used for numbers, instructions and general working are arbitrary. The locations numbered 10–999 have been divided into three sections to emphasize the different purposes for which the stores are used. The different purposes are further emphasized by the use of colours which also facilitate SAM's operation.

The language used in the following description is the Mnemonic Code defined by the City and Guilds of London Institute, for educational purposes. Its use on the Atlas Computer at the University of Manchester is due to G. Riding whose work and infectious enthusiasm have helped several establishments to make a start in Computer Education.

Designing SAM (Simulated Arithmetic Machine)

If a class is asked to name the components which a computer must have they usually suggest a memory, an arithmetic unit, input and output devices and some kind of overall control. As each component is named, with or without prompting, it can be produced and placed in position. The order is not important and it is best to follow the order of the class suggestions.

Memory   It is convenient to divide SAM's memory into three parts:

(a) Number Store   (red)   Locations   10–99
(b) Program Store   (green)   Locations 100–199
(c) Working Store   (brown) Locations 200–999

The three stores are represented by large white cards divided into

O	O			
Number store				
10	14	18	22	26
11	15	19	23	27
12	16	20	24	28
13	17	21	25	29
Red				

Fig. 5.2   Number Store. The Program Store (green: Locations 100–199) and the Working Store (brown: Locations 200–999) are similar

locations with thick felt markers of the appropriate colour. Small cards are hung in various locations by means of magnetic strip.

Arithmetic unit (accumulator) An electronic desk calculator makes a most suitable arithmetic unit, but any sort of calculator will do. If no mechanical aid is available, numbers should be kept simple so that one of the more able pupils can perform as a reasonably quick arithmetic unit. The accumulator, as it is called, is the centre of operations. All numbers which are being processed in any way pass through it. For this reason it should be situated near the control unit with which it is associated.

Input and output The reader is a large white card with five coloured rectangles on it. The first rectangle (black) receives the complete program, a set of cards, and these are passed in sequence to one of the other rectangles which are named:

- (a) DIRECTIVE (purple)
- (b) NUMBER (red)
- (c) INSTRUCTION (green)
- (d) DATA (orange)

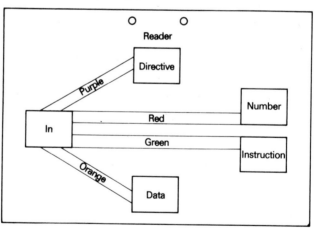

Fig. 5.3 Reader

and from here appropriate action is taken.

Results are recorded (after the program title) by a printer which is a green card with a holder for the title card and a note pad for recording results.

Control All the components described above must perform their various tasks in the correct sequence. The control of a computer is highly technical but SAM gives some indication of what happens by means of his control unit which is a white card with ten locations numbered 0–9. 0 is for a permanently stored zero and 1 is the register for the arithmetic unit or accumulator. Numbers 2 to 9 are index registers which can contain only positive whole numbers. They are used mainly for controlling the program and location 4 is reserved for a special purpose to be described later.

Data store The working store is completely flexible in the sense that numbers can be put in, copied, or overwritten at will but this flexibility is technically complex and therefore expensive. For this reason computers use other types of storage which are less versatile but much cheaper.

It is also important to separate the data for a calculation from the program of instructions so that an identical problem with different data can be solved by the same program. These two points are recognized by the City and Guilds code which provides for data to be added to the end of a program. It is not as easy to introduce data in this way and at first children should work only with the number store. The data store can be introduced at a later stage.

SAM's data store is simply a card with a note pad to receive a set of numbers. Since the numbers come in and out only once they can be written down and crossed off as they are used.

When each component has been mentioned and discussed it can be hung in its place—two panel pins for each component knocked into a piece of 1″ × 1″ timber. Two such pieces are necessary, to support nine cards: Reader, Control, Number Store, Program Store, Working Store, Printer and three cards for recording the code and meaning of instructions and directives. The accumulator should also be in place on a table near the control unit. At this point all is ready for the introduction of the basic computer operations.

Using SAM

Storing and loading The instruction

STA 200

means store the number copied from the accumulator into location 200. If three or four children with their names on cards hanging round their necks are invited to stand at the front of the class the necessary points can be made effectively. The above instructions can be rewritten

STA SUSAN

Susan is then requested to copy on to a card the number in the accumu-lator. The class will quickly grasp two points. Firstly, the important distinction between a number and its address. Susan is the address. Secondly, the number 42, say, remains in the accumulator after it has been stored into its new address. It is now easily seen that the instruction

STA 200

has the effect of copying the number 42 from the accumulator into location 200 without removing the number 42 from the accumulator.

Pupils will very quickly see that the inverse operation

LDA PAT

causes Pat's number 75, say, to be copied into the accumulator without taking it away from Pat.

One further point needs emphasizing: an incoming number either to a numbered location or to the accumulator will first cause a number already there to be wiped out. Thus

LDA 10

causes the number 75 in location 10 to be copied into the accumulator.

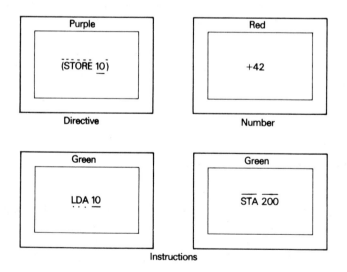

Fig. 5.4   Program cards

The number previously in the accumulator is wiped out. Children need to play or watch storing and loading, first using names for addresses. When they understand the principles, the cards can be turned round and address numbers written on the back. Clarity is also aided by the use of colour. STA 200 is brown to indicate that the number concerned is destined for the working store. LDA is blue to denote its reference to the accumulator, while the address 10 is red to show that it relates to the number store. Both instruction cards are bordered in green because they will initially be stored in the program store.

Arithmetic   Addition is easily achieved by the instruction

ADD SUSAN

which means add Susan's number to the accumulator and leave the result in the accumulator. Of course the correct form is

ADD 200

and, as always, after the addition has been performed the number 42 remains in location 200.

Similarly the instructions

(a) SUB 201
(b) MLT 203
(c) DIV 207

will cause respectively

(a) the number in location 201 to be subtracted from that in the accumulator
(b) the number in location 203 to be multiplied by the number in the accumulator
(c) the number in the accumulator to be divided by the number in location 207.

In every case the result is put into the accumulator and the number originally in any location remains there.

Simple programs can be gradually introduced by giving numbers to children. If we start with the situation

PAT	SUSAN	PAUL
75	42	3

then the program

LDA PAT
SUB SUSAN
ADD PAUL

97

is easily seen to perform the calculation

$$75 - 42 + 3 = 36$$

leaving the result in the accumulator.
If the numbers are now placed in the number store thus

10	11	12
75	42	3

the program

LDA 10
SUB 11
ADD 12

performs the same calculation, and the psychological compulsion to take the meaning as

$$10 - 11 + 12$$

is avoided.

Children can be given numbers and the opportunity of obeying various instructions. They will soon realize that they are actually simulating the execution of simple computer programs although nothing has yet been done about input or output. Before discussing these topics it should be noted that clarity is again improved by colouring the letters of arithmetic instructions blue to associate them with the accumulator, but the location addresses 10, 11, and 12 should be red to refer them visually to the number store.

Printing   Output is obtained by the instruction

PNT 2,0

which means print the number in the accumulator with two places before the decimal point and none after. At this stage it is useful to take the printer from its hanging position and place it on a table in such a position that a pupil given the job of printing can see a number in the accumulator from which he will always have to copy.

It can be pointed out that it is unnecessary to predict how large a result will be. If the accumulator showed the number

3576

when the above instruction, PNT 2,0, was encountered, the whole number is printed but the spacing of large amounts of output would be disturbed. If there is any doubt the instruction

PNT 4,4

will cover most results.

Print instructions should be green on pale green cards to connect them with the printer. Although green is also the colour of the program store the two functions are not confused and well judged repetitions of striking colours are preferable to introducing less attractive or less readable ones.

Reinforcement About half a dozen numbers can now be placed in the first few locations of the number store and children can be asked to work through a few simple programs, one or two of which should be placed in sequence in the program store. See Fig. 5.4. The last two problems could usefully involve intermediate storage using the working store. For example, the program

LDA 10
SUB 11
STA 200
LDA 12
ADD 13
MLT 200
PNT 4,4

given the initial state of the number store

10	11	12	13
8	6	4	2

will perform the calculation

$(8 - 6) (4 + 2)$

and print the result. The point here is that the working store has been used to preserve an intermediate result.

Children can now be invited to write simple programs, some of which can be tested by other children working through them with SAM. Before they do this it is useful to place in position the large cards on which are defined the various instructions, drawing attention to those which have already been discussed.

Input and control Digital Computers would not be very effective if they had not the ability to store instructions as well as numbers. The stored program enables a computer to read and obey instructions at speeds comparable to its calculating speeds which are measured in microseconds (millionths of a second). Other important capabilities derive from the stored program concept and these will be discussed in the following sections. In previous examples a program has consisted of

NUMBERS (in the Number Store) and

INSTRUCTIONS (in the Program Store)

A 'directive' is also an order to the computer but it must be obeyed at the input stage when the program is being stored.

The directive

(STORE 10)

causes SAM to store whatever follows in locations 10, 11, 12 . . . until another directive is encountered. Thus

(STORE 10)
+75
+42
+ 3
(STORE 100)

would produce in the number store

10	11	12
+74	+42	+ 3

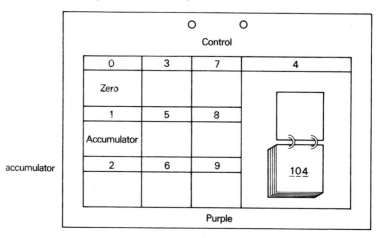

Fig. 5.5.   Control

Directive cards are edged in purple to exhibit their connection with control. The brackets also distinguish them from ordinary instructions. 'Store' is purple as well but the address 10 is red. The address 100 relates to the program store and is therefore green. Two further directives are necessary:

(TITLE)
SIMON EXAMPLE 1

tells SAM to print the words

SIMON EXAMPLE 1

so that the output can be related to the right problem.

(EXECUTE 100)

tells SAM to commence obeying the fully stored program starting with the instruction in location 100.

A complete program ready for punching and processing would take the form:

(TITLE)
SIMON EXAMPLE 1
(STORE 10)
+75 ⎫
+42 ⎬ Up to 90 numbers
+ 3 ⎭
(STORE 100)
LDA 10 ⎫
SUB 11 ⎪
ADD 12 ⎬ Up to 100 instructions
PNT 4,4 ⎪
JST 100 ⎭
(EXECUTE 100)

The last instruction JST 100 simply means stop. Its form will be explained later.

O   O
INSTRUCTIONS

LDA 10	LOAD ACCUMULATOR WITH NUMBER COPIED FROM ADDRESS 10
STA 201	STORE NUMBER COPIED FROM ACCUMULATOR INTO ADDRESS 201
ADD 10	ADD THE NUMBER IN ADDRESS 10 TO THE NUMBER IN THE ACCUMULATOR
SUB 204	SUBTRACT THE NUMBER COPIED FROM ADDRESS 204 FROM THE NUMBER IN THE ACCUMULATOR
PNT 2,1	PRINT THE NUMBER COPIED FROM ACCUMULATOR WITH 2 PLACES BEFORE THE DECIMAL POINT AND 1 AFTER
JST 100	JUMP TO STOP INSTRUCTION

Fig. 5.6   Instructions

```
        O        O
       INSTRUCTIONS

MLT  13        MULTIPLY THE NUMBER IN THE ACCUMULATOR BY
               THE NUMBER COPIED FROM ADDRESS 13

DIV  202       DIVIDE THE NUMBER IN THE ACCUMULATOR BY
               THE NUMBER COPIED FROM ADDRESS 202

RNT  110       READ THE NEXT NUMBER FROM DATA STORE INTO
               THE ACCUMULATOR. (ESCAPE ADDRESS 110)

JUN  104       JUMP TO THE INSTRUCTION IN ADDRESS 104

               IF THE NUMBER IN THE ACCUMULATOR IS
JEQ  104       EQUAL TO ZERO JUMP TO THE INSTRUCTION
               IN LOCATION 104
```

Fig. 5.7   Instructions

```
        O        O
       DIRECTIVES


(TITLE)        PRINT THE TITLE OF THE PROGRAM

(STORE 10)     STORE THE NUMBERS STARTING AT
               ADDRESS 10

(STORE 100)    STORE THE INSTRUCTIONS STARTING AT
               ADDRESS 100

(EXECUTE 100)  EXECUTE THE INSTRUCTION STORED AT
               ADDRESS 100
```

Fig. 5.8   Directives

SAM

SAM can be regarded as a series of short plays. The characters, played by children, are in order of appearance:

READER
CONTROL
PRINTER
NUMBER STORE
PROGRAM STORE
ACCUMULATOR

Another character, WORKING STORE, will appear later. At the commencement of the play, READER takes the pack of cards which constitute a program and places them in the Input rectangle. The play then proceeds.

(TITLE)	*READER:* The first directive is 'Title'. (Hands card to CONTROL) *CONTROL:* Pass the next card to Printer. (READER does so) *PRINTER:* The title is 'Simon Example 1'. (Prints it)
(STORE 10)	*READER:* Directive. Store 10. (Hands card to CONTROL) *CONTROL:* Store all the red bordered cards that follow in the Number Store commencing at location 10. (READER hands next three cards to NUMBER STORE who stores them) *NUMBER STORE:* The numbers are stored.
(STORE 100)	*READER:* Directive. Store 100. (Hands card to CONTROL) *CONTROL:* Store all the green bordered cards in the Program Store commencing at location 100. (READER hands cards to PROGRAM STORE who stores them) *PROGRAM STORE:* The Program is now stored.
(EXECUTE 100)	*READER:* Directive. Execute 100. (Hands card to CONTROL) *CONTROL:* Obey the instruction at location 100.
LDA 10	*PROGRAM STORE:* LDA 10. *NUMBER STORE:* The number at location 10 is 75. (ACCUMULATOR loads 75) *ACCUMULATOR:* 75 loaded.
SUB 11	*PROGRAM STORE:* SUB 11. *NUMBER STORE:* The number at location 11 is 42. (ACCUMULATOR subtracts 42) *ACCUMULATOR:* 42 is subtracted.
ADD 12	*PROGRAM STORE:* Add 12. *NUMBER STORE:* The number at location 12 is 3. (ACCUMULATOR adds 3) *ACCUMULATOR:* 3 is added.
PNT 4,4	*PROGRAM STORE:* PNT 4,4.

JST 100

ACCUMULATOR: The number in the Accumulator is 36.
PRINTER: 36 is printed.
PROGRAM STORE: JST 100.
CONTROL: Jump to the stop instruction.
Program Ends.
PRINTER: Output is 'Simon Example 1 36' (Holds up page)

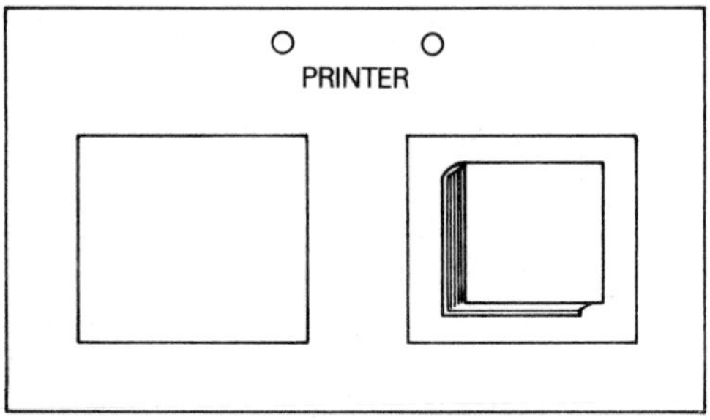

Fig. 5.9   Printer

A few more programs can now be played on SAM by different children. WORKING STORE can be introduced when a program requires the storage of an intermediate result, for instance, as in the calculation (4 + 7) (11 − 6). The stage should be reached where children can work through a program which they haven't seen before. They will then be ready to write some complete programs themselves which can be tested on SAM.

Once familiarity with SAM's operation has been gained and consolidated, another method for the input of data can be introduced. By this method a glimpse can be given of the power of a computer to deal with large amounts of data.

Development

The data store   Instead of putting numbers into the number store they can be brought into use from the data store. The data store is simply a set of numbers, without specific locations, which are read one at a time in sequence into the accumulator by the instruction

RNT

which means read the next number in the data store into the accumulator. Once there it can be used or put into the working store for future use. Numbers cannot be put back into the data store or brought out in any order other than the natural sequence. One advantage of this method of input reveals itself when it is combined with a jump instruction to form a loop.

Jumps and loops Instructions in a program are normally obeyed in strict sequence, but the instruction

JUN 100

interferes with this and causes the instruction in location 100 to be obeyed instead. In order to add, say, a hundred numbers the following instructions stored in locations 100–103 are used.

RNT
ADD 200
STA 200
JUN 100

As they stand these four instructions are inadequate since the computer would eventually attempt to read a number which was not there and the program would fail. The easy way of overcoming the difficulty is to put an 'escape address' after RNT. Control is then transferred to this location. The section of the program would now read

RNT 104
ADD 200
STA 200
JUN 100
PNT 4,4

The first four instructions form a loop which is obeyed repetitively until something breaks the sequence. To simulate this concept on SAM it is necessary to consider again the sequential obedience of instructions. Location 4 has been mentioned as a special location, and its purpose can now be specified. It always records the address of the currently obeyed instruction. In fact it causes that instruction to be obeyed, adds one to its value, and causes the next instruction to be obeyed. The instruction

JUN 100

causes the 103 in location 4 to be removed and 100 substituted, which in turn brings the RNT instruction into play again. Similarly if an RNT instruction fails because the data store has been emptied of numbers, the computer seeks an escape address, and this number is then put into location 4, transferring control to location 104 which contains the print instruction. The operation of location 4 can be simulated by a large counting device such as a set of numbered cards which can be turned over one at a time. This vital function should be performed by a child who has no other duties which might distract him. One card at the end of the sequence should read STOP which explains why

JST 100

has the form of a jump instruction. The 100 is not significant but it must be there to preserve the correct form.

Another play can be used to demonstrate loops with an extra character, LOCATION FOUR, who can be asked to speak whenever a jump instruction or an escape address is encountered.

Further development

The City and Guilds code provides for considerable further development of programming techniques and includes provision for conditional jumps, address modifying, mathematical functions, subroutines and character processing. SAM can be extended to simulate any of these processes. Some extra organization will be necessary when functions are used. The character, FUNCTION, will need to be provided with tables to enable him to respond appropriately. Obviously the amount of development possible depends on the age and ability of the class. A modified list of the instructions available in the City and Guilds code is given in Appendix 5.1. Appendix 5.2 contains some simple programs in increasing order of difficulty.

Appendix 5.1

City and Guilds mnemonic code   (Extract from the Minimum Instruction Set given in City and Guilds Prospectus Mn 319. Address modifiers are omitted for simplicity.)

Instruction		*Effect*
LDA	n	$(n) \to A$
ADD	n	$(A) + (n) \to A$
SUB	n	$(A) - (n) \to A$
MLT	n	$(A) \times (n) \to A$
DIV	n	$(A) \div (n) \to A$
LDAN	n	$n \to A$
ADDN	n	$(A) + n \to A$
SUBN	n	$(A) - n \to A$
MLTN		$(A) \times n \to A$
DIVN	n	$(A) \div n \to A$
JUN	n	$n \to$ location 4
JGR	n	If $(A) \geqslant 0$, $n \to$ location 4
JEQ	n	If $(A) = 0$, $n \to$ location 4
JSR	n	[Jump to Subroutine]
JST	n	[Jump to STOP]
SQT	n	$\sqrt{(A)} \to A$ [Escape address n]
EXP	n	$\exp (A) \to A$ [Escape address n]
LGN	n	$\ln (A) \to A$ [Escape address n]

SAM (simulated arithmetic machine)

SIN		sin (A) → A
COS		cos (A) → A
RNT	n	[Number from data → (A)] [Escape address n]
PNT	n, m	[Print number]
PNL		[Print 'Newline']

Notes
1. Square brackets indicate a statement not in the City and Guilds Prospectus Mn 319.
2. (n) means 'contents of location'.
3. (A) means 'contents of the accumulator'.
4. → means 'is transferred to'.
5. *n* means 'the number n'.
6. The above instruction set is not a complete list and has in any case been superseded by an amended set.
7. Permission to use the City and Guilds code is gratefully acknowledged.

Appendix 5.2

Example 1   Calculate (17 + 15) (12 − 8) using the number store.

```
(TITLE)
ATHERTON USE OF BRACKETS 1
(STORE 10)
+17
+15
+12
+ 8
(STORE 100)
LDA 10
ADD 11
STA 200
LDA 12
SUB 13
MLT 200
PNT 4,4
JST 100
(EXECUTE 100)
```

Example 2   Repeat example 1 using the data store.
    The advantage of this method is that the calculation could be repeated on a computer with different numbers by simply splicing a different data tape on the end of the program tape.

```
(TITLE)
ATHERTON USE OF BRACKETS 2
(STORE 100)
RNT
STA 200
RNT
ADD 200
STA 200
RNT
STA 201
RNT
STA 202
LDA 201
SUB 202
MLT 200
PNT 4,4
JST 100
(EXECUTE 100)
17   15   12   8
```

Example 3 Write a program to calculate each pupil's average percentage mark resulting from two examinations with maximum marks of 100 and 25 respectively.

Calculations of the form $\frac{53 + 14}{125} \times 100$ are repeated until there are no more data. The escape address 108 then causes exit from the loop.

```
(TITLE)
ATHERTON PERCENTAGES 1
(STORE 10)
+125
+100
(STORE 100)
RNT 108   ←┐
STA 200    │
RNT        │
ADD 200    │
DIV 10     │
MLT 11     │
PNT 2,0    │
JUN 100   ─┘
JST 100
(EXECUTE 100)
53   14   64   19   45   12
```

Example 4 Example 3 is repeated here but the loop is obtained by a conditional jump

JGR 103

If the number in the accumulator is greater than zero (i.e. positive), control jumps to the next but one instruction. Otherwise the next instruction, which is a jump to the end of the program, is obeyed. Any negative number at the end of the data will cause exit from the loop.

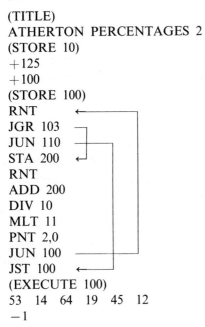

(TITLE)
ATHERTON PERCENTAGES 2
(STORE 10)
+125
+100
(STORE 100)
RNT
JGR 103
JUN 110
STA 200
RNT
ADD 200
DIV 10
MLT 11
PNT 2,0
JUN 100
JST 100
(EXECUTE 100)
53   14   64   19   45   12
−1

Example 5 Calculate the mean of n numbers.

This is another simple loop with exit by means of an escape address. The first number in the data is n, in this case 5.

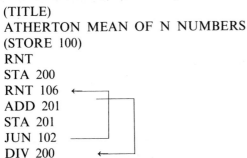

(TITLE)
ATHERTON MEAN OF N NUMBERS
(STORE 100)
RNT
STA 200
RNT 106
ADD 201
STA 201
JUN 102
DIV 200

PNT 4,4
JST 100
(EXECUTE 100)
5 23·6 21 25·3 22·8 23·4

Example 6   This is a repeat of example 5 introducing several new ideas.

(a) Words following the symbol / are for explanation only and are ignored by the computer. Such words are called comments.
(b) Exit from the loop is obtained by using location 2 as a counter. The instruction

ADDN 1

causes one to be added to the number in the accumulator. An N on the end of ADD, SUB, MLT, DIV or LDA means that the number following is not an address but the actual number to be used. It must be a positive whole number.
(c) The counter which is set to zero by LDA 0 (which contains a permanently stored zero) at the start is increased by one each time round the loop. On each occasion the count is tested by subtracting five. As soon as the result is zero, exit from the loop is obtained by the instruction

JEQ 114

which causes control to jump to the end of the program if the number in the accumulator is equal to zero.

The techniques illustrated in example 6 are of fundamental importance in computer programming.

(TITLE)
ATHERTON MEAN OF N NUMBERS
(STORE 100)
RNT
STA 200
LDA 0
STA 2   / COUNTING REGISTER CLEARED
STA 201   / SUMMING REGISTER CLEARED

SAM (simulated arithmetic machine)

```
RNT      ←──────┐
ADD 201         │
STA 201         │
LDA 2           │      / COUNTER INCREASED
ADDN 1          │      / BY ONE
STA 2           │
SUB 200         │      / TEST FOR JUMP
JEQ 114   ┐     │      / OUT OF LOOP
JUN 105   ┘─────┘
LDA 201   ←┘
DIV 200
PNT 4,4
JST 100
(EXECUTE 100)
5   23·6   21   25·3   22·8   25·4
```

6
Simulation in international relations

Paul Smoker

Paul Smoker holds joint appointments as Fellow in Conflict Research at the University of Lancaster, England, and Assistant Professor of Political Science at Northwestern University near Chicago in the United States. He has a teacher's certificate from Chorley College and the M.Sc. and Ph.D. degrees in politics from the University of Lancaster. His main publications have been in mathematical models of arms races, empirical analyses of conflict behaviour, and simulations of international relations. His present research interests include simulations of alternative global futures and total systems models of planet Earth.

This paper was prepared as part of the activities of the Simulated International Processes project (Advanced Research Projects Agency, SD 260) conducted within the International Relations programme at Northwestern University. Copyright © 1969 by Northwestern University.

Varieties of simulations

Simulations of international relations have been used for both educational and research purposes during the last ten years. Developed in part from traditional war games and in part from laboratory experiments of social scientists, simulations of international relations are constructed from theory about international relations. Sometimes this theory is concerned with a small segment of international relations, as in the case of war games, diplomatic games,[1] and international business games,[2] and sometimes with the total international system.[3]

In the gradual evolution of simulations of international relations, variants of five or six simulations have been used in much of the educational and research work.[4] The Inter-Nation Simulation, now a classic historical model, is perhaps the best known of the standards.[5] Developments from this simulation have included the World Politics Simulation[6] and the International Processes Simulation (IPS)[7]. The second section of this chapter describes the construction and use of the International Processes Simulation.

Like the Inter-Nation Simulation and the World Politics Simulation, the International Processes Simulation uses human decision makers and a computer simulated environment. Other simulations, such as the Political–Military Exercise,[8] are 'all-man', and use a panel of judges or a control team of experts to keep the game moves in check. A third format is the all-computer simulation, of which the Technological, Economic, Military, and Political Evaluation Routine (TEMPER)[9] is the best known example. In this simulation a theory of international relations is completely programmed and used to calculate future states of the international system. TEMPER has subsequently been modified and is now used as a man–machine simulation.[10] A complete review of simulation in international relations is now available.[11] This review, published in a shortened form elsewhere,[12] presents details of all major international relations simulations.

There are many definitions of simulation in international relations. For some a simulation is a model;[13] for others it is experimentation on a model.[14] The matter is further complicated by varying interpretations of the concept *model*. As Ackoff points out,[15] *model* as a noun implies a representation, as an adjective perfection, and as a verb to demonstrate or show or reveal. All three interpretations are used in international relations, since simulations try to represent social entities and events, are idealized and simplified to include just those aspects of theory considered relevant, and, in addition, attempt to demonstrate or reveal properties of a theoretical construction.

Guetzkow conceives of simulation as a theoretical construction consisting not only of words and mathematical symbols, but of words, mathematical symbols, and surrogate or replicate components all set in operation over time to represent the phenomena being studied.[16] However one defines simulation, it is important to remember that simulation is not necessarily a representation of a 'real world' or possible 'real world' situation. It is a representation of a theory or set of theories about a 'real world' or a possible 'real world' situation. The adequacy of implicit and explicit theoretical assumptions about the perceived reality is central in understanding any simulation of international relations. For example, the TEMPER simulation implicitly assumes that a nation will increase its own armaments in response to an increase in the armaments of a potential enemy. The explicit assumptions are concerned with the relative size of the increase. A student of non-violence might legitimately question not only the explicit assumptions concerning the relative size of armament increase but also the implicit assumption that such an increase is an appropriate response.

Problems of validity

A number of workers in international relations simulations are concerned with *validity*. The concept validity, like the concepts simulation and model, has a number of different interpretations in international relations. Hermann, for example,[17] suggests five classes of validity—internal validity, face validity, variable parameter validity, event validity, and hypothesis validity. For Hermann, internal validity is determined by comparing the output of a series of simulations, each beginning with identical conditions. For perfect internal validity, all simulations would behave in the same way. This is seldom the case in international relations simulations, since many relationships are at best probalistic and considerable variance between simulations occurs. Face validity is a strictly subjective evaluation of how the simulation 'feels', and while it can be argued that face validity lacks explicit criteria and 'objectivity', there is no doubt that from an educational or experiential point of view, face validity taps an essential dimension of simulation. Variable parameter validity, on the other hand, attempts to provide an 'objective' evaluation of simulation. Here a statistical comparison of simulation behaviour with 'real world' behaviour is undertaken. While variable parameter validity concentrates on relationships between variables, event validity considers specific events, such as the outbreak of the First World War, and the ability of a simulation to reproduce that single event.[18] Hypothesis validity compares simulation behaviour to predictions from international relations theory. For example, hypotheses concerning the conflict behaviour of complex global systems were investigated using the International Processes Simulation, the results supporting the structural peace model proposed by Johan Galtung.[19]

For simulations of international relations, validity is often regarded as the correspondence between a simulation and a 'reality'. The greater the correspondence of phenomena in the two situations, the greater the assumed validity of the simulation. Thus Guetzkow conceives of validity as the correspondence of simulation processes and outcomes to 'real world' processes and outcomes.[20] The greater this correspondence, the greater the credibility of simulation theory. He also points out that although correspondence may exist for certain variables, this does not mean that correspondence has been achieved for a wider sample of variables. Correspondence in political development, say, may or may not be relevant to correspondence in foreign policy.

Strictly speaking, correspondence for any aspect of man–machine

114

simulations can be assumed only when empirically demonstrated, for differing from formal mathematical models, deductions from a man–machine simulation are not merely calculations of logical consequences of an explicitly defined system. Man–machine simulations are not explicitly defined, since a number of human beings are involved and no total general theory of human behaviour exists. Indeed, this fact is one of the important arguments in favour of using man–machine simulations.

Apart from this problem, complete correspondence of all aspects of simulation behaviour to all aspects of the 'reality' represented by the simulation would require any defined variable or set of variables to be identical in both model and 'reality', and the model to be precisely as complex as 'reality'. In social systems this is rather a tall order. Assuming that we must be satisfied with something less, it is necessary to accept behavioural distortions in a model relative to a 'reality'.

So while it seems reasonable to argue that greater correspondence between model and 'reality' encourages us to have more confidence in the theory represented by the simulation, it is worth remembering that complex models have complex properties. Distortions and omissions are to be expected in the behaviour of any complex model relative to the perceived reality because of the simplifications involved in model construction.

Using the perspective that simulation is operating theory, Guetzkow postulates an increase in the credibility of the theoretical constructions of simulations as internal processes and outputs of a simulation in-increasingly correspond to 'real world' processes.[21] This perspective equates correspondence with validity in the sense that the greater the number of correspondences between simulation output and 'real world' behaviour, the greater the assumed validity of the simulation.

Another approach to validity[22] defines validity in terms of the model building process itself. In those places where the simulation model accurately represents a theory, one anticipates high correspondence; where the simulation model fails to represent a theory, one would anticipate low correspondence. If this view is taken, correspondence does not necessarily imply validity, for a simulation model might deliberately emphasize a certain type or area of behaviour through fine modelling at the expense of another area of behaviour where the simulation is less focused. To give a simple analogy from physics, a child might be puzzled on seeing out-of-focus areas in photographs taken with his father's camera. He might conclude that something was wrong with the camera since distant objects were out of focus when close-ups were clear, and vice versa. But with an understanding of lenses and the principles of optics, distortions in the image (model) of reality become understandable and controllable. For close-ups one focuses on near objects; for landscapes on distant ones.

The validity problem is further complicated if the fundamental nature of social science is considered.[23] It is possible to view human nature and human behaviour as fixed and law-like and to assume a simulation is 'realistic' if it adequately replicates behaviour observed in some 'reality'. If, however, human behaviour is not viewed as law-like, or if the laws themselves are subject to change, then the validity problem becomes increasingly complex. To model a largely unknown system in which the laws are constant is difficult enough, but when the laws themselves are subject to change, the prospect becomes almost unthinkable. Social scientists themselves are not agreed upon this question. Some adopt the perspective that human behaviour is at least sufficiently law-like to enable prediction and validation at a general level. Others argue that simulation is more appropriately used as a technique of social creation where alternative forms of social organization and behaviour can be explored.[24]

Using simulation to explore alternative futures can lead to an action-research perspective in social science. Most empirical social scientists overcome a discrepancy between model and 'reality' by adjusting the model. But it is possible to take a complementary position and evaluate a 'real world' relative to the 'model world' incorporated in a simulation. With this perspective, the model world becomes an attempt to demonstrate or show or reveal the way parts of reality could or should be, and differences between the two worlds are rectified by changing aspects of 'reality' through social and political action. Such an approach is not only important in social creation of desired futures, it suggests an alternative perspective for empirical social science that differs from the 'realistic' position of 'telling it the way it is'.

Difficulties and prospects

Although great strides have been made in the simulation of international processes during the last decade, these simulations are still extremely primitive when compared to the technological sophistication of simulations in the applied physical sciences. At least three factors contribute to the primitive nature of international relations simulations. First, theory about international relations is highly under-developed, fragmented, and primitive. Possibly this is due to the inherent complexity of global social processes. At least in part, it is due to the relatively small number of man hours of work devoted to systematic theory building in this area. A second factor contributing to the present state of international relations simulations concerns the human and economic resources currently available. Even if it is possible to create simulations that adequately correspond to 'global realities', it is likely that such a task is at least as difficult as putting a man on the moon and requires a corresponding allocation of man hours of work. A third contributing factor concerns the technological sophistication that social scientists have been able to bring to bear. Simulations of social processes are inherently complex phenomena, yet only within the last five or six years have we begun to utilize computer technologies that in principle are capable of handling this complexity.

The immense problems inherent in simulating international relations are readily apparent. But it is also possible to see the potential pay-offs simulation offers. Simulation is one of the few research techniques now available for studying complex social systems where many known and unknown factors interact in many known and unknown ways. Even with the vast computational powers of modern high-speed digital computers, numerical solutions to many of the problems of international relations are just not feasible. Similarly, many complex aspects of large social systems defy verbal analysis. When used as an educational device, simulation offers the student an experimental basis for thinking about international relations that is at least as valuable as the traditional outsider's view gained from formal lectures. This is particularly true if the simulation is a valid expression of the 'reality' it represents. For this reason questions of validity are as important to educational users as to researchers in international relations theory.

When using simulation either as an educational or a research device, it is well to be aware of the numerous shortcomings that still exist in all the international relations simulations currently available. One can then gain maximum advantage from the rich educational and research environments simulation offers without getting too carried away with the significance of the results.

International Processes Simulation

An overview The International Processes Simulation, a simplified model of a system of nations, national and international corporations, and international organizations, gives participants the experience of making decisions in a miniature prototype of a complicated international system. During the simulation, governments can engage in diplomatic activity, form coalitions, give aid, sign treaties, and even on occasion wage war like their counterparts in the international community. At the same time citizens and governments negotiate with national and international corporations for a variety of products.

The simulation is played in eighty-minute periods and lasts two days.

Each day there are five or six periods. At the beginning of the first period the Simulation Director provides each government with information about its nation's wealth, basic resources, form of government, and defence position. Each Executive Director of a corporation is given information on his corporation's factories and inventory. Citizens are told their income for the period, and International Organization Delegates are briefed on the current state of international affairs. Using this information, the leaders of each government, the directors of each corporation, and the citizens of each country plan their goals and strategies for the period.

The *Head of State* is the chief government official in each nation. He is concerned with developing long-range domestic and foreign policies, planning short range programmes consonant with these policies, and selecting appropriate means to carry out policies and programmes. In some nations the decision of the Head of State is final; in others the collective decisions of the whole government are required.

The *Domestic Adviser* is responsible for the internal affairs of his nation. His work encompasses the duties of such United States officials as Secretary of Labour; Secretary of Commerce; Secretary of Health, Education and Welfare; Secretary of the Interior; and Secretary of Agriculture. He considers the long-range prospects of his nation for such matters as consumer demands, capital depreciation and development, research and development projects, and maintenance and internal deployment of military forces. He gives advice and supervision on all internal affairs, including the chances for his government staying in office. Although he is not concerned directly with foreign policy, he is a member of the National Council (Cabinet) because a government's foreign policy and capabilities in international affairs depend in part upon internal conditions.

The *Foreign Affairs Diplomats* have positions similar to that of an ambassador to a 'real world' nation. Although their duties do not involve them directly in the policy making process, they contribute indirectly through negotiating on behalf of their government and reporting the results of every negotiation to their government. They have the important task of interpreting their government's position to other governments. To do this effectively they must thoroughly understand the positions of their own government and state these positions clearly and diplomatically. In addition, they must estimate the intentions and capabilities of other governments and report the results of their negotiations to their government.

An *International Organization Delegate* represents his government at an international organization. Like the Foreign Affairs Diplomats, his duties do not involve him directly in the policy making process although

118

he contributes indirectly by reporting the proceedings of the international organization to his government. He has the important task of stating publicly the position of his nation in the international organization and he attempts to influence world opinion in favour of his government's policy. In order to do this, he must understand the positions of his own government, state these positions and define them in the light of world opinion, interpret the statements and positions of other governments in the international organization, and report back to his government on events in the international organization. Because he operates in the glare of world publicity, the difficulties of projecting his nation's policies in a favourable way can sometimes be great.

Citizens can participate in a number of different activities, although a basic concern is improving their standard of living. They can, for example, own stock, call local or general strikes, participate in international non-governmental conferences, demonstrate, vote, riot, engage in guerrilla warfare or assassination attempts, or travel to foreign countries. In all cases the programmed or unprogrammed environment responds in some way. For example, a general strike stops production and wages, and owning stock brings extra (taxable) income.

The *Executive Director* is the chief official in each corporation. He is concerned with such problems as developing long-range policies for his corporation, planning short-range programmes consistent with these policies, and selecting appropriate means to carry out policies and programmes. The policies and programmes he selects should maximize the profit and growth of the corporation during the simulation.

High-ranking decision makers in government and industry rarely have as much time as they would like to make important decisions. Simulation decision makers operate under analogous time pressures, and the information cycles of the simulation are designed to maintain the continual demand for decision. To be politically effective, governments must balance such competing demands as consumer needs, long-term economic development, national defence, and alliance obligations. National characteristics such as public opinion, world opinion, and national security are continually calculated by the computer simulated environment and are reported to decision makers and the press.

Similarly, national and international corporations must continually make decisions on such questions as product mix, research and development strategies, geographical distribution of capital investment, profit margins, and distribution of profits.

Operating the International Processes Simulation Because of the complexity of the International Processes Simulation[25] the Simulation

Director supervises a staff of five or six people. In addition, some ten couriers are required to facilitate communications between the twenty-five to fifty participants. The simulation staff has two major functions: running the training session and operating the simulation. During the training session staff members conduct four separate training groups, each group concentrating on one or two decision making positions and the particular decision-making procedures relevant to those positions. During the actual simulation runs, each staff member is responsible for operating one part of the simulation machinery. The Simulation Director co-ordinates the activities of the simulation staff.

Before taking part in the simulation proper, participants must attend a two or three hour training session. Even though participants have previously studied the 'Participant's Manual',[26] effective manipulation of the complex set of decision forms requires a role specific training session. The training session is usually held in four distinct groups. The first group includes Heads of State and Domestic Advisers for each government; the second, Executive Directors and their financial assistants in the international corporations; the third, Citizens of each nation; and the fourth, Foreign Affairs Diplomats and International Organization Delegates. After these sessions at least one trial period is held in which participants make practice decisions that help them understand how the simulation works. The importance of a training session cannot be overstressed. Future simulations might use programmed instruction[27] to improve the quality of initial decision making in a man–machine simulation.

The physical arrangement of the simulation is illustrated in Fig. 6.1. Simulation staff work at a Message Centre, a microphone, a Data Centre, two computer consoles, and a high-speed photocopying machine.

The Message Centre is best located in the middle of the floor space to minimize communication distance between cubicles, each cubicle housing either a National Council, Citizens, an Executive Director, or Foreign Affairs Diplomats. As couriers may have to deliver messages from any one of the cubicles to any other cubicle, the Message Centre is conveniently situated to process all messages *en route*. The twenty-three cubicle layout shown in Fig. 6.1 is used for a six-nation, five-corporation simulation. The number of nations, corporations, and international organizations used in a given simulation depends on the object of the simulation and the limitations imposed by the size of the computer's memory.

As in the Inter-Nation Simulation,[28] written messages are an important means of communication. If the simulation is undertaken for research purposes, for example to study possible consequences of nuclear pro-

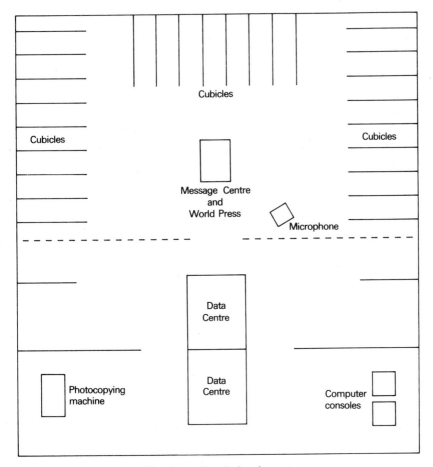

Fig. 6.1   Simulation layout

liferation upon alliance structure,[29] the message pad produces each message in triplicate. A courier collects the top two copies of the message from the out tray on a decision maker's table (the decision maker keeping the bottom copy for his files) and goes straight to the Message Centre. At the Message Centre all messages are placed in a tray and time-stamped by the simulation staff, who retain the second copy for research purposes, while a courier delivers the third copy to the addressee. The average time for delivering messages is two or three minutes, although when information overload occurs, for example at times of crisis when many communiqués are exchanged, a message can be delayed up to five minutes. The Message Centre can also be used to delay messages between governments who do not recognize each other diplomatically. In some simulations[30] messages have been deliberately delayed to simulate communications difficulties between parties in a conflict situation. As in the Inter-Nation Simulation, both restricted and unrestricted messages are sent, the decision maker selecting the appropriate message pad from his files. The World Press usually sits at the Message Centre and has immediate access to all unrestricted messages, using the research copy to avoid delaying messages. A random sample of the restricted messages is leaked to the Press by simulation staff.

A second function of the Message Centre is to co-ordinate conferences. A decision maker wishing to have a conference with another decision maker fills out the Conference Request Form and instructs a courier to circulate the form to other intended conferees. If any of the invited decision makers decline the request, the courier returns to the originator and asks if the conference should still be held. If the answer is yes, the courier once again consults with those invited. The fully signed-up Conference Request Form is then returned to the Message Centre and conferences are arranged in order by a member of the simulation staff. Again, it is possible to arrange conferences on a priority basis, depending upon the particular political structure of a simulation. For example, conferences between allied governments may be arranged on a quicker turn around than conferences between governments not formally allied. In the one series of research runs undertaken with the International Processes Simulation to date, four conference rooms were used, each conference lasting four minutes. Again, this should not be regarded as a hard and fast rule, and the Simulation Director should use his judgement concerning the duration of important conferences.

The World Press provides a major source of information and misinformation in a simulation. Many possibilities exist for intertwining the World Press within the structure of a simulation. In one television simulation using a version of the International Processes Simulation adapted to create the Czechoslovakian crisis of 1968 six weeks before the real event,[31] a global news agency as well as national ideologically biased news media were used. National news media were in many cases staffed by professional journalists, and a great variety of interpretations became apparent in the subsequent analysis. The simplest use of the World Press is for a single news desk to disseminate information to all participants in a simulation. Again, the basic model is sufficiently flexible to allow many different structures. In the research runs undertaken with the International Processes Simulation, an average of ten issues of the World Press per seven-hour day was published.

A microphone sometimes proves useful for informing participants of decision making deadlines, since in the excitement and involvement generated by a simulation, mundane decisions, such as allocating the nation's resources, can be overlooked. Couriers can sometimes provide the necessary degree of control, and in simulations undertaken purely for educational and experiential purposes, indirect control through couriers is to be recommended. For the more rigorous demands of international relations research, when standardization over a number of different simulation runs is a desirable goal, direct control through a microphone is often of great value.

Man–computer interface The programmed component of the International Processes Simulation uses 'on-line' computing facilities for interaction between participants and a computer simulated environment. On-line computers are designed so that many people can use the same computer at the same time, each user communicating with the computer through his own typewriter-like console. The consoles are connected to the computer through an ordinary telephone, and a user is able to get an immediate typed response from the computer. For the International Processes Simulation, two consoles are used to link the decisions of participants to the computer simulated international system. By this procedure consequences of participants' decisions can be calculated in a few minutes.

Apart from the advantages of fast feedback to participants, the programs are written in such a way that those not familiar with computers are still able to operate the simulation. On-line facilities offer the further advantage that a number of commercial firms now exist,[32] and groups who do not normally have access to such facilities may rent them on a short-term basis. For one two-day simulation computing costs are roughly £100. Programs are available in a self-instructional package for two of the largest commercial on-line companies, General Electric and International Business Machines. The self-instructional package includes an instruction program, and eight other programs. The instructional program gives details of the other programs and describes procedures for entering a program into the computer's memory. The first program loads the starting data into twenty previously empty data files. This data includes all the economic, political, and military characteristics of the nations, corporations, and international organizations. When this is done, the second program is run from one of the terminals to generate appropriately labelled statistics for the participants. For example, each nation is told its current political characteristics, such as governmental stability and public opinion, the existing military situation, and its various economic capabilities.

Having run these first two programs, by simply typing the command 'run' into one of the terminals, the computer component of the simulation is ready for operation. The remaining six programs are operated in two sets, one set from each terminal. The programs interact with each other through the twenty data files. Any person of average intelligence can learn to operate a computer console in two or three hours. All of the programs are self-instructional in the sense that each program specifies the exact information it requires to run.

Simulation schedule The information cycles of the simulation are illustrated in Fig. 6.2. During the first ten minutes each government meets to plan policy for the coming period. In the first period policy is developed from a *scenario* that participants have previously read. Great flexibility exists with regard to the *scenario*. It is possible to give all participants the same *scenario*, or members of each nation can be given a *scenario* written from the national point of view. Ideological bias can in this way be incorporated so that the same situation looks quite different to two different governments.

As soon as the government meetings are over, each participant completes a World Opinion Form evaluating the performance of each government. (During the first period participants' evaluations are based on the *scenario*.)

Roughly fifteen minutes after the beginning of the period, each government must make an important complex of decisions. These decisions are principally concerned with fiscal questions and allocating the nation's resources. Governments record their decisions on a Budget Allocation Form, National Investment Forms, and a Profits After Tax Form. Couriers take all decision forms to the Data Centre. An analogous set of decisions are required from corporations ten minutes later. These decisions are recorded by Executive Directors of corporations on a Corporation Plan for the period. Knowing the profits available after taxation, an Executive Director can decide how to reinvest in his company and, knowing the current and projected sales, how to plan company production. At this time the research and development computer program is run on Terminal One. This program simulates outcomes of research and development and capital investment using governmental and company decisions.

From the very beginning of a simulation, trade agreements and trade terminations are possible. These are entered on Terminal Two through a pair of interlocking computer programs. Terminal Two provides a book-keeping capability, checking on existing agreements and up-dating agreements as they are negotiated between decision makers. The informa-

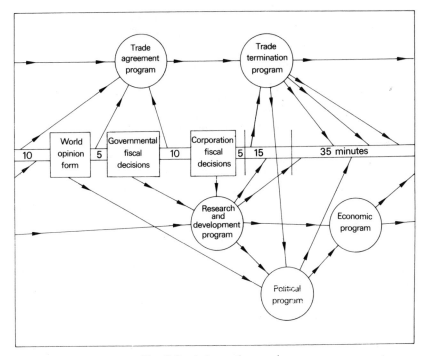

Fig. 6.2　Information cycles

tion cycles of a simulation become continuous at this time in Period
One. Five minutes after the Corporation Plan has been collected, the
trade agreement deadline is reached. This marks the point in time after
which trade agreements are no longer valid for the current period or
year. Agreements may still be negotiated of course, but they will not
become effective until the next period.

All print-out from the computer terminals contains some information
that is role specific—that is, only one decision maker has access to it.
For example, the print-out from the research and development program gives production costs for a particular company to manufacture a
particular product for a particular customer. Only the company Executive Director gets this information. Other information, such as the geographical distribution of companies, or the occurrence of a revolution
in a particular nation, is given to all participants. Thus, some parts of
each print-out are distributed directly to particular decision makers,
while other parts are photocopied or duplicated and distributed to all
participants. Stencils can be cut directly from a computer terminal at
the time the program is running, or a paper tape copy of a program

output can be made. Then, using the terminal as an ordinary teletype, it is possible to cut a stencil of the print-out at any time.

As can be seen from Fig. 6.2, when the research and development program is complete on Terminal One, a program concerned mainly with political and economic characteristics of nations is put into operation. Output from this program provides the starting data for the next period. When this program is complete a program concerned with the trade structure of the simulation and the profit and loss account of corporations is put into motion.

The actual length of a period can be varied to suit the individual needs of students and teacher. While the information cycle illustrated in Fig. 6.2 assumes one hour and twenty minutes as the length of a simulation period, some runs have used periods of two or two and a half hours quite successfully. Much depends on the purpose of the simulation and the proficiency of participants. Initially, participants are hard pressed even to operate the system effectively. But after five or six periods of play the routine decisions illustrated in the information cycle become less time consuming.

It would be misleading to assume that these routine decisions represent the core of a simulation. On the contrary, Table 6.1 illustrates a sample of 'free activity' open to various participants. Governments, for example, in addition to trading and giving aid, can establish diplomatic relations, expel diplomats, expel ambassadors, sign cultural or military agreements, place limitations on citizens' travel, impose tariffs, go to war, mobilize forces, or even support the U.N. Citizens, apart from attempting to satisfy ever increasing consumer needs, can indulge in anti-government or anti-foreign demonstrations, riots, revolutions, strikes, assassinations, expo's, international non-governmental activity, elections, and a host of political behaviour relevant to international relations.

As a general rule each simulation lasts two whole days, with an additional half day set aside for training. Again, great flexibility exists here, and sometimes a simulation can be run with one period each day over a period of a week or more. To run continuously over two days has the advantage that involvement becomes rather intense due to continuous immersion in a simulated environment. The simulation has, however, been used on a one-period-a-day basis, and participants appeared to benefit from the experience.

Prospects for education

Educational aspects of international relations simulations can be considered in relation to various interpretations of validity. If validity is seen as correspondence of model and 'reality', then participation in a

126

Simulation in international relations

Table 6.1   Activities open to simulation decision makers

Name of form	Colour	From	To	Type of decision
*Trade Agreement Form	Goldenrod	NC and Executive Director of a Corporation	Simulation Director	Trade agreement between National Council and Corporation to provide Basic Resources or Force Capability to National Council
*Trade Termination Form	Goldenrod	NC	Corporation	Terminates trade agreement
Force Utilization Plan	Blue	NC	Simulation Director	Deployment or redeployment of Forces, or declaration of war
**Budget Allocation Form	Blue	NC	Simulation Director	Allocation of nation's economic resources for the period
**World Opinion Form	Green	NC	Simulation Director	Evaluates policies of own and other nations
Conference Request Form	Green	NC	Any other participant	Requests conference
Diplomatic Relations Form	Blue	NC	Simulation Director	Alters diplomatic relations of nations
*National Investment Form	Blue	NC	Executive Director of Corporation	Allocation of nation's resources to specific corporations for capital investment or research and development
International Agreement Form	Blue	NC	Courier	Makes international agreement or aid agreement
Internal Control Form	Blue	NC signed by Domestic Adviser	Simulation Director	Breaks strike, discovers and destroys internal subversive forces
Negative Sanctions Form	Blue	NC	Simulation Director	Establishes or removes trade embargo, withdraws aid, limits or frees travel of individual citizens, imposes or removes tariffs

Note: Those forms marked ** must be used each period; those marked * usually are used each period; and the remainder are used if necessary.

simulation could provide a student with a subjective and practical set of experiences that he otherwise might not encounter. There are relatively few presidents and prime ministers in the 'real world', but large numbers of children and adults might be 'king for a day' in a simulation, and through this experience come to better understand the incredible political and social complexity of the twentieth century.

With this perspective, the educational value of a particular simulation is in large part determined by just how closely it replicates the 'real world'. A number of validity studies have been undertaken with the International Processes Simulation, and behaviour in the simulation compared to behaviour in 'real' international systems. These studies are

127

reported elsewhere,[33,34] and it is sufficient to summarize some of them here.

When 'real world' professional decision makers were used in a series of research runs, correspondence with 'reality' was high when the conflict behaviour from six weeks of simulation was compared to international conflict during three years in a 'real' international system. Statistically it proves very difficult to differentiate between these simulations and 'reality' in terms of conflict behaviour. But when a sixteen-year-old student sample was used, a completely different pattern of conflict behaviour emerged from the simulation. Similarly, when the simulation was used to model an alternative future in which there were many superpowers, large multi-national corporations, a strong international organization, and much international non-governmental activity, totally different styles of conflict behaviour were produced. The students were much less violent than the professionals, and the alternative future much less violent than the present.

These results bring us to a second interpretation of validity. While it is possible to evaluate the validity of a model relative to a 'reality', the complementary position can be adopted. In this case the model is interpreted as a desirable state of affairs, or at least a more desirable state of affairs than the present 'reality', and efforts may subsequently be made to alter the 'reality'. Politics here becomes the art of the possible, and the simulation a device for defining and creating a range of alternatives. Given the first concept of validity and its associated philosophy of education, simulation is a teaching machine and the high school students were, thank goodness, 'poor learners', since their conflict behaviour in identical structural surroundings was totally different from that of both the 'adult' participants and the 'real world'. It could be argued that the high school students were being 'unrealistic'. On the other hand, the fact that they were placed in an identical structural setting with identical programmed restraints suggests that the ensuing worlds developed by the students are at least as tenable as the current 'reality'. Simulation viewed in this sense becomes a device for creating and exploring alternatives, and validity of models can no longer be gauged relative to 'reality'.

This use of simulation has educational pay-offs both for students and for teachers. Properties of alternative futures can be examined and, depending upon one's criteria, ranked in terms of desirability. Within a school setting a teacher using simulation in this way is not giving answers, he is providing an environment for generating alternatives.

In a field as underdeveloped and complex as the study of global society and international relations, simulation provides a vehicle for learning, discovery, and exploration. It complements the outsider's view of politics that comes from lectures or seminars with an insider's perception that can come only from practical experience. By compressing the time dimension in simulation, intensity increases, and terms such as 'information overload' and 'decision making in crisis' become *right now* experiences. While today's simulations of international relations are crude and inadequate in many ways, the advent of modern computer technology makes it possible in theory to bring large, complex international systems—past, present, and future—into the smallest classroom. The same technology can catapult the smallest classroom back into the world.

REFERENCES

1. Benson, O.: 'A simple diplomatic game'. In J. N. Rosenau (ed.) *International Politics and Foreign Policy*, Free Press, 1961, pp. 504–511.
2. Thorelli, H. B.: *International Operations Simulation*. Free Press, 1964.
3. Smoker, P.: 'International Processes Simulation: a Man–Computer Model'. Northwestern University, 1968.
4. Guetzkow, H.: 'Simulation in International Relations'. *Proceedings of the IBM Scientific Computing Symposium on Simulation Models and Gaming*, Thomas J. Watson Research Centre, 1964.
5. Guetzkow, H., Alger, C. F., Brody, R. A., Noel, R. C., and Snyder, R. C.: *Simulation in International Relations: Developments for Research and Teaching*. Prentice-Hall, 1963.
6. Coplin, W. D.: 'World Politics Simulation II'. Industrial College of the Armed Forces, 1968.
7. Smoker, P.: 'International Processes Simulation', op. cit.
8. Bloomfield, L. P., and Whaley, B.: 'The Political-Military Exercise: A progress report'. *Orbis*, 8, 4, 1965.
9. Raytheon Company, 'TEMPER: Technological, Economic, Military, and Political Evaluation Routine'. 1965.
10. Industrial College of the Armed Forces, 'TEMPER: Technological, Economic, Military, and Political Evaluation Routine'. 1965.
11. Smoker, P., and MacRae, J.: 'Peace Research Reviews'. Forthcoming article on simulation in international relations, Canadian Peace Research Institute, 1970.
12. Smoker, P., and MacRae, J.: 'Simulation in International Relations'. In H. Guetzkow and P. Kotler (eds.) *Simulation in Social and Administrative Science*, Prentice Hall, forthcoming, 1970.
13. Brody, R. A.: 'Varieties of Simulations in International Relations Research'. *Simulation in International Relations: Developments for Research and Teaching*, Prentice Hall, 1963. (Book co-authored by H. Guetzkow, C. F. Algar, R. C. Noel, and R. C. Snyder.)
14. Ackoff, R. (with collaboration of S. K. Gupta and J. S. Minas): *Scientific Method: Optimizing Applied Research Decisions*. John Wiley & Sons, 1962.
15. Ackoff, R. *Scientific Method*.
16. Guetzkow, H.: 'Some Correspondences between Simulations and "Realities" in International Relations'. In M. A. Kaplan (ed.) *New Approaches to International Relations*, St Martin's Press, 1968.

17. Hermann, C. F: 'Validation Problems in Games and Simulations with Special References to Models of International Politics'. *Behavioral Science*, 12, 3 May 1967.
18. Hermann, C. F., and Hermann, M. G.: 'An Attempt to Simulate the Outbreak of World War I'. *The American Political Science Review*, 61, 2 June 1967.
19. Galtung, J.: 'Entropy and the General Theory of Peace'. *IPRA Studies in Peace Research*, Vol. I, Van Gorcum, 1968.
20. Guetzkow, H.: 'Some Correspondences between Simulations and "Realities"', op. cit.
21. Guetzkow, H.: 'Some Correspondences between Simulations and "Realities"', op. cit.
22. Smoker, P.: 'Simulation for Social Anticipation and Creation'. *American Behavioral Scientist*, July 1969.
23. Devereux, G.: *From Anxiety to Method in the Behavioral Sciences.* Mouton & Co., 1967.
24. Waskow, A.: 'Looking Forward: 1999. Who Plans Your Future?' *New University Thought*, 6, 3, spring 1968.
25. Smoker, P.: 'Analyses of Conflict Behaviours in an International Processes Simulation and an International System, 1955–60'. Northwestern University, 1968.
26. Smoker, P.: 'Participant's Manual: International Processes Simulation'. Northwestern University, 1967.
27. Bitzer, D. L., and Braunfeld, P. G.: 'Description and Use of a Computer Controlled Teaching System'. *Proceedings of the National Electronics Conference*, 1962.
28. Guetzkow, H., et. al.: *Simulation in International Relations.*
29. Brody, R. A.: 'Some Systemic Effects of the Spread of Nuclear Weapons Technology: a Study through Simulation of a Multi-nuclear Future'. *Journal of Conflict Resolution*, 7, December 1963.
30. MacRae, J., and Smoker, P.: 'A Vietnam Simulation: a Report on the Canadian/English Joint Project'. *Journal of Peace Research*, 1, 1967.
31. Biery, J.: 'Playing Games with the Future'. *Northwestern Review*, winter 1969.
32. Colburn, L., and Magnell, J. P.: 'Time-sharing Services'. *Modern Data*, October 1968.
33. Smoker, P.: 'Analyses of Conflict Behaviours', op. cit.
34. Smoker, P.: 'International Processes Simulation', op. cit.

7

Simulation and media

Paul A. Twelker

Paul A. Twelker is Associate Research Professor, Teaching Research, Oregon State System of Higher Education. He obtained his doctorate in Educational Psychology at the University of California, Los Angeles in 1964.

For six years, Dr Twelker has conducted research, development, and training activities on instructional simulation. He is perhaps best known for his work on classroom simulation in teacher education. Dr Twelker currently directs the Simulation Systems Programme at Teaching Research, whose activities cover both media-oriented simulation and simulation and non-simulation games. He is President of the American Council on Educational Simulation and Gaming, and editor of a 1,500-reference annotated bibliography on simulation.

One can make a case for the conventional being the norm in education. Arguments for instruction that consist of a teacher equipped with blackboard, and perhaps an overhead projector, lecturing to thirty or more students may be made. Proponents of the conventional might point to its adaptability ('instruction can proceed anywhere, anytime'), its low cost ('with school budgets in danger of defeat, we can't buy expensive hardware or instructional materials'), its long history of use ('why, if it's good enough for my generation, it's good enough for the present . . .'), its apparent degree of success ('who's failing school in our community?'). Perhaps these arguments hold for some students in some places. But the thesis of this chapter is quite the opposite. If one permits the assumption that instruction is only as effective as the methods and technology used to instruct, and that the technology of education has now progressed to the point that it is useful for the solution of problems that cannot be solved through the application of the conventional, then it behoves the instructor to move away from the 'hand tools' of education—the blackboard, the lecture, the paper-and-pencil examination—to more powerful tools, including simulation. Richard Braby of the Naval Training Device Center in Orlando, Florida, makes a telling case for using these more 'powerful' instructional tools in place of the conventional 'hand tools' in military training.

Paul A. Twelker

I don't think we could ever talk a pilot into having the behavior that he must perform in that aircraft. You could talk to him for 30 years and he would never be able to perform under the stress of actual flight. In other words, in the classroom you don't have the stimuli that will actually trigger the behavior . . . I think you have to experience it.[1]

In the light of the very complex systems that are now used in the military and in industry, it is not surprising that there exists a requirement for better learning systems. One characteristic of these unconventional learning systems is that the student is actively engaged in the learning process. Instruction occurs in a context that is learner-centred rather than instructor-centred. To use the example cited by Braby, the pilot practises the operations required in the flying of an aircraft in a less-than-real-life setting rather than by simply listening to rules, procedures, and principles of flying in a classroom. In addition, feedback —information about the appropriateness of the pilot's moves—is provided for primarily in the context of on-going instruction and only secondarily from the instructor. In this highly controlled situation made possible by machine/media components, where life-like responses may be made to a number of standard as well as emergency situations, not a drop of fuel is burned, mistakes are not fatal (lives are never lost in simulators), and rare events may be made commonplace. This is simulation.

This chapter is divided into nine sections. In order to orient the reader to what follows, they are described here:

(a) The essence of simulation for instruction—answers the question, 'What is simulation?'
(b) Media-ascendant simulation—distinguishes between simulations that emphasize media and machines, and simulations that emphasize player interaction.
(c) Military applications—explores the multi-million dollar efforts of the military.
(d) Civilian applications—examines a wide range of applications in public and professional education.
(e) Testing uses of media-ascendant simulation—since instruction also includes assessment, this section examines this use.
(f) Learning outcomes—selects some important cognitive and affective outcomes for examination.
(g) Advantages and limitations of media-ascendant simulation—summarizes some advantages and limitations of the technique.
(h) Two crucial issues: transfer and motivation—examines these two

strengths of simulation with particular emphasis on some questions that are as yet unanswered.

(i) Some new horizons in simulation—explores several new directions that media-ascendant simulation might be taking in the future.

As various simulations are described, the reader is encouraged to translate or apply what is being discussed to his own field. In some cases, suggestions will be made about the wider use of a particular technique. But to the extent that this chapter tantalizes the reader into an active translation role rather than pacifies him into a passive information-reception role, the goals of this writer will be realized.

The 'essence' of simulation for instruction

The unique advantage of simulation is summed up by Thomas and Deemer:[2] 'To simulate is to obtain the essence of, without the reality.' Harman[3] points out that the substitution of 'essence' for 'appearance' which is in most dictionary definitions is a vital distinction. Simulations contain the important parts of, but not all of, reality. Simulations do not have to look like the real-life counterpart, but they do have to 'act' like the real thing.

What does it mean to obtain 'the important parts of'? First, it is clear that when a simulation includes important aspects of reality, it *omits* other elements of the real life situation. When simulations are designed, unimportant elements from real life are subtracted. In the case of simulated displays, there is a reduction of information from the real life source, information that is in some sense unnecessary for the learning of the task. Simulation might be thought of in the following terms:

$$\text{simulation} = (\text{real-life}) - (\text{task-irrelevant elements})$$

where real life, in an instructional sense, is composed of task-relevant as well as task-irrelevant elements.

The simulation not only omits certain elements of real life, but it represents some of the elements that are included. In one sense, a simulation is a caricature in that some of the attributes of real life are not realistically represented. This representation may appear as a distortion or magnification or exaggeration. For example, a simulation of the atomic structure of a DNA helix may represent (distort) size. That is, simulation might be built to a scale, for example, of two centimetres to one Angstrom unit, so that a group of students may examine certain features of the DNA helix without the aid of magnification or special apparatus. On the other hand, the representation may reflect more the characteristics of substitution or addition. The model of a DNA helix may use lengths of plastic to represent ionic bonds. In real life, these bonds are invisible, and are certainly not composed of plastic. In this sense, the represented link is a caricature of a real bond. With this in mind, we may think of simulation in these terms:

simulation = (real life elements) + (represented elements of real life)

It is clear that a simulation designer not only has a task of choosing what elements of real life to include and what elements to omit, but he also has a task of deciding how task-relevent elements are to be represented. In the literature, these considerations usually fall under the general topic 'fidelity of simulation, or, precision of representation'.

Media-ascendant simulation

Generally speaking, all of the various techniques that are labelled 'simulation' fall into two categories:

(a) those that emphasize the role playing, decision making, and player interaction common in simulation games such as CONSUMER,[4] CRISIS,[5] and MANCHESTER;[6] and

(b) those where the instructional burden is carried by media (e.g., slide-tapes, motion pictures, programmed instruction, and computers).

Representatives of the former category may be termed 'interpersonal-ascendant' simulations while the representatives of the latter category may be given the label 'media-ascendant simulation'.[7] The latter category is focused upon in this chapter, and includes such representatives as the well-known driver education trainers, flight trainers, weapon system simulators, and classroom simulation for teacher education. It should be noted that these categories are not meant to imply that media-ascendant simulations may not involve decision making, role playing or team interaction. Not at all. Many weapon system simulators, for example, in fact do exercise whole teams in a rather complex series of interactions. But the basic characteristics of these simulations is that the machine or media portion of the training system is (or is thought to be) indispensable.

Military applications

In the military, the word 'simulator' is commonly associated with equipment. The Naval Training Device Center defines a simulator as: 'A machine or facility which "simulates" the combat environment to a trainee as realistically as possible, enabling him to perform a combat procedure just as he would if he were in action.'[8]

Many simulators are multi-million dollar devices and are mediated by analogue and digital computers. Although no one probably can tell for sure, it has been estimated that there are over 3,000 different simulators that have been used, or are currently in use by the military, the space agencies, and commercial aviation. Expenditures on prototype simulation devices exceed $27 million annually in the United States.

It should be made clear that there is nothing new about simulators as instructional devices. It has been reported in *Naval Research Review*[9] that in the Middle Ages, soldiers trained on mock-up battlements, and that knights learned to joust by charging a wooden figure on a pivot called a quintain. If the rider struck it squarely it would fall over, but if he glanced it, it would swing round and hit him.

However, it was not until the Second World War that simulation was used to train huge numbers of recruits, many of them non-academically inclined. The United States Navy Department responded to this challenge by organizing a Special Devices Division in the Bureau of Aeronautics in 1941. This division later evolved into the Naval Training Device Center. The Navy obtained the services of Admiral Luis de Florez, a civil engineer and inventor, to direct the new division. In these early years, the division drew upon the progress that the British had already made in the development of training devices. The Naval Training Device Center now is the only U.S. governmental agency concerned exclusively with the application of simulation to training equipment. Let us examine a few of these applications to understand better how simulation is applied in the military.

Ship handling simulator   Instruction in the handling of ships may proceed either at sea, using real ships, or on land, using simulation. By using a land-based simulator for training, many problems are alleviated, such as the high cost of operating ships, ship unavailability, and hazard to the trainee and crew. The Visual Simulation Laboratory of the Naval Training Device Center has been investigating a new ship handling trainer using a visual display produced by a wide-angle television projection system and an analogue computer that is programmed to simulate ships' motions.[10] In this simulator, the trainee stands in a mock-up of a destroyer's bridge. The instructor takes the role of the pilot house personnel and adjusts input to the ship's motion computer according to the verbal commands issued by the trainee. In simple manoeuvring problems, rudder angle and engine orders are given by the trainee as commands (input information). In more complex problems involving manoeuvring in harbours, wind speed and direction, water current speed and direction, and water depth comprise the information that the instructor may choose to imput to the computer. In order, visually, to give the trainee the experience of seeing the effect of his commands, the output of the motion computer controls a wide-angle television camera mounted above a model of a destroyer which also moves within a model of a harbour in exactly the same way that the real life destroyer would move. Thus, the television image which is picked up by the camera is observed as a simulation of a real scene. The trainee sees the image on a spherical screen which surrounds the destroyer bridge mock-up. The projected image is carefully designed so that the trainee sees a moving scene which simulates what he would see when observing from the real life ship.

The same technique of taking pictures of a model in action that simulates the real life effects of the trainee's moves is also employed in certain aircraft simulators (e.g., the SST simulator 'flown' at Boeing Aircraft in Seattle, Washington).[11] As in the case of the ship handling trainer, the camera's position and motion are determined by how the pilot 'flies' the simulator. The pictures are projected on a screen in front of the mock-up of the cockpit and make the simulated landing appear real.

Weapon system trainer The Attack Trainers Division of the Naval Training Device Center has developed a weapon system trainer which simulates the A-7A Corsair II, a single-place, light-attack, jet aircraft.[12] This simulator is used to train jet pilots in the procedures and techniques that they must know in order to establish and maintain maximum weapon system capabilities of the aircraft. This simulator is representative of a broad class of flight simulators that permit a wide variety of training programmes including cockpit familiarization, instrument flying, normal and emergency procedures, navigation, communication procedures, etc. The flight aspects of the simulator may be integrated with tactics training so that the trainee must 'fly' an integrated mission where his skills in handling the aircraft as well as skills in attack operations are exercised. The simulation of the aircraft systems is so complete that even the fuel system, including in-flight refuelling procedures, is functional. Realism (fidelity) is so complete that the computer program provides for the changing of the aerodynamics of the aircraft when weapons and armament are released. With the use of this and similar simulators, it is possible to train pilots in operations that would be extremely costly to exercise in real life, not only in terms of operating costs, but also in terms of hazard to life.

Simutech trainer Kristy[13] describes a training environment that staggers the imagination of those who spend most of their time lecturing to students. The Simutech Trainer was conceived of to train Air Force electronics technicians in a manner that provides tutorial teaching capabilities integrated with realistic (but simulated) on-the-job experience. The specification of the system which Kristy describes calls for computer-controlled programmed learning to integrate several types of display: (a) animated schematics, (b) textual and diagrammatic teaching material that includes quizzes and branching sequences. A high speed, quick access, video-taped presentation system provides informal lectures, 'cookbook' advice, and tutorial support for the student. All this is linked with a simulation of an electronic system which the student is responsible for maintaining. This system, also linked with the computer, senses and responds to the student's maintenance actions. Another component in the trainer system is a simulation of the 'operations room' of an Air Force site. This is accomplished by a 'squawk box' communication tie between the operator and the maintenance room.

With this training system, the students:

(a) can receive video instruction on fundamentals of electronics;
(b) can receive clarification and reinforcement from the computer-controlled programmed instruction console;
(c) can practise what they have learned by performing 'on the job' by means of the simulated hardware;
(d) can receive remedial help when they wish or when the computer deems it necessary;
(e) can be quizzed on their progress;
(f) can proceed at their individual paces;
(g) can be monitored so as to inform instructors of their progress and difficulties that may be examined during small, live-group sessions.

From studies of the efficiency of computer-assisted instruction and simulation training, it is estimated that training time may be cut by two-thirds using this equipment. If the system is implemented to accomplish electronics training in the Air Force, the cost would be about $130 million. Although this cost represents a huge sum, Kristy points out that if the trainers were capable of actually reducing training time by two-thirds, the Air Force would save a large fraction of the funds expended on training, and these savings would pay for the system engineering, hardware development, and installation costs of $130 million in only eighteen months. Thereafter, the Air Force would save in training costs up to $75 million per year.

Auto-instructional simulators In the military, simulation applications range from the exceedingly simple to the exceedingly complex. At one end of the continuum, a simulator may cost as little as ten cents, while on the other end of the continuum, one single simulator may cost as much as $11 million. The Simutech Trainer discussed above was a complex system that taught, among other things, the proper steps and procedures of trouble shooting (a cognitive objective) as well as how to carry out the task operationally (a cognitive/psychomotor objective). The former involves the teaching of certain decision-making skills, discrimination skills, problem solving, and so forth. The latter involves the student in using these skills on the simulated job which demands physical manipulation. Although simulation may be used to exercise both types of objectives, the cost may vary tremendously. A class of auto-instructional devices termed Trainer-Tester Simulators that cover many subjects illustrates this admirably. For illustration, a motor trouble-shooting Trainer-Tester Simulator developed by Van Valkenburgh, Nooger, and Neville, Inc. will be examined.[14]

Several courses at the U.S. Army Ordnance School at the Aberdeen Proving Ground in Maryland require servicemen to remove, install, trouble-shoot and adjust six-cylinder engines. One means to accomplish this is to have a series of engines rigged to exhibit certain defects, and teach the servicemen the correct procedures to use in trouble-shooting and correcting the fault. Needless to say, this is expensive. An alternative is to simulate the cognitive operations involved in motor trouble-shooting. The Trainer-Tester Simulator provides this exercise of cognitive operations, all in a self-paced auto-instructional manner. Pictorial review sheets are used in conjunction with specially designed worksheets to familiarize the trainee with the location of various components, to show the inter-relatedness of the components, and to assist the trainee in determining correct procedures to be followed in performing the simulated tasks given in the problems. Trouble-shooting and repair worksheets include columns that list a specific problem (e.g., 'Engine will not start and there is no spark at the spark plugs'), a symptom section, and a corrective-action section. The data in the symptom and corrective-action sections are concealed by a silver overlay and are revealed by using a pencil eraser. The data uncovered reflect deviations from normal operation with the equipment operating under the indicated trouble symptom. The trainee must be familiar with the equipment to select those checkpoints from which he wishes to obtain data so that he may arrive at a correct solution. Indiscriminate erasures indicate that the trainee has analysed the problem incorrectly.

The pocket blinker and war wound moulage kit Lest the reader get the mistaken idea that the lower the cost, the more limited the simulator, let us examine two ingenious techniques that represent low cost simulators. One costs about ten cents and is called a pocket blinker, and it certainly meets all of the requisites to be classified as a simulator. This little cardboard device has been used for years and simulates the operation of a ship's blinker.[15] Two seamen, sitting across a table from each other, may practise sending Morse Code messages back and forth using two of these little devices. They are so constructed that hand pressure moves a sliding cardboard in and out of a slot, thus simulating the alternate black and white patterns emanating from a ship's blinker light.

The second simulation is the War Wound Moulage Kit,[16] which represents relatively high fidelity but low cost. The wound moulage serves two principal purposes:

(a) it enables the wearer to apply first aid treatment to himself, witnessed by students for a first-hand demonstration of proper first-aid procedure, and

(b) it enables the wearer to be placed in the field as a casualty, enabling students to perform first-aid measures under simulated battle conditions.

The wound moulage consists of a thin, flexible, flesh-coloured overlay which simulates as closely as possible actual wounds in pertinent adjacent areas of the human anatomy. Each individual moulage is full size, depicts all of the characteristics of a wound, including details such as torn flesh, broken bone, severed veins and arteries, and even blood flow. Bone structure and flesh are shown in relief on the surface of the moulage. Each moulage is capable of being attached to the appropriate area of the wearer's body, and is readily removable without the use of tools. Included in the kit is a veinous puncture moulage and a hypodermic needle insertion moulage to train students in withdrawing blood and injecting medication into the body. The kit contains twenty moulages, several of which are mentioned below:

(a) gun shot wound of the palm of the hand;
(b) phosphorous burns of the hands;
(c) second and third degree burns of the forearm;
(d) compound fracture of the lower leg;
(e) amputation.

The technique has been adapted for first aid and medical training in numerous hospitals.

Simulated tutoring George Brown of the Human Resources Research Office of the George Washington University has been experimenting with a self-instructional method for foreign language learning that seems to offer a genuine communication experience that is motivating and rewarding in an area that often uses notoriously boring and monotonous programmed courses.[17] The technique, termed 'simulated tutoring', is created by having an experienced language teacher tutor a subject in the pronunciation of a short dialogue. Rather than recording both student and tutor, only the tutor's voice is recorded. This results in a tape which contains all of the tutor's comments, instructions, and explanations, with intermediate pauses which approximate the time required for a student to respond. When the tape is subsequently played in an instructional situation for a student, that student has the experience of interacting with a 'tutor'. Students have reported that, with properly prepared tapes, the illusion is so realistic that they think a live tutor is located behind a screen.

A second technique being explored at the Human Resources Research Office is 'simulated conversation.'[18] The basic idea is to provide a student with a communication partner that will enable the student to exercise the use of the foreign language in a realistic and motivating way. In simulated conversation, the student is confronted with a situation in which he must respond to unpredictable communications, typical of real life situations. Yet, the student's partner is simulated using a tape recorder.

Dr Brown describes one possible exercise of this type. The student is told that he is to imagine himself in a shop buying a pair of shoes. He is given information that is relevant to this purchase: for example, the colour of shoe desired, its size, its style, the maximum price he wishes to pay, and mode of payment. This information is given to enhance the probability that the student may interact freely and smoothly in the simulated conversation. The student then turns on the tape recorder and interacts with the simulated shoe assistant which starts the conversation with a greeting. In English, a typical conversation in this setting might resemble the following:

TAPE: Good morning, sir.
SUBJECT: Good morning.
TAPE: May I help you?
SUBJECT: Yes, I want to buy a pair of shoes.
TAPE: Any particular style, sir?
SUBJECT: Something modern, please.
TAPE: What size do you wear?
SUBJECT: Size 11.
TAPE: Here is a nice pair, size 11, and they are the latest style.
SUBJECT: How much do they cost?

TAPE: Only 18 pesos, sir.
SUBJECT: Too expensive. I don't want to spend more than 15 pesos.
TAPE: Here is another nice pair and they cost only 13 pesos.
SUBJECT: Fine, I'll buy these.
TAPE: How do you wish to pay, sir?
SUBJECT: With a 20-dollar traveller's cheque.
TAPE: Fine. Sign here please.
SUBJECT: All right.
TAPE: Here is your change and thank you very much.

Following the first encounter with the simulated conversation, the student is given further instruction including typical utterances that might be given at each step. Then the simulated conversation is replayed.

Implications for educators   The Simutech Trainer, the Trainer-Tester Simulator, and the other techniques mentioned are but a few applications currently being used or investigated by the military. What does the military think about simulation? An Arthur D. Little Inc. report states that:

The growing emphasis on cost/effectiveness in military training programs will result in much greater use of simulation training. NTDC personnel suggest that the use of simulation is in its infancy and that there may be almost total dependency on simulation in several training areas in the not-too-distant future. Typical areas which lend themselves to simulation techniques are cockpit and operational flight training, in-flight training, and training in electronic warfare and weapon systems.

In order to teach personnel to operate in the conceptual, psycho-physical environments of the present and those anticipated for the future, new technologies are used to simulate such environments visually. A simulator involves any one or a combination of the training environment, computing and associated simulation systems, and instructor station and display systems. Electronics and optics represent major elements in the fabrication of a simulator. However, the market is not limited to electronics and optics companies; industrial organizations having educational technology capabilities should realize a considerable share of this market.[19]

Will the military experience in simulation be translated effectively to the education of civilians in school settings? Few simulators have been used in occupational education. The civilian application of simulator trainers is discussed in detail by Kristy. In summary, several important points are made:

141

(a) the major area of application appears to be in large federal training and retraining programmes;

(b) On-the-job training seems necessary for retraining efforts, but poses serious problems;

(c) A high-efficiency training system such as the Simutech Trainer can provide simulated 'on-the-job' training;

(d) The application of the Simutech Trainer to the federal programmes would occur simultaneously with its application in industrial training programmes;

(e) The application of the system to vocational high schools has serious problems with respect to the large capital investment required.

Regarding the last point, Kristy shows that the cost of training students in an optimal installation in six to ten different technical areas might run $450 per trainee per year, figuring a ten year period to amortize the capital investment. This is two or three times the average investment in training students. Do the benefits or potential of such devices as the Simutech Trainer demand such expensive training? Is it necessary to build a 'simulator-trainer-tutorial environment' that even senses human actions to a sensitive degree and presents 'diverse, alternative programmed situations leading toward teaching and learning objectives'?

Probably not, at least for some types of objectives. The Trainer-Tester Simulator represents a low cost, but effective technique for motivating students and for teaching both identification skills and operational procedures when used with supporting operational equipment.[20] Note that these operations are at the cognitive level, and do not involve psycho-motor skills *per se*. Of course, in the operational situation, the trouble-shooter would then be required to remove engine components, replace defective parts, and so forth. Yet a properly designed auto-instructional simulator effectively shortcuts an inefficient and time-consuming trouble-shooting operation if real equipment were involved at early stages of instruction. It is important that the trainee knows what to trouble-shoot, and in what order, before he actually begins the messy business of removing engine components and the like. These skills could just as easily be performed or practised on the job. This illustrates an important advantage of simulation: when actual on-the-job performance would be costly or hazardous, use simulation. Auto-instructional simulators are inexpensive to produce (although not necessarily inexpensive to design) and are admirably suited for cognitive objectives. What better way would there be to have biology students 'practise' dissection before actually beginning the work? After reading the text, they could go through the procedure using an auto-instructional simulator. Or the technique could be applied to medical education, where medical students would be required to diagnose certain problematic symptoms of a patient. This, in fact, has been done in the area of orthopaedic surgery, and will be discussed below.

In summary, such techniques as the pocket blinker and the auto-instructional simulator illustrate the fact that simulation exercises or devices do not have to be expensive to be effective. As long as the educational objective is consistent with the operations demanded by the exercise, low-fidelity, low-cost devices are satisfactory, especially in early stages of training. Even if the objective for a seaman learning Morse Code is to have him identify patterns under adverse conditions such as bad weather or combat, variation in the way the pocket blinker is used could provide such training. However, for educational objectives that simply reflect the learning of the Morse Code and identifying visually Morse Code patterns, the pocket blinker used in the simplest circumstances is a suitable simulation exercise. Low fidelity, in this case, does not sacrifice learning effectiveness and efficiency.

Civilian applications

Classroom simulation   Civilian applications of media-ascendant simulation are becoming increasingly familiar, especially in higher education. One example is found in the unique and pioneering application of simulation in teacher education as developed at Teaching Research, a Division of the Oregon State System of Higher Education. In 1961, Bert Y. Kersh[21], funded under NDEA Title VII, built a simulation facility and initiated the development of a variety of simulated classroom situations. It was Dr Kersh's direct experience with various military applications of simulation, including those developed at the System Development Corporation, that led him to investigate its use in civilian applications. He was impressed with the highly effective way that simulation trained men for duty in very complex man–machine systems. It seemed that this high degree of transfer from the instructional situation to the real life operational situation could be attributed directly to simulation.

It is interesting to note that Dr Kersh's first experiment with the facility, prior to his development of classroom simulation materials for training pre-service teachers, involved children.[22] He was interested in seeing if an individual, in this case a small child, would react to a projected image of another person as he would in a real life situation. To test his hunch that learners would indeed react to a filmed individual as though he were talking with the person in real life, he developed some motion-picture clips of himself asking a few questions and giving a few simple commands such as, 'What is your name?' and 'Write your name.' Other motion-picture clips contained scenes of his repeating the questions and commands more emphatically or presenting statements of praise and encouragement. One by one, he brought fifth grade subjects into the simulation facility without revealing to them what was to happen. After asking the subject to state his name, write his name, and do some other things, Dr Kersh went behind a oneway glass screen and observed the subject's reactions to the same commands that were now projected life size on a large rear projection screen. It was found that the children's reactions were almost identical to their previous behaviour in the real life setting. He then proceeded to test whether he could control the intensity of the subjects' voices and elaboration of their responses by presenting feedback films of either the repeated request or praise and encouragement. Three projectors were used to present these motion picture clips, one for the initial stimulus, and two projectors for the feedback clips. The equipment was so designed that the experimenter was able to switch from one projector to another at will. Again, he found that simulation training did indeed influence the intensity of the children's voices. They reacted as though the experimenter were in the room rather than on film. These encouraging experiences led to the preparation of a research proposal and subsequent awarding of a grant to explore the possibilities of simulation in teacher education. This grant allowed the development of classroom simulation episodes for the training of elementary teachers in classroom management and control as well as the experimenting with the technique in an effort to determine if realism of the projected image was an important factor in achieving the desired outcomes.

The prototype classroom simulation technique creates for the student teacher many of the relevant features of a single classroom situation called 'Mr Land's Sixth Grade'. Mr Land is the hypothetical supervising teacher with whom the student-teachers work during the simulated experience. A complete cumulative record file is available for each child in the simulated classroom in addition to printed descriptions of the hypothetical school and community. The technique of filming the youngsters in the simulated class so that they appear to be reacting to the student-teacher during the sequences is employed in sixty different problem sequences on sound, motion picture film. In each case, the student-teacher is expected to react to the film as though he were in a real classroom.

'Mr Land's Sixth Grade' is limited as an instructional vehicle since it requires a simulation facility equipped with several projectors, a complex electronic control system, and a rear projection screen. Further, ideally only one student can be trained at a time, and an experienced teacher is required to tutor the student. These limitations led to the development of new 'low-cost' simulation packages that could be used in a variety of circumstances: individualized laboratory (tutorial) instruction, conventional classroom instruction, and self-instruction.[23] These new materials take into account previous research concerning size of image, mode of feedback, mode of response, motion in image, and the effects of prompting that has been carried on at Teaching Research in recent years.[24,25,26,27]

It is thought that the classroom simulation technique may be appropriately used for several types of training:

(a) transition training,
(b) pre-service training,
(c) in-service (refresher) training.

Transition training   When a teacher moves from one school to another, or from one type of school to another (e.g., from a suburban school to an inter-city school), he might profit from a simulation experience of the new environment. This training might include becoming acquainted with new teachers, faculty, curriculum, procedures, regional characteristics, students, problems and so forth.

Simulation might also be used to illustrate unique problems in dealing with culturally different students. Jack Gordon of Wayne State University has proposed that simulation be used in realistic decision forcing episodes interspersed among actual footage of situations typical to the educational environment of culturally different children.* In this way, these materials would be used to focus upon the similarities and differences teachers might encounter when working with these groups. Adjunct materials might include: (a) films showing an exaggerated view of the new teacher as depicted by picture and stories of the children, (b) both beginning teacher blunders and experienced teacher moves that are unique to the particular group, and (c) a semi-documentary of the home life of a typical child with an interview with parents portraying their attitudes toward education. Especially relevant areas of application might be in the educational systems of emerging countries.

Pre-service training   One main advantage of simulation as applied in this teacher education circumstance is that it bridges the gap between textbook learning and the operational real life situation. Usually, students
*Personal communication.

are bombarded with principles of classroom management and yet given little opportunity to exercise or apply these principles in realistic circumstances. Under these conditions, students may be very able to verbalize the principles and pass tests which ask for statements of the principles as taught. The problem is that students do not have sufficient opportunity to practise or exercise the application of the principles in a variety of situations. If this opportunity is not given, students may not be in a position to transfer adequately knowledge gained from the classroom situation to the operational situation. As stated above, simulation offers a valuable technique for increasing the probability of this transfer occurring. In essence, simulation is based on the old adage that 'experience is the best teacher'. Classroom simulation is a technique that allows a prospective student-teacher to gain the benefits of 'direct experience' and at the same time have the advantage of discussions about the experience with skilled instructors. The effect of this training is to provide an environment whereby the student can practise the discrimination of cues which signal problems requiring immediate attention, and practise management and instructional strategies without fear of censure or embarrassment. Through systematic practice in a simulated classroom, the student may learn the decision-making role of the teacher in the classroom by participating in a comparable role in the simulated situation. In brief, the instructional simulation technique forces the student to focus on a situation and devise different modes of responding. In summary, simulation offers the student an opportunity:

(a) to build and to practise his own strategies of searching for cues that signal a decision-making process on his part;
(b) to test hypotheses he has about how to respond to these problems;
(c) to change his behaviour in view of the feedback he receives.

Refresher training Teachers might profit from time to time from participating in simulation training experiences involving topics such as classroom management, the use of various innovative procedures and even professional negotiation techniques. Many of the problems associated with using innovations such as team-teaching and modular scheduling might be alleviated with proper training.

There are numerous other examples of media-ascendant simulation in civilian education, some still under development. Some are briefly discussed below.

Teaching problems laboratory These materials developed by Donald Cruickshank and others,[28] and published by Science Research Associates, simulate an elementary school in which the participant assumes the role of Pat Taylor, a new fifth grade teacher at Long Acre Elementary School. Dr Cruickshank's initial experience with simulation was also in the military setting, as was Dr Kersh's. These experiences, together with the experience of teaching college professors how to use the Whitman School materials of the University Council on Education Administration led to the development of the Teaching Problems Laboratory.

These materials create a fictitious but life-like elementary school through the use of film strips, motion picture films, cumulative record folders, a faculty handbook, and other resource materials. Each simulation participant assumes the role of Pat Taylor and is given an opportunity to react to problems selected from a list of those reported crucial by experienced teachers. Besides the use of critical teaching problems presented on film, role playing techniques are also used in the Teaching Problems Laboratory. Among other things, the experience is intended to provide opportunities for students to examine their own motives and values. The Inner City Teaching Problem Laboratory represents a major revision of the Teaching Problems Laboratory and recreates significant problems of teaching in inner-city schools.[29]

Professional decision simulator The Learning Systems Institute at Michigan State University under the direction of Ted W. Ward has developed and researched the Professional Decision Simulator I (PDS-I) Programmes designed primarily to teach student-teacher trainees to use available cues from the instructional environment as an aid in decision-making involving plans of action.[30] The simulator brings the student trainee to a point of decision and commitment concerning relevant action to take on a particular problem. A sound-film presentation is used to present:

(a) the essential situation leading up to a decision making problem;
(b) verbal suggestions of alternative plans of action;
(c) either negative feedback in the form of aural instruction tracks or positive feedback in the form of a reinforcing continuation of the sound-film.

The positive feedback presents a preferred decision being acted out that is followed by relevant and desirable consequences. Films are not used to present the negative feedback. Instead, 'coaching' is given to help the student understand the suggested outcomes of the choice made and to help him perceive the problem environment more adequately. After coaching, part or all of the original problem sequence from the film is repeated. The professional decision simulator is based on what is termed the 'SAC' model which stands for:

(a) *situation*;
(b) *action* of the teacher making the 'model' decision;
(c) *consequences* of the decision made.

Simulation for counsellor education   Beaird and Standish[31] developed a
simulated environment to train counsellors to:

(a) discriminate between cognitive and affective client responses;
(b) use counsellor response leads in ways to facilitate more client
    affective responses.

The materials use a pre-programmed tape recording that simulates the
client and provides a context for the counsellor to practise the above-
mentioned skills. The simulation materials use a continuous flow pattern
or 'contiguous sequencing'. That is, instead of using a stimulus-response-
feedback-halt condition (single-cycle simulation) typical of the classroom simulation materials discussed above, the counsellor-education
simulation materials are so sequenced that the feedback situations
become the next stimulus situation in a series of interactions between
the subject and the simulated environment.

In an experiment that was designed to provide evidence relevant to the
effectiveness of the simulation technique in counsellor training, subjects
were randomly assigned to an experimental group that received two
hours of individual instruction with the simulated interview, and a
control group, which received similar amounts of time role playing
counselling interviews. After training, all subjects were required to
counsel a role playing client while their performances were evaluated.
These evaluations became the dependent variable of the study. The
analysis revealed that subjects receiving simulation training demonstrated
significant gains in their performance from the pre-training to post-
training interview, while subjects in the control group demonstrated a
small but statistically non-significant decrease in their performance.
While the materials were limited in their scope, the evidence clearly
suggests that other simulated interview techniques might be prepared
and integrated into a comprehensive counsellor programme. In fact,
David Delaney of the University of Illinois has proposed that simulation
materials be used to assist counsellors-in-training to develop certain
basic competencies such as:

(a) reinforcing speaking behaviour in a non-communicative client;
(b) increasing counsellors' awareness of responding to clients' non-
    verbal cues;

(c) increasing counsellors' effectiveness in working with clients who desire test-reinforcing support; and

(d) shaping affective client verbal behaviour.

In some cases, training might rely on video-taped programmes that provide both visual and auditory stimuli.*

Needless to say, numerous problems are involved in designing contiguously sequenced materials. The counsellor training interview along with the simulated tutoring interview and simulated conversation interview, share the common problem of predicting what should be given as feedback to the student. The skill of the simulation designer is crucial in that the hypothetical simulated situation must be structured in such detail that student responses are delimited and that the programme feedback is appropriate for as wide a range of responses as possible. If the number of possible responses were too large, the feedback would become meaningless and any possibility of switching to other tracks, containing feedback or comments, would be hopeless. Yet, these three techniques do represent an attempt to incorporate meaningfulness and realism into the instructional situation, and should be explored further.

Music education simulation   John Gustafson of the University of Oregon is currently developing simulation materials for use in music education.* It is Dr Gustafson's belief that conventional methods of training prospective music teachers are inadequate in that students are not able to extract cues from complex situations, to integrate them, and to make appropriate responses to them. With the simulation materials employing video-taped incidents and adjunct manuals, it is hoped that an opportunity may be given for students to practise skills and to listen for errors committed by individuals in the music class, to detect shades of variance in intonation and to attempt to achieve balance and blend, all within the context of keeping students aware of the overall effect. From preliminary task analysis studies, Dr Gustafson has found that approximately 80 per cent of rehearsal time is devoted to activities characterized by students playing given selections while the teacher listens. After the weakness is diagnosed, students play again as a total group or in sections to try to improve one or more of the performance aspects such as rhythm, technique, articulation and phrasing. The simulation materials that are being developed are directed to these diagnostic and remedial performance activities.

Dental emergencies simulation   A real advantage of simulation over the use of an operational situation is the opportunity to present rare events.

*Personal communication.

149

This advantage is aptly illustrated by the simulation materials that have been developed by Teaching Research to teach dental emergencies.[32] For the most part, dental students have little opportunity to practise handling emergencies that might occur throughout the dentist's professional career. These emergencies are sufficiently infrequent that the probability is small that dental students will experience them in the clinic setting. Even if they are experienced, they would usually be handled by supervising personnel. In this way, the training which the student receives in the handling of dental emergencies is often inadequate and incomplete, and usually limited to textbook learning.

The simulation materials which have been developed, and are currently being used in many dental schools throughout the United States, offer a unique opportunity for students to receive practice as well as instruction in diagnosing various emergencies and coping with them. Sound motion pictures and accompanying written materials enable the dental student to experience most of the types of emergencies that might occur in the surgery: allergy reactions, asthma, hysteria, insulin shock, angina pectoris, anxiety, epilepsy, and syncope. As in the case with the classroom simulation materials, alternative feedback films may be shown that show either the patient recovering from the emergency due to fast and effective treatment or becoming worse.

Forest service training simulator   The United States Forest Service has been using successfully since 1963 a forest fire simulator that is used with campaign fire exercises to train fire bosses and staff, and initial attack crews.[33] Previous to the use of the simulator, campaign fire exercises have utilized maps, blackboards and topographical models that did not provide sufficient dynamic realism, time pressure, and active trainee participation. The fire simulator, designed by the International Electric Corporation, Paramus, New Jersey, allows trainees to see:

(a) a moving fire perimeter with clearly visible flames and smoke;
(b) burned-over areas;
(c) movement of fire lines in accordance with wind, topography, fuel type and effectiveness of staff decisions;
(d) aerial and oblique views of the fire area; and
(e) fire fighting equipment and forces shown by symbols.

Imaginative design enables this simulator to be relatively inexpensive as well as portable. The simulator enclosure, 30 ft wide × 24 ft long, includes a training area accommodating up to twelve trainee observers, and a control area for a projection booth and simulation operator positions. The projection system uses various types of projectors to simulate the flame, smoke, wild land scene, and symbols. All of the equipment fits into a standard tandem wheel trailer that is moved about from one forest service centre to another. The forest fire exercise allows U.S. fire control personnel practice in sizing up the fires, ordering and assigning resources, planning attack strategies, making on-the-spot decisions as conditions dictate, dealing with emergency control problems, directing fire forces, and monitoring and evaluating decisions.

Reading methods education simulation   Instructional films and materials termed *The Informal Reading Inventory Instructional Process* were developed by Utsey, Wallen, and Beldin to alleviate problems of providing students in reading methods courses with instruction on the use of the informal reading inventory.[34] The developers found that when they brought children out of the classroom setting to demonstrate the use of the informal reading inventory, they presented atypical performances. Further, the demonstration could not be repeated in the same way, thus an opportunity for students to practise the informal reading inventory repeatedly was not provided. The simulation materials that were developed solved many of these problems in that students were given an opportunity to practise in a realistic situation the marking code and the application of the criteria of the three functional reading levels. Further, the simulation materials could be repeated time and again, giving students the opportunity to see the child repeat his errors enabling the students to evaluate their own skills. Filming of the materials was done in such a way that the student gains the impression that he is sitting at a teacher's desk across from a student. As far as possible, the student is placed in the teacher's role to heighten the impression that the student is in fact administering an informal reading inventory to a child. Other simulation films have been developed to teach prospective teachers to identify and provide for specific deficiencies in comprehension, rate of comprehension, and word attack skills.

'Sim One'   In the civilian applications examined above, relatively low-cost techniques were used in the simulation. Perhaps the most sophisticated simulation tools that represent rather high-cost techniques may be found in such computer-mediated simulators as 'Sim One', an anthropometric manikin developed by the University of Southern California.[35] Sim One is a very life-like dummy possessing plastic skin that resembles a real human being both in colour and texture. Sim One lies on an operating table, with his left arm extended ready for an intravenous injection, and his right arm fitted with a blood pressure cuff. The dummy is capable of reacting exactly like a real human being: 'he' breathes;

possesses a heart beat, temporal and carotid pulse, and blood pressure; moves his mouth and blinks his eyes; responds to administered drugs and gases and even vomits.

The patient simulator which is used to train residents in anaesthetics at the Los Angeles County General Hospital, was designed with the supposition that training on the simulator would allow students to achieve criterion levels of performance in less time and with fewer operating-room trials than conventional instruction. Data collected in an experiment showed that the mean number of trials necessary to achieve satisfactory ratings for the experimental group was about half that required for the control group. In fact, it is pointed out that if all the skilled tasks to be learned by anaesthetists could be taught by simulation, one could speculate that a saving in time of training might be as high as three-quarters of the time now needed. It was also pointed out that the use of the patient simulator leads to significantly less threat or hazard to patient welfare. Again, this points up the advantage that in using simulation, lives are never lost. Simulators such as Sim One have a capacity to 'bounce back' after otherwise fatal mistakes.

Training simulation for special education administrators   In recognition of the proliferation of school programmes for exceptional children and the increasing requirement for competent administrative personnel to provide leadership for such programmes, Sage has developed materials to simulate the problem situations facing a typical administrator of special education.[36] These materials were developed to utilize in a maximum way two advantages of simulation: fidelity (realism) and the provision of a controlled practice setting. The materials allowed students to assume a role in a simulated special education directorship of a school district with given characteristics and to react to problem situations presented in a standardized manner. Although the simulation exercise developed, termed the Special Education Administration Task Simulation (SEATS) Game, is based on the in-basket model of the Whitman Elementary School materials described by Hemphill, Griffiths, and Frederiksen,[37] they departed from the almost total reliance on written communication that the typical in-backet technique uses by:

(a) providing slide-tape materials for orientation;
(b) providing audio tapes of conversations of groups with which the administrator must work;
(c) providing problem input through telephone calls and visual presentation with motion pictures;
(d) allowing for group role playing of case conferences;

(e) providing opportunities for students to respond to filmed materials in a face-to-face role playing interview.

From the evaluative study of the materials, Sage concluded that the simulation could be used profitably both as a training and research tool.

Computer-based simulation games Computer-based instructional games have been used in business, the military, political science, and even in elementary schools. In the latter case, the technique has been researched by the Center for Educational Services and Research of the Board of Cooperative Educational Services (BOCES) in Northern Westchester County, New York.[38] These simulations involve one person playing 'against' a computer program. Possibly, the greatest potential in these games is their ability to provide individualized instruction, not only in terms of self-pacing but also variation in content, difficulty of problems, style, and mode of presentation. The SUMERIAN GAME is designed to teach sixth graders basic principles of economics applicable at the time of the Neolithic revolution in Mesopotamia. The SIERRA LEONE DEVELOPMENT PROJECT simulates the economic problems of a newly-emerging nation. In one experiment, these games were played on three IBM 1050 terminals, two of which were equipped with modified Carousel Projectors and a third with an experimental random-access film-strip projector. A total of about seventy-five pictures were projected during each game. About 15,000 lines of instruction and approximately 37,000 memory places were used in the computer system. In an experiment comparing the computer games with the conventional classroom teaching, it was found that 'students in the experimental group attained approximately the *same amount of learning* with considerably *less investment of time*'. The researchers concluded that in this sense of learning effectiveness, that is, amount of learning by pupil time, 'the games appear superior to conventional classroom teaching'.

One other example of the use of computer-based games might be cited to illustrate the unique advantages of the computer. The Industrial College of the Armed Forces (ICAF) uses an international relations game known as the WORLD POLITICS SIMULATION that places the student in a foreign policy decision-making environment.[39] The game is conducted in morning sessions, while in the afternoon and evening sessions, individual students work at a computer terminal to test out various strategies that are important in the conduct of the game. Students 'poll' the computer for information, but only a limited number of polls are allowed. (Otherwise, students would be able to deduce the model in its entirety). This polling feature provides more feedback to the student than is ordinarily possible in simple game participation. The student may gain information on budget decisions, policy decision, resource allocations, and so forth without having to resort to repeated cycles of the game itself to test out the effects of a particular plan of action.

Testing uses of media-ascendant simulation

Now that the military and civilian uses of simulation for instructional uses have been examined, we shall turn our attention to the use of simulation for assessment. In designing the form of a test, an individual has a number of possibilities available to him, such as:

(a) elicit a related behaviour that must be inferred on the basis of logical relations;

(b) elicit 'what I would do' behaviour, where the student states what action he would take to solve a problem, given a brief description of a problem situation;

(c) elicit life-like behaviour, where the student gives life-like responses in non-real life (simulated) settings; and

(d) observe real life behaviour.

These and others are discussed in detail by Frederiksen.[40]

Frederiksen states that the 'observation of real life behavior is ordinarily not a suitable technique for measurement'. (Nor is it usually practical, especially with large groups of students.) Frederiksen claims that the measure that is 'recommended for just consideration in a training evaluation study is the type that most closely approximates the real life situation'.

Simulated physician–patient encounters Let us begin our examination of simulation tests by exploring the work of the American Board of Orthopaedic Surgery, which has revolutionized its in-training examination with a procedure that simulates the physician–patient encounter.[41] The Patient Management Problem test has several unique features:

(a) It presents a simulation problem in patient management that carries the examinee through a series of sequential, interdependent decisions representing various stages in the diagnostic work-up and management of a patient.

(b) It provides realistic feedback about the results of each decision as a basis for subsequent action, and does not allow the examinee to retract his decision once it is made.

(c) It allows both for variations in medical approaches and in patient responses appropriate to several approaches.

The procedure used in the Board examination is quite similar to that employed in the auto-instructional simulators described above.

This simulation test is characterized by a series of branching problems that require the examinee to make decisions from a large number of strategy routes, several of which lead to an acceptable conclusion. For example, one case involves a 62-year-old woman who fell and fractured her hip. A mild cardiac failure was detected and controlled. The examinee is now asked to specify treatment of the fracture. Pictures of the fracture are provided. First of all, the examinee is asked to choose among six alternatives. Should he:

(a) initiate non-operative therapy;
(b) perform a closed reduction and internal fixation;
(c) perform a closed reduction, valgus osteotomy and fixation;
(d) perform an open reduction and internal fixation;
(e) insert a prosthetic replacement;
(f) remove the femoral head and neck.

The examinee indicates his choice by erasing an opaque overlay on a specially designed answer sheet. This reveals an instruction for him to erase another response that is appropriate to his choice. For example, if the examinee chose to perform a closed reduction and internal fixation, the feedback would read, 'After two attempts at reduction, X-rays were obtained. (Figures 5 and 6.) Turn to Section III E.' In Section III E, the examinee is asked if this is an acceptable or unacceptable reduction on the basis of the X-rays. Depending on his response, he moves along to another decision point, decides on the next course of action, and discovers the outcome of this action, until the end of the problem is reached. In some problems, the use of high fidelity tape recordings allows examinees to listen to such features as the patient's heart beat, something that is entirely impossible with conventional symbolic tests. Since each decision is permanently exposed, a record is kept of each action on the part of the examinee which may be subsequently scored.

Other examinations employing simulation techniques that have been developed for the evaluation of performance in medicine include simulated diagnostic interviews, simulated proposed treatment interviews and simulated patient-management conferences.[42,43,44] These techniques all use role playing, where the examiner is 'programmed' to play the role of a patient.

Motion picture testing   The use of motion pictures for testing is not new. Using motion pictures as test stimuli dates back to 1947 when James Gibson directed a series of studies for the Army Air Forces.[45]

A search of the literature reveals that little work using motion pictures as assessment devices has been accomplished in comparison with using motion pictures for instruction. Carpenter and others suggest that film testing advantages may be apparent in the assessment of personality characteristics.[46] This is confirmed by Lhotsky who suggests that motion picture sequences may be used as stimuli for projective measures.[47] But McIntyre places these suggestions in doubt. In his research, he used motion picture sequences based on cards from the 'Thematic Appreception Test',[48] and concluded that the realistic nature of the film might be in opposition to the desired ambiguity that is necessary for projective tests and that the actions depicted in the films structured responses to a greater extent than was desirable in the situation. The net effect was reduced ambiguity, an undesirable consequence. In another study, Van Horn's data did not seem to confirm McIntyre's, but led to the conclusion that verbal and visual items could be used interchangeably.[49] However, Van Horn warns that if the question can be asked in other ways that are less expensive or require less mechanical complexity, then the method should be used over motion picture testing which demands excellent technical quality. If more conventional techniques are not effective, then the experimenter must 'equip himself abundantly with funds, patience, and ingenuity, and be willing to accept nothing but the best of materials —conceptually and technically—that can be produced'.

Another line of research dating back to 1964 has been conducted by Schalock, Beaird, and Simmons,[50] and replicated by Schalock and Beaird.[51] These two research studies examined the use of motion picture tests to predict the classroom behaviour of teachers. The general hypothesis of the first study was that

> in order to predict complex human behavior the tests to be used as predictors had to reflect in their composition the complexity of the behavior to be predicted. Specifically, the hypothesis tested in the study was that as test stimuli increased in their representativeness of the behavior to be predicted, and as the opportunity for response to those stimuli approached 'life-likeness' in their freedom, the predictive power of tests would increase accordingly.[52]

To test this hypothesis, motion picture sequences of classroom behaviour were used to simulate the complexity involved in the real life operational teaching environment. Four predictor tests bearing on a continuum of stimulus and response complexity were used in the study:

(a) Paper and pencil attitude scale where the test stimulus was a statement describing an orientation to a teaching function and the response was agreement or disagreement of the examinee to the statement (The Minnesota Teacher Attitude Inventory).

(b) A situational response test which used written descriptions of filmed classroom situations and response was again agreement or disagreement to statements made in relation to the descriptions (a Word Test).

(c) A situational response test where test stimuli were motion picture sequences of classroom situations and the response was similar to the Word Test (The Film Test).

(d) A situational response test where motion picture sequences were used but the response was free, i.e., examinee responded to the simulation episode as though he were the teacher in the situation (The Simulation Test).

The hypothesis stated that the predictive power of the MTAI would be weakest while the predictive power of the simulation test would be most powerful. In both studies, the hypothesis was supported. Multiple correlations of ·69 to ·87 were obtained between predictor and criterion measures which were specific behavioural measures obtained through the use of a systematic observational system.[53]

Schalock summarizes the research to be pursued in relation to the application of simulation to educational psychological measurement. He cites four primary problems:

(a) the range of measurement problems for which the methodology is applicable,

(b) the relative power which the methodology brings to various measurement tasks,

(c) the extent to which situations must be sampled in order to make reliable statements about constructs or behaviour in situation, and

(d) the point at which a trade-off between cost of increasing the fidelity of test stimuli (setting portrayal) and the effectiveness of assessment or prediction is reached.

Suggestions for research in each of these areas are offered elsewhere by Schalock.[54]

From the examples cited above, it appears that media-ascendant simulation is indeed useful in assessment. Simulation offers a unique opportunity to assess performance in a life-like setting that is often times untestable by other means. For example, it is difficult to think of a paper-and-pencil test as being adequate to test the performance of astronauts in a space vehicle coupling activity. The use of simulation for performance evaluation is discussed further by Gagne,[55,56] Thorndike,[57] and Weislogel and Schwartz.[58]

Learning outcomes

Why use media-ascendant simulation? What does the learner gain by participating in such a simulation exercise? If there are certain benefits or 'pay-offs', then how can an instructor in biology or history or psychology, for example, realize these benefits in his own instruction? Are some training functions better served through simulation than other training functions?

One problem that is faced in answering these questions is the great variety of simulations available. One would not expect that benefits derived from the appropriate use of one exercise to be necessarily valid for another exercise. A second problem that is apparent when attempting to identify the learning outcomes served by simulation is that a particular benefit may or may not be realized in a particular simulation, depending on such factors as exercise administration, learner abilities and characteristics (entry behaviour), and even instructor competence. Presenting a media-ascendant simulation exercise to a student does not automatically insure the fulfilment of the intended objectives, just as the reading of a book does not necessarily insure the acquisition of facts.

In order to illustrate the variety of learning outcomes that may be achieved through the use of simulation, the following learning functions are presented as examples of what may be achieved. It should be recognized that in many cases, little or no evidence is available to support what amounts to intuitive hunches. It should also be noted that the examples are given for illustrative purposes only and are not meant to be inclusive of all simulations that may be used for a particular training function or of all training functions.

Cognitive outcomes

Principles and relationships Although it is possible to use simulation for the acquisition of cognitive knowledge, the learning of factual knowledge (e.g., the meaning of words and symbols, rules and principles, and relationships) is considered by some authorities (who deal mainly with aircraft simulators) as a secondary training function of simulators. Parker and Downs[59] list the understanding of principles and relationships as a quite appropriate use of a simulator granted it is programmed properly. It should be noted that the use of a highly complex and costly simulator for learning conceptual information may not at all imply that it is the best way to use such a piece of equipment. In many cases, an instructional film or even a chart may teach a principle as well as a complex simulator and at much less cost. Gagne[60] points out that the optimal use of a simulation is in the later stages of training, not in the early stages when the learning of prerequisite knowledge is probably most important.

Decision-making skills Demaree[61] points out that complex decision making mission-oriented decisions under real time simulation of instrument readings is probably best trained by exercising these behaviours in a lifelike setting where the student may receive immediate feedback as to the adequacy of his response. Parker and Downs[62] also report that a simulator that includes all the necessary cues and occasions for the training of decision-making is useful if it is properly programmed. This writer has also noted that increased decision-making skills may be one benefit of classroom simulation training. Students may make decisions about how to handle typical classroom problems, often weighing the consequences of one response against the other.[63] Several studies have shown a definite improvement in the student's handling of the problems after training, as measured by responses to novel filmed episodes. Little evidence is available however to show that this decision-making skill is transferred to real life situations.

Identifications An important skill that may be taught by the use of media-ascendant simulation is the learning to identify important cues, signals, and other stimulus situations. Parker and Downs[64] define 'learning identifications' as the 'pointing to or locating objects and locations, naming them, or identifying what goes with what—either physically or in words or symbols'. Demaree places the learning of perceptual identifications, and naming and locating as a secondary training function of simulators, which essentially means that a simulator may be used for such purposes, but it may not necessarily represent the most economical approach to this training.[65] It cannot be argued that the identification of cue patterns may be taught by means other than media-ascendant simulation. A chart may be quite adequate for teaching a student to identify, for example, various varieties of resistors. However, when this skill must be used in the operational situation, and all sorts of 'noise' is likely to be encountered in the system, a simulator may be useful in exercising the student in these discrimination skills in the operational situations. It is one thing for a novice to 'read' Morse Code in the classroom. It is quite a different thing to require that individual to perform when unusual messages are presented during various disturbances that may occur on the battlefield.

Procedural sequences Parker and Downs[66] suggest that this training function represents the most effective use of a typical simulator. They point out that it is especially effective in the training of emergency procedures where practice on the simulator may bring the learner to a high state of proficiency. Demaree[67] also lists the procedural sequences as a primary function of simulators. However, the term, 'integrated task performances' is used rather than procedural sequences. No evidence is presented in either report that would serve to substantiate the use of a simulator rather than other techniques.

Skilled perceptual-motor acts   A discussion of learning outcomes would not be complete without the inclusion of this training function. By and large, the two most widely used applications of simulation for this training function would be (simulated) aircraft flying and motor-car driving. There is some data to show that gains do result from the use of simulation, although not necessarily in increased proficiency. For example, Flexman, Townsend, and Ornstein[68] report that students trained in an aircraft simulator received thirty hours less flying time than a non-simulator trained group. Thirty hours flying time represents a substantial saving in money with no appreciable decrease in effectiveness. The authors do point out, however, that the simulator was better suited for training certain manoeuvres heavily loaded with procedural components. This limitation could have been a function of the particular simulator and training programme.

Affective outcomes
Involvement   Without question, individuals confronted with media-ascendant simulations are shown to have an amazing capacity to 'throw themselves into the situation'. Even though the simulation is clearly seen as not real life, still the student behaves as though it were real life. (At least that is what is hoped by the designer.) This phenomenon is remarkably illustrated in one particular sequence shown on the popular television show *Candid Camera*. This episode involved an individual delivering a key to a particular doctor's office. The individual was requested by the nurse to sit in the waiting-room until the gentleman to whom the key belonged appeared. The television set in the waiting-room was then turned on and the messenger observed what he thought was the middle of a 'soap opera', but in fact was a staged plot involving the key which he was attempting to deliver. The doctor was irate because he had not been brought the key on time, and was complaining to another nurse about the situation. Although the stimulus was presented by means of television, the messenger began interacting with the simulated situation as though it were real.

It has been observed repeatedly in classroom simulation training that some individuals become so involved in the simulation that they break down and weep, or become extremely frustrated, and even, on occasion, simply refuse to respond.[69,70,71] It has been noted by more than one observer of such situations that the prototype classroom simulation training which includes discussions between the student and a tutor, may involve more therapy than instruction.

The author has observed pilots in complex computer-controlled weapons simulators where involvement was so tense that the individuals perspired freely. In these situations, it is clear that the stress is an important factor in creating the environment that produces this involvement. In fact, the student's perception of stress may make the difference between his perception of the simulation as relevant and realistic or irrelevant and unrealistic. It goes without saying that a characteristic of simulators such as flight trainers is the amount of stress that is placed on the student to perform, sometimes in difficult circumstances and in limited periods of time. In these cases, stress is probably most increased by learner overloading; that is, by presenting the student with too much information that demands him to make an excessive (but realistic) number of responses or decisions in a given period of time. The rate at which a student may receive information is dependent upon input difficulty, learner ability, and the rate at which the input is presented. For example, in classroom simulation training, stress may be increased simply by increasing the number of cues to which a student must respond. Whether or not the instructor wishes to do this is dependent upon his objectives. If the instructor's objective is to exercise the student in making quick decisions under adverse conditions, such techniques of learner overloading that produce stress may be used. It should be noted, however, that research has not revealed the optimal level of information overloading for various cognitive or affective outcomes. It might be that excessive student involvement may actually lead to a decrement in cognitive outcome.

The author does not want to leave the impression that *all* media-ascendant simulations produce such involvement as described above. Even creating the proper amount of stress does not guarantee satisfactory involvement. Smode[72] describes a situation where an aircraft simulator resembled quite closely the operational aircraft in function. However, students perceived it as being unrealistic; they claimed it was too unstable and hence more difficult to fly than the real aircraft. Tests showed this to be false, and pointed up the problem as one of motivation and involvement. Students did not give their undivided attention to 'flying' the simulator as they would have in a real aircraft. A momentary lapse of attention caused the student to 'get behind' the craft and cause it

Paul A. Twelker

to go into instability. Such lapses occurred in the simulation experience because involvement was low. These lapses would not occur in the real life aircraft because involvement would be total (it is hoped).

It should probably be noted that involvement may not only affect students; in many cases, it affects the designer even more. That is, the simulation designer in many cases becomes so involved in designing the simulation to be realistic that he goes to extremes. By increasing the realism, many think that the simulation becomes more effective. Probably the most extreme example of this type of designer involvement may be found in the University of Missouri's Nepali House, where Peace Corps volunteers have duplicated the average peasant abode even to the extent of 'bringing in cow dung each week and replastering the floor with it'.73 The relation between fidelity or realism of simulation and motivation will be discussed in greater detail below.

Emotion   Closely related to involvement as discussed above is the factor of emotion with those behaviours such as the expression of joy, frustration, and unhappiness that may relate to or follow involvement. Cited above is the example of students in classroom simulation training, when becoming involved to the point of frustration, break down and cry. In fact, it is often noted in these cases that students experiencing this frustration will move out of involvement with the simulated problem circumstance. The removal of one's self from the simulated (and potentially threatening) situation has been aptly illustrated by Kersh74 in his early work in simulation with children. Kersh not only found that the children's reactions to the films were almost identical with their behaviour in real life, he observed a most interesting affective outcome with one child (which, in fact, led to the halting of further work with children). When the child was confronted with the filmed stimuli, he became so disturbed that he withdrew and assumed a foetal position in the corner of the laboratory. Kersh has reported that it took quite a while to work with the child to bring him back into the real life situation.

The reader is probably well aware of the emotions elicited by motion pictures. Who can resist crying, or minimally swallowing a tear or two when confronted with cruel treatment given to the canine heroes of *Lassie Come Home* or *Dog of Flanders*. Or who can resist laughing over some of the antics shown in comedy films and even some of the advertisements (admittedly only a few) shown on television screens. Is there any less chance that media-ascendant simulation can at least equal the intensity of these emotions, if not surpass them?

Attitudes towards self, others, and country   A good example of the potential use of media-ascendant simulation for changing attitudes

162

toward self as well as other objects and people is in the area of cross-cultural training. Foster and Danielian[75] point out that an American's awareness and understanding of the foreign culture with which he is working helps improve communication and his overall effectiveness. This is only part of the story, however, since the American should understand the values and assumptions of his own culture since they inevitably influence his thinking, attitudes, perceptions, and behaviour towards the other country. They suggest that insight to, and understanding of, the motives, values, thought patterns, and assumptions of self as an individual American are required.

Often, the training approach in bringing about this behaviour consists of the presentation of information about culture, that is, American culture, history, and so forth. Often, it would seem that content is peripheral to the goals of understanding one's self. Another approach assumes that more favourable attitudes and appreciation come through increased knowledge, especially from a historical perspective. This approach seems limited in helping the American to be more effective in communicating and interacting with foreign nationals. A third approach might involve the preparing of the trainee to be better able to discuss the United States with foreign nationals and answer various questions about it. This approach emphasizes the importance of being well versed in world affairs and American policy.

Since cultural characteristics are found to be deeply rooted as a determinant of behaviour, simulation has been chosen as one of the most promising methods of this type of training which involves among other things the perception of, or empathy towards others. Stewart[76, 77] and Danielian[78] report several simulation exercises utilizing the 'Contrast American' approach that could be adapted for use with media. Presently, the simulation, which requires a behavioural event, assumes the form of role playing scenes. One American adviser and his counterpart meet in a cross-cultural encounter. The scenes are constructed so that culturally derived behaviour is evoked from the subject playing the role of the adviser. It is conceivable that in time, the role of the counterpart could be filmed and a computer-controlled system be designed to train large numbers of personnel at one time, rather than the one-to-one approach now used.

Another direction of innovation is the PACKAGE programme approach developed by Grace and Hofland.[79] PACKAGE involves the use of a variety of media to present information about an area or culture. Maps, picture cards, filmstrips, audio tape, video tape, and motion picture films are used. It should be noted that simulation is not a part of this approach, however, at least as defined by the author above. However, it would probably be easy to modify the system to capitalize on the strengths of simulation where appropriate.

One other example of the use of media-ascendant simulation for developing attitudes towards others might be mentioned. It has been proposed by Teaching Research staff that an important aspect of the training of teachers and administrators in special education is the sensitization of these individuals to the problems of exceptional children. It is suggested that media-ascendant simulation, as well as other role playing techniques, be used to develop an awareness of the exceptional child's problems, handicaps, and everyday life patterns, whatever the case may be. Through such training the teacher could develop attitudes and sensitivities to deal with the child.

Two crucial issues: transfer and motivation

Now that some learning outcomes of simulation have been examined it would be well to explore two areas that bear on these outcomes. In its conventional usage, transfer occurs whenever a previously learned skill or habit or behaviour influences the acquisition, performance, or re-learning of another skill at a later time. When performance on the second task (the 'transfer task') is facilitated, it is said that 'positive transfer' has occurred. When performance on the second task is inhibited, it is said that 'negative transfer' has occurred.

Gagne[80] talks about two types of transfer. One type makes it possible for the individual to perform in a way that is not directly learned, but is in some sense similar to what was learned. Consider a population of situations, all of which represent only one class in terms of the operations involved. For example, imagine a population of cryptograms, all of which are different in terms of the symbols used, but which could be solved by applying the same rule or principle. Or consider a population of toggle switches, all of which require the same movement to activate a machine. In terms of this type of transfer, a 'one to many' relationship is involved: *one* operation pertains to *many* situations. Gagne terms this type of transfer 'lateral transfer', since it refers to a kind of generalizing over a broad class of situations at about the same level of complexity.

A second type of transfer Gagne terms 'vertical transfer', which involves the application of subordinate principles previously learned to the learning of additional principles at higher levels. The key to satisfactory vertical transfer is the mastery of the subordinate principles or capabilities.

It would seem appropriate, when considering simulation, to think in terms of a third type of transfer that might be termed 'horizontal' or 'parallel' transfer. This involves the transfer from the instructional conditions to the testing or transfer conditions when the situation and operation required in the second task is equivalent to that taught previously. That is, the operation required in the transfer situation, which may be the operational situation, by the way, differs from that taught in the instructional situation only in terms of what might be called a simulation continuum. For example, if the instructional conditions used an iconic (pictorial) situation and involved enacted (life-like) responses, the transfer situation might also involve the same modes. In this case, no parallel transfer would be required since the transfer conditions and the instructional conditions were essentially equivalent. On the other hand, if the transfer condition involved the real-life situation (and hence a real-life operation) then parallel transfer would be involved since the subject was instructed under different conditions (that used simulation). Also, if the transfer situation were a paper-and-pencil test, parallel transfer would be involved since the subject must then transfer from the enacted response to the symbolic response, and from the iconic stimulus to perhaps a symbolic stimulus. In short, parallel transfer involves the student in simply moving from the instructional situation to a parallel transfer situation which involves the same situation, and the same operation. The only difference is that when the skills or knowledge were learned, the stimulus and response conditions were different than when the subject was tested.

The characteristics of the three types of transfer, lateral, vertical, and parallel, are summarized in Fig. 7.1.

Type of Transfer	Situation	Operation	Characteristic
'Parallel'	Informationally equivalent	Operationally equivalent	Learner applies same operation to same situation in the transfer condition as in instructional condition. Testing condition may be more or less realistic.
'Lateral'	Member of class of situations	Operationally equivalent	Learner applies same operation to members of a class of situations.
'Vertical'	Member of new class of situations	Different	Learner generates new operation from previously learned operations.

Fig. 7.1

Now it is not too difficult to see how the consideration of parallel transfer is important when a media-ascendant simulation exercise is developed. A prime objective of such a simulation is to have the learner operate as though he were in a real life situation so that he will perform in the operational situation adequately.

For example, after classroom simulation training as developed at Teaching Research, the student is expected to behave in a classroom in such a way that disorders are handled with a minimum of disruption of instructional continuity. Note that successful, even perfect performance in the simulator, will not guarantee successful performance in the operational situation. Clearly, the classroom is a great deal more complex and unpredictable than the controlled environment created by the simulator. The complexity of the operational situation, as compared with the simulation, has led some simulation designers to go 'all out' and attempt to recreate exactly the operational situation. Usually, such extreme realism (fidelity) costs millions of dollars, involves the use of computers, and is commonplace in the military training sphere.

These 'high-fidelity' simulations do have a theoretical base. Some studies on transfer of training have shown that the more similar two situations are the more transfer will occur from the first situation to the second situation. For example, Bugelski concludes that '. . . experimental findings indicate that positive transfer is a function of the degree of similarity between stimuli (if responses are the same)'.[81] This would seemingly justify the use of the so-called 'high fidelity simulations', some of which are so complex that entire teams of operators are required to monitor the experience.

Later studies on fidelity have placed doubt on the maxim: 'For maximum transfer of training, use perfect fidelity or realism.' There is some evidence to indicate that for complex skills, greater transfer is produced by a systematic arrangement of *practice* than by high-fidelity *physical* simulation (Gagne,[82] Cox et al.,[83] Gryde,[84] Crawford,[85] Grimsley,[86] Smode,[87] Newton[88]). In fact, for tasks of great difficulty, it is probably more advantageous to use simulation to simplify the instructional conditions than it is to use a real life situation in the hope of increasing positive transfer. By using simulation, time may be compressed or expanded, feedback may be augmented, emergencies may be introduced, guidance may be used to limit learner errors, task variety may be introduced (as an aid to lateral transfer), and practice may be distributed.[89]

Unfortunately, even if a simulation designer did know how to design the system for maximum positive transfer, other factors must be considered. For example, the designer must consider a trade-off between transfer and cost, primarily. Further, a trade-off between transfer and safety, and special training provisions for feedback must also be considered.

The trade-off between transfer and cost or economy is illustrated in Fig. 7.2. The curve shown is a hypothetical relationship between amount

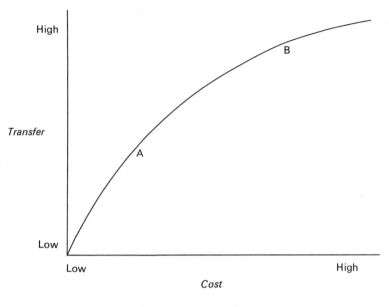

Fig. 7.2

of transfer and cost of a simulation. Point A illustrates a trade-off between providing for a medium amount of transfer at a relatively low cost. If economy is not an important factor, the designer may choose to accept a high cost-high transfer relationship as shown at Point B.

It should be made clear that this discussion has not attempted to define either cost, or the way that transfer is measured. These are problems that must be worked out by the simulation designer. Needless to say, there is no easy way to define cost, since it may involve cost per student hour, cost per unit to produce, cost per unit to sell, and so forth.

In summary, it should be realized that exact physical duplication does not guarantee maximum positive transfer. Gagne insists that the most important thing is to determine the operation to be taught, and then specify the conditions to bring about the learning of that operation so that the student will perform in the real life situation satisfactorily. Muckler et al.[90] also point out that transfer will be greatest when there is psychological fidelity, that is, when the skills taught in the simulation experience are the same as in the real-life situation. For a more complete overview of the state of the art in regards to transfer and simulation design, the reader is directed to discussions by Miller,[91] Gagne,[92] and Gryde.[93]

Motivation   Another factor that seems to lie at the heart of simulation is motivation. Why is simulation motivating? Clark Abt suggests that the reason is that there is increased student motivation because subjects of topical relevance to the student's own life are selected and because students actively participate in the simulation. Although his remarks are primarily directed towards learning games, they are appropriate here.

A great deal of our substantive content is not perceived by the student as relevant to his own life, however much we might feel that it is and should be so perceived. A great deal of the material, whether perceived as relevant or not, is not actively responded to by the student. We would like to introduce the active response mode that has been so successful in the area of the physical sciences into the social studies area. We would like to introduce essentially a laboratory method, and we would like to do this with material that is perceived as substantially relevant to the student's own life.[94]

Smode et al.[95] introduce the term, 'motivational similarity', as that which is concerned with the feeling or attitude of the student in a simulation experience as compared with a feeling experienced in real life. Smode's orientation is principally that of a military trainer of aircraft operations. As such, a primary factor in motivational similarity is the realism of the simulation. It is conceivable that a simulation might be designed that would produce optimal transfer except for the fact that its lack of realism causes the learner to disregard the instructional experience because of its obvious falsity. If lack of motivation results, then measures must be taken to assure the proper conditions for instruction to be effective. To this end, physical similarity must be added to the two factors of relevance and activity mentioned by Abt. It goes without saying that this does not contradict the emphasis given by Gagne to the specifying of operations to be taught before physical conditions of realism are considered. It does point up the fact that even though operations are the crucial thing in designing simulations, the fidelity of the stimulus and feedback situations must not be ignored lest the conditions be inadequate for eliciting the desired responses on the part of the learner.

One word of caution must be given when considering the physical similarity of a complex media-ascendent simulation, and this is relevant in designing a learning game as well. The design of simulations is often influenced by a desire to make them 'more appealing' and 'interesting' to learners and this usually takes the form of increased realism of non-essential elements. If properly done, it adds to the effectiveness of a simulation. It motivates the student, and he regards the experience as meaningful and relevant. On the other hand, simulation designers often resort to 'gimmicks' or what Lumsdaine refers to as 'fancying up' the device or technique which may cause distractions that may 'interfere with the attention of the student to the essential task to be learned, and thus have an adverse effect on learning rather than a beneficial one'.[96]

Smode et al.[97] point out that motivational similarity is a function of the entire instructional programme. Thus, a fourth factor emerges: administrative or management considerations of instruction. The way in which the simulation experience is scheduled, the way in which the experience is utilized, the competence of the instructor, the 'set' given to the students by the instructor, the 'de-briefing', and the development of the syllabus all affect motivation. Parker and Downs[98] present evidence that points to the importance of pre-simulation activities in the context of a flight simulator. They cite an unpublished study by Solarz et al.[99] where one group of students was told how the differences in fidelity between the simulator and the operational aircraft made the trainer practically worthless. Another group of students was told that these differences existed but were of negligible importance in the value of the experience. Thus, the 'set' given to the two groups of students differed and, in fact, an attitude scale showed that the groups' acceptance of the simulator was indeed quite different. In actual performance on the aircraft, however, the negative attitude and the positive attitude groups performed equally. But, the negative attitude group required more trials to criterion and hence more training time. While lack of simulator acceptance lengthened training time, it was shown to have little effect on parallel transfer from the instructional situation to real life.

Now it is difficult to speculate on the implications of the study to the conduct of simulations. Muckler[100] points out that the pilots were highly motivated to perform at a very high level of competency and this motivation may have overridden any decrements from the negative attitudes toward the simulator. It would be interesting to repeat the study with different classes of students, some of which were highly motivated in the general sense to succeed, and some of which were potential dropouts. In this case, the factor of set may be shown to be quite important for transfer performance as well as instructional performance. In any event, the evidence presented by Solarz is but an indication of the importance of attending to pre- and post-simulation details. Certainly, careful attention must be shown for all of the administrative considerations of conducting a simulation exercise.

A fifth factor that should be mentioned in regard to motivation is that of stress. Stress was mentioned above as an important contextual variable. The learner's perception of stress may make the difference between his perception of simulation as relevant and realistic or irrelevant and unrealistic. It goes without saying that a characteristic of many simulators is the amount of stress that is placed on the student to perform, sometimes in difficult circumstances in limited periods of time.

Stress may be produced in the instructional simulation in several ways. First, learner overloading may produce stressful performance. The learner may be overloaded by presenting him with too much information that demands him to make an excessive number of responses or decisions in a given period of time. Second, stress may be generated by means of unexpected stimuli and emergencies. These situations require immediate attention over and above that required in the normal functioning in the simulation experience. Third, stress may be generated by an emphasis on competition, either with peers or with a predetermined standard of performance.

Advantages and limitations of media-ascendant simulation

Before examining some new directions of simulation, it might be profitable to summarize the advantages and disadvantages of simulation as suggested in our discussion above. As already stated, it is impossible to generalize among classes of media-ascendant simulations. However, a few overall guides might be stated with the understanding that their appropriateness or relevance may vary from simulation to simulation.

Advantages

Reproduceability Input can be constructed to specification using media-ascendant simulation. Films, slides, and other media may be designed to fulfil practically any intent. Once designed, media presentations are reproduceable.

Planned variation If variation is desired, it may be obtained over selected instances throughout a wide range of problems. For example, in the classroom simulation materials developed at Teaching Research, the classroom management problems extend across an empirically derived range of situations. Planned variation may be used to enhance transfer of learning.

Realism Often the input needed cannot be conveyed other than by a machine/media component. Complex visual stimuli such as those presented to an aircraft pilot attempting to land cannot be transmitted by word or by action. In this case, one picture is indeed worth a thousand words. It has been suggested that about 85 per cent of learning is through the visual sense.

Integration of psychomotor and perceptual learning As was cited earlier, such simulations as the driver education simulator, the aircraft simulators, and the vast numbers of other military trainers, exemplify this advantage. No other instructional technique, including practice on the operational equipment, offers the advantages of simulation training.

Learner competence Low entry skills of the learner and limited response repertoires can prevent conventional instruction from functioning adequately. Machine simulation systems may be designed to provide competencies necessary for adequate learning of the terminal performance. Also, in military training very often the non-academically inclined student who does not enjoy learning is being dealt with. Simulation which confronts this learner with a relevant, meaningful, motivating environment that can be manipulated is useful in this circumstance.

Traditional teacher control over students Traditional teacher control is not usually threatened by machine systems. Although the foci of control may be located at the machine, it seems an acceptable temporary substitute as compared with techniques such as learning games where the control is shifted to the learner participants. In addition, media-ascendant simulations may be easily monitored by the instructor.

The next eight advantages have been suggested by Braby.[101] The advantages of simulation are compared with training in the real life situation.

Cost of training Training in the operational situation may be very costly. For example, aircraft may be worn out, fuel is consumed, and maintenance is necessary. Simulation may be less costly.

Safety of personnel One must accept that the operational situation may cost the trainee and others their lives. There has been no record of anyone ever losing his life in a simulator.

Effectiveness of learning The simulation environment may be so structured that learning effectiveness is assured through careful sequencing, instructor control, monitoring, and so forth.

Availability of rare events With simulation, the probability of rare events occurring may be reordered. For example, clinical emergencies that rarely happen in the dentist's surgery may be reproduced time and again with simulation.

171

Ease of experimenting with new procedures Simulation is a natural means of trying out new ideas and of assessing the feasibility of new procedures without disrupting the operational situation.

Measurement of readiness If an individual can't perform well in a simulator, he probably will not be able to perform any better in real life. Although successful performance in a simulator does not guarantee similar performance in the operational situation, simulation training does increase the probability of this transfer occurring.

Availability of operational equipment In many cases, the operational situation is not available for training uses. If application-type training is required, simulation holds the answer.

Damage to the operational situation Even if the real life situation is available, it may be undesirable to use it because of the potential of damage to it. For example, a forest fire would never be set for training purposes because of the loss potential. Thus, the forest fire simulator is used.

Limitations

Complexity and expense For the most part this is a distinct disadvantage of media-ascendant simulation. For example, when film tests are used, research suggests that sequences of the highest quality are imperative. Although it was shown above that media-ascendant simulations do not have to be expensive, they generally are.

Human interaction emphasized in model Dynamic models which do not emphasize human interaction are easiest to transpose into media-ascendant simulation. For example, aircraft functioning may be pro-grammed by a computer since it is predictable and the variations are known. It is much more difficult and costly to predict and programme models that involve human interaction. To date, there has probably been more research done on the effects of a specified force on an airplane wing at a given speed than there has been on the effect of a given com-munication on a given group of learners under specified conditions.

Adaptation to individual differences Although this is possible with media-ascendant simulation, it is often costly. In providing alternative branches to a learning sequence not only additional media is required but also a mechanism to monitor the learner and present the alternative decision points and tracks.

Continuous feedback In the review of the uses of simulation, it was noted that a characteristic of media-ascendant simulation is the provision of feedback in the ongoing context of instruction. With computer-mediated systems, this is practical over an extended period of time. On the other hand, feedback is usually limited to one or two sequences in such applications as classroom simulation. Further stimulus-response-feedback cycles in classroom simulation are prohibitive in cost and the necessary research to construct such sequences is largely non-existent.

Some new horizons in simulation

It is fitting to conclude our discussion of media-ascendant simulation with an exploration of some selected new directions that indicate its potential for education has yet to be realized. Three directions will be considered:

(a) The use of television for supplementing or complementing simulation;

(b) Environmental simulation for exploring new areas;

(c) Holography for presenting a true three-dimentional image from a two-dimensional medium.

Television-mediated simulation Simulation need not be limited to a trainer, a classroom, or a series of rooms in which students interact in teams. One of the most unique experiments involving simulation used home audiences of WGBX-TV, a special service UHF channel in Boston. In the autumn of 1967 a 5-programme simulation game, called *The Most Dangerous Game*, was broadcast.[102] It was a fictional-name simulation of the Korean crisis of 1950. Studio participants represented statesmen of six major nations involved in the simulated dispute. The home audience took the part of the political *élite* of one of the teams. They advised the statesmen through telephone calls and letters. Further, home viewers interacted with each other and discussed issues raised in the simulation.

Roger G. Mastrude of the Foreign Policy Association, with whose co-operation the series was developed, summarized the goals of the experiment:

(a) to enlist a new participating audience not enlisted through proper community organizing efforts;

(b) to motivate a relatively large audience of intelligent television viewers sufficiently to: (i) induce them to view a world affairs programme, and (ii) induce them to act as participants in simulation by inter-personal discussion and/or by telephone to the station;

173

(c) to reshape simulation into a *visual* medium (for its normal character as a process wholly constructed for the experience of the players who enact it);

(d) to construct a learning situation effectively combining the 'media' of the simulation exercise, television, discussion, and telephone feedback;

(e) to communicate substantive lessons with important educational value for this audience.

The results of the experiment have been resported in detail elsewhere.[103] For purposes of this discussion, it is sufficient to note that audience response was overwhelming. By far the most appealing aspect of the programme reported by home viewers was 'audience participation'. Sixty-nine per cent of the audience called the station more than once on the last programme. It is also interesting to note that the majority of viewers watched the programme (or more accurately, participated in the simulation) as family groups or with informal groups.

This unique experiment represents a most significant wedding of a technique with a medium. There is little doubt the success of *The Most Dangerous Game* will not be forgotten. It revealed that television audiences need not be passive receptors. The experiment dramatically illustrated how television can involve home viewers.

In the experiment, the home audience played the role of advisers to one studio team. Clearly, this limitation did not reduce home participation involvement. However, the home participants need not be limited to an advisory role for only one team. Lee suggests that the simulation might be played in several cities, each city representing a country. Through a flexible interconnected network system, cities could break away from the interconnection and broadcast locally to only its own constituents. This, in fact, has now been done. *Cabinets in Crisis*, a simulation involving the 1950 Yugoslav crisis with Russia, was played in the spring of 1968 in three cities—Boston, Philadelphia, and Rochester, New York. The studio audience took roles of executives while the home audience acted as the legislature who sent back replies to the executives to try to influence them. It was played for one day per week for five weeks. This game has also been played with English speaking high school students in Singapore, Kenya, and Chicago.

The use of television as a medium for simulation need not be limited to international relations and world affairs. What better use could be made to involve all parts of society in an examination of urban problems, civil rights, and educational and local issues. For example, in an examination of poverty, could home viewers develop empathy with real-life

174

counterparts in such a manner that their behaviour would be permanently changed? Since television is so universally watched and enjoyed, the implications of using television, not as an information-imparter, but as a response eliciter, are staggering. What better way is there to unite a family for an evening in a school-related simulation in history, civics, or social problems. Simulation exercises need not be limited to class hours in a schoolroom. The day might even come when periodic simulation specials are conducted over networks in prime time spots.

Environmental simulation　In Warminister, Pennsylvania, is the Everett A. McDonald Elementary School, which represents a significant departure from the norm. The facility houses children with a complete range of educational ability from the physically handicapped through the gifted and, because of the design of an unusual learning centre called the Special Experiences Room, provides the pupils with a unique opportunity to participate in sensory experiences that may in time form the core of the curriculum.[104] The Special Experiences Room provides for the integration of the perceptual and cognitive domains of learning that is usually not available in typical elementary schools. The room is circular, about 40 feet in diameter, with a hemispheric dome. Provision has been made for 360 degree projection, both still and motion, as well as hemispheric projection. In addition to sound experiences, provision is being made for the introduction of olefactory stimuli into the room. Finally, the air conditioning system is so designed that room temperatures may be varied over such a range as to simulate cold and warm temperatures to help pupils to sense such geographical features as desert and arctic climates. With the Special Experiences Room, pupils may be totally involved in a seal hunting expedition in the Arctic, for example, or an intercultural programme that will bring new dimensions of understanding and sensitivity to various cultures to the elementary school.

Silber and Ewing define environmental simulation as the 'selection, manipulation and/or modification of any number and combination of human channel inputs and/or outputs to create an experience which simulates an environment—real and/or imaginary'.[105] The authors cite a rationale for the use of environmental simulation given by David Orcutt, who suggests that information which is associated with supportive environmental input is more apt to be recalled than information which is not. Even more important, he suggests that the ability of a learner to experience the subject ('feel' what it is like to live in an adobe hut in Mexico, for example) requires that the desired environment be simulated by a system of rear projections from all sides and integrated

175

with appropriate sounds as well as the handling of tactile objects. The goal, then, in using environmental simulation is to 'produce affective-cognitive-psychomotor outcomes which can be set, modified, changed or eliminated, either before, during or after the experience by an environmental designer, by the participants in the experience, or by both together'. Silber and Ewing have operationalized the concept of environmental simulation by constructing a prototype physical facility in which a total environment could be simulated. In concept, their Total Environment Room is similar to the Special Experiences Room described above. The major difference, however, is in its technical approach to the problem. A five-sided theatre, rather than a 360 degree circular theatre was constructed. This provides a practical and economical structure for the presentation of media without the use of special lenses and equipment needed for spherical or circular projections. The designers state that the primary consideration in their Total Environment Room is portability to aid in its adoption and demonstration in schools. Each of the five walls is seven feet high and eight feet wide, thus creating a pentagon with a diameter of approximately 12 feet. The audience size is limited from one to five people. Initial efforts have concentrated on the senses of vision and hearing and only secondarily on the senses of touching and smelling. Rather than using high cost motion pictures, 35 mm slides are used which enables students in the audience to actually manipulate and change the environment during the presentation. The audience sits or lies (and in some cases walks around the room) on a rug.

The designers' initial efforts in programming a presentation to be used in the Total Environment Room include topics ranging from the birth of a baby to a walk through the forest, complete with pine scent and the raining down of pine cones and needles. Other possibilities for using environmental simulation as cited by the designers include:

(a) placing the learner inside the human body to experience the heart action, lung action, and so forth;
(b) placing learners inside physical substances in the midst of chemical reactions;
(c) placing learners in different geographical climates and settings;
(d) placing learners in different historical settings;
(e) placing learners in the countries of which they are studying either the language or the geography;
(f) relating art to the world in which it was created;
(g) placing learners studying a novel in the time and situation in which that novel was created;
(h) placing student teachers in a simulated classroom and having them interact with students;

(i) providing stimulus material to 'loosen up' a group for sensitivity training.

With the Total Environment Room, the major costs in programming these presentations appears to be the production of 35 mm slides. Just possibly the greatest hindrance to the effective implementation of environmental simulation, both in terms of the Special Experiences Room of the McDonald Elementary School, and the Total Environment Room, is the lack of creative imagination to develop the programmes necessary for the room. The designers of the Special Experiences Room at Warminister, Pennsylvania, have found technical solutions to practically all of their problems. Silber and Ewing, by settling for a less sophisticated and elaborate technical set-up, have demonstrated the applicability of environmental simulation in a relatively low-cost manner. Yet without the programmes to be used in environmental simulation theatres, the innovation may well be neglected.

Holography A most fascinating technical field that is fast emerging is that of holography which is defined as 'a process for photographic recording of a stationary interference fringe field produced by a reference beam and reflections from an object'.[106] In non-technical terms, holography holds the promise of presenting to learners a true three-dimensional image from a two-dimensional medium without the use of special lenses or other optical aids. It is said that the three-dimensional image of the object that is thus recorded possesses all of the properties attributed to the real life object or scene. For example, one can view an image which can be turned around to the opposite side. Objects hidden from view can be seen by simply moving around the projected image just as in the real world.

The Naval Training Device Center is currently investigating the application of three-dimensional properties of the hologram to training devices.[107] Because the hologram image is projected in space out in front of the recording medium, the image has no substance and provides a unique opportunity for the learner to walk around the image or probe the image. NTDC is confident that holography holds great promise in visual simulation including the utilization of three-dimensional holographic motion pictures and television, 360 degree holograms viewable from all directions, and complete landing and docking simulators using holograms as the visual display. The NTDC report fails to mention, however, the problems involved in recording holographic images. For example, the laser, which is used as the light source, must operate perfectly. Out of adjustment operation cannot be tolerated. Also, such mechanical vibrations as caused by talking, people walking, and the opening and closing of doors cannot be tolerated when exposures are made. Equipment must be massively supported on a stable base that isolates vibration. The Naval Electronics Laboratory uses massive polished granite slabs that float on inflated innertubes to isolate vibration. Also, air convection has been found to cause low intensity images and must be eliminated. Another problem involves thermal equilibrium which is absolutely necessary throughout exposure. Granted that these and other problems may be solved feasibly, there exists a fantastic potential for the use of holography in visual simulation. Instead of using motion pictures to recreate a classroom scene, imagine a holographic image which allows the student participating in the experience to move about a classroom interacting with pupils. Or imagine recreating a forest, complete with logging operations and the like to expose pupils to this interesting industry. In the latter case, even simulated logs could fall on the pupil to illustrate the dangers in logging operations, with no physical harm. The reader is left to his own imagination to conjure up other applications of three-dimensional holography to visual simulation.

Certainly the three new directions discussed above, television-mediated simulation, environmental simulation, and holography, are but three exciting horizons in the area of media-ascendant simulation. As these and other horizons are explored, the innovation of media-ascendant simulation will move from its present pioneering state to a mature, sophisticated technique that will be as commonplace in education as the lecture is today. In essence, what will be produced in the area of media-ascendant simulations in the next decade will make what is now available look like mere 'hand tools' as compared with the more powerful techniques yet to be designed, to use the analogy presented in the opening paragraphs of this chapter. This is not to minimize the contribution of existing simulations in use today. However, it is clear that as our technology progresses, as research findings are applied in the field, and as design procedures are integrated with sound, instructional principles yet to be made explicit, the innovation will evolve into a much used and very useful technique.

REFERENCES

1. Braby, R.: 'An Interview with Richard Braby of the Naval Training Device Center'. Monmouth, Oregon, Teaching Research Division, Oregon State System of Higher Education, 1968 (reproduced with the permission of R. Braby and J. H. Beaird).
2. Thomas, C. J., and Deemer, W. L., Jr.: 'The Role of Operational Gaming in Operations Research'. *Operations Research*, 5, 1, 1957.

3. Harman, H. H.: 'Simulation: a Survey'. *Proceedings of the Western Joint Computer Conference*, Los Angeles, California, 1961.
4. Zaltman, G.: 'Degree of Participation and Learning in a Consumer Economics Game'. *Simulation Games in Learning* (eds. S. Boocock and E. Schild), Sage Publications, 1968.
5. Western Behavioral Sciences Institute, 'CRISIS'. La Jolla, California, 1967.
6. Abt Associates, Inc.: 'MANCHESTER: an Historical Simulation'. Cambridge, Massachusetts, Abt, 1965.
7. Twelker, P. A.: 'Simulation: An Overview'. *Instructional Simulation: a Research Development and Dissemination Activity* (ed. P. Twelker), Monmouth, Oregon, Teaching Research Division, Oregon State System of Higher Education (U.S. Office of Education, Project No. 7-1-045), 1969.
8. U.S. Naval Training Device Center, *Naval Research Review*, XXI, 4, 1968.
9. U.S. Naval Training Device Center, *Naval Research Review*, XXI, 4, 1968.
10. Chea, F.: 'Visual Simulation for Ship Handling Trainers'. *Naval Research Review*, 21, 4, 1968.
11. Columbia Broadcasting System: 'Tomorrow . . . Today'. *21st Century Documentary Program*, New York, 1968.
12. Burns, J., and Omar, E.: 'A Modern Weapon System Trainer'. *Naval Research Review*, 21, 4, 1968.
13. Kristy, N. F., 'The Simutech Trainer for Technical and Vocational Training'. *Inventing Education for the Future* (eds. W. Z. Hirsch, et. al.), San Francisco, California, Chandler Publishing Company, 1967.
14. Van Valkenburgh, Nooger, and Neville, Inc.: 'Trainer-Tester Auto Instructional Device: Six Cylinder Engine (Reo)'. New York, VVN&N, 1960.
15. U.S. Naval Training Device Center: 'Pocket Blinker Device 12ww'. Orlando, Florida, Naval Training Device Center, 1963.
16. Woolley, F. L., and Audet, C. W.: 'Training Aid: Wound Moulages, Device 29-JD-1'. Orlando, Florida, Naval Training Device Center, 1956.
17. Brown, G. H.: *Providing Communication Experience in Programmed Foreign Language Instruction.* Alexandria, Virginia, Human Resources Research Office, 1968.
18. Brown, G. H.: *Providing Communication Experience in Programmed Foreign Language Instruction.* Alexandria, Virginia, Human Resources Research Office, 1968.
19. Little, A. D., Inc.: *The Government Instructional Market.* Cambridge, Massachusetts, Little, 1968. Reproduced by permission.
20. Van Valkenburgh, Nooger, Neville, Inc.: *An Evaluation of Trainer-Tester Devices.* New York, VVN&N.
21. Kersh, B. Y.: *Classroom Simulation: a New Dimension in Teacher Education.* Monmouth, Oregon, Teaching Research Division, Oregon State System of Higher Education (U.S. Office of Education, NDEA Title VII, Project No. 886), 1963.
22. Kersh, B. Y.: *Simulation with Controlled Feedback: a Technique for Teaching with the New Media.* Monmouth, Oregon, Teaching Research Division, Oregon State System of Higher Education, 1962.
23. Teaching Research: 'Low-cost Instructional Simulation Materials for Teacher Education: Classroom Management'. *Instructor Manual*, Monmouth, Oregon, Teaching Research Division, Oregon State System of Higher Education, 1969.

24. Kersh, B. Y.: *Classroom Simulation: a New Dimension in Teacher Education*, op. cit.
25. Kersh, B. Y.: *Classroom Simulation: Further Studies on Dimensions of Realism*. Monmouth, Oregon, Teaching Research Division, Oregon State System of Higher Education, 1965.
26. Twelker, P. A.: *Prompting as an Instructional Variable in Classroom Simulation*. Monmouth, Oregon, Teaching Research Division, Oregon State System of Higher Education (NDEA Title VII, Project No. 5-0950), 1966.
27. Twelker, P. A., Kersh, B. Y., and Pyper, J. R.: *Successive vs Simultaneous Attainment of Instructional Objectives in Classroom Simulation: Final Report*. Monmouth, Oregon, Teaching Research Division, Oregon State System of Higher Education (U.S. Office of Education, Project No. 5-0774, Grant No. OE-7-47-9015-283), 1968.
28. Cruickshank, D. R., Broadbent, F. W., and Bubb, R. L.: *Teaching Problems Laboratory*. Chicago, Illinois, Science Research Associates, Inc., 1967.
29. Cruickshank, D. R.: *Inner City Simulation Laboratory*, Science Research Associates, 1969.
30. Michigan State University: *Professional Decision Simulator*. East Lansing, Michigan, Department of Education, MSU.
31. Beaird, J. H., and Standish, J. T.: *Audio Simulation in Counselor Training*. Monmouth, Oregon, Teaching Research Division, Oregon State System of Higher Education (U.S. Office of Education, NDEA Title VII, Project No. 1245), 1964.
32. Lund, V. E.: *Teaching Dental Emergencies Through Simulation Techniques: Final Report*. Monmouth, Oregon, Teaching Research Division, Oregon State System of Higher Education (Public Health Service, Contract Project No. Ph 108-64-77 [P], 1965.
33. U.S. Forestry Service: *Fire Control Simulator*. Washington, D.C., Forestry Service, U.S. Department of Agriculture, 1963.
34. Utsey, J., Wallen, C. J., and Beldin, H. O.: 'Simulation: a Breakthrough in the Education of Reading Teachers'. *Phi Delta Kappan*, 1966.
35. Denson, J. S., and Abrahamson, S.: 'A Computer-Controlled Patient Simulation'. *Journal of American Medical Association*, 208, 3, 1969.
36. Sage, D. D.: *The Development of Simulation Materials for Research and Training in Administration of Special Education: Final Report*. Washington, D.C., Bureau of Education for the Handicapped (U.S. Office of Education, Project No. 6-2466, Grant No. OEG-1-6-062466), 1967.
37. Hemphill, J. K., Griffiths, D. E., and Frederiksen, N.: *Administrative Performance and Personality: a Study of the Principal in a Simulated Elementary School*. New York, Bureau of Publications, Teachers College, Columbia University, 1962.
38. Wing, R. L.: 'Two Computer-based Economic Games for Sixth Graders'. *Simulation Games in Learning* (eds. S. Boocock and E. Schild), Beverly Hills, California, Sage Publications, 1968.
39. Industrial College of Armed Forces: WORLD POLITICS SIMULATION: *Participants Manual*. 1969.
40. Frederiksen, N.: 'Proficiency Tests for Training Evaluation'. *Training Research and Education* (ed. R. Glaser), Pittsburgh, Pennsylvania, University of Pittsburgh Press, 1962.
41. University of Illinois: *Simulation Technique in the Evaluation of Clinical*

Judgement. Chicago, Illinois, Center for the Study of Medical Education, College of Medicine, 1967.

42. University of Illinois: *Materials for the Evaluation of Performance in Medicine*. Chicago, Illinois, The Evaluation Unit, Center for the Study of Medical Education, College of Medicine, University of Illinois, 1967.

43. Levine, H. G., and McGuire, C.: 'Role-playing as an Evaluative Technique'. *Journal of Educational Measurement* (ed. R. E. Schutz), 5, 1, 1968.

44. McGuire, C.: 'An Evaluation Model for Professional Education—Medical Education'. *Proceedings of the 1967 Invitational Conference on Testing Problems*, Princeton, New Jersey, Educational Testing Service, 1968.

45. Gibson, J. J. (ed.): *Motion Picture Testing and Research*. Washington, D.C., Army Air Forces (Research Report No. 7, Aviation Psychology Program), 1947.

46. Carpenter, C. R., Greenhill, L. D., Hittinger, W. F., McCoy, E. P., McIntyre, C. J., Murin, J. A., and Watkins, R. W.: 'Development of a Sound Motion Picture Proficiency Test'. *Personnel Psychology*, 7, 1954.

47. Lhotsky, J.: 'Film Test and Test Films'. *Psychological Abstracts*, 20, 7293, 1955.

48. McIntyre, C. J.: 'Sex, Age, and Iconicify as Factors in Projective Film Tests'. *Journal of Consulting Psychology*, 18, 1954.

49. Van Horn, C.: *An Investigation of the Applicability of Motion Pictures to Education Testing: Final Report*. Urbana, Illinois, University of Illinois (Project No. 665, Grant No. 7-23-1020-125), 1967.

50. Schalock, H. D., Beaird, J. H., and Simmons, H.: *Motion Pictures as Test Stimuli: an Application of New Media to the Prediction of Complex Behavior*. Monmouth, Oregon, Teaching Research Division, Oregon State System of Higher Education (U.S. Office of Education, NDEA Title VII, Project No. 971), 1964.

51. Schalock, H. D., and Beaird, J. H.: *Increasing Prediction of Teacher's Classroom Behavior Through Use of Motion Picture Tests: Final Report*. Monmouth, Oregon, Teaching Research Division, Oregon State System of Higher Education (U.S. Office of Education, Project No. 5-0836, Grant No. OE-7-47-9015-284), 1968.

52. Schalock, H. D., Beaird, J. H., and Simmons, H.: *Motion Pictures as Test Stimuli: an Application of New Media to the Prediction of Complex Behavior*. Monmouth, Oregon, Teaching Research Division, Oregon State System of Higher Education (U.S. Office of Education, NDEA Title VII, Project No. 971), 1964. (Reproduced with the permission of the authors.)

53. Schalock, H. D.: *An Overview of the Teaching Research System for the Description of Behavior in Context*. Monmouth, Oregon, Teaching Research Division, Oregon State System of Higher Education, 1967.

54. Schalock, H. D.: 'Situational Response Testing: an Application of Simulation Principles of Measurement'. *Instructional Simulation: a Research and Development Activity* (ed. P. Twelker), Monmouth, Oregon, Teaching Research Division, Oregon State System of Higher Education, 1969.

55. Gagne, R. M.: 'Simulators'. *Training Research and Education* (ed. R. Glaser), New York, Science Editions, Wiley and Sons, 1965.

56. Gagne, R. M.: 'Training Devices and Simulators: Some Research Issues'. *American Psychologist*, 9, 1954.

57. Thorndike, R. L.: *Research Problems and Techniques*. Washington, D.C., Army Air Forces, Aviation Psychology Program (Report No. 3), 1947.
58. Weislogel, R. L., and Schwartz, P. A.: 'Some Practical and Theoretical Problems in Situational Testing'. *Educational and Psychological Measurement*, 15, 1955.
59. Parker, J. F., Jr., and Downs, J. E.: *Selection of Training Media*. Arlington, Virginia, Psychological Research Associates, Matrix Corporation, 1961.
60. Gagne, R. M.: 'Simulators'. *Training Research and Education*, op. cit.
61. Demaree, R. G.: *Development of Training Equipment Planning Information*. Arlington, Virginia, Psychological Research Associates, 1961.
62. Parker, J. F., Jr., and Downs, J. E.: *Selection of Training Media*. Arlington, Virginia, Psychological Research Associates, Matrix Corporation, 1961.
63. Twelker, P. A.: 'Classroom Simulation and Teacher Preparation'. *The School Review*, 75, 1967.
64. Parker, J. F., Jr., and Downs, J. E.: *Selection of Training Media*. Arlington, Virginia, Psychological Research Associates, Matrix Corporation, 1961.
65. Demaree, R. G.: *Development of Training Equipment Planning Information*, op. cit.
66. Parker, J. F., Jr., and Downs, J. E.: *Selection of Training Media*, op. cit.
67. Demaree, R. G.: *Development of Training Equipment Planning Information*, op. cit.
68. Flexman, R. E., Townsend, J. C., and Ornstein, G. N.: *Evaluation of a Contact Flight Simulator When Used in an Air Force Primary Pilot Training Program: Part I: Over-all Effectiveness*. USAF, AFPTRC Technical Report 54-38, 1954.
69. Kersh, B. Y.: *Simulation with Controlled Feedback: a Technique for Teaching with the New Media*, op. cit.
70. Kersh, B. Y.: *Classroom Simulation: a New Dimension in Teacher Education*, op. cit.
71. Twelker, P. A.: 'Classroom Simulation and Teacher Preparation'. *The School Review*, op. cit.
72. Smode, A. F., Gruber, A., and Ely, J. H.: *Human Factors Technology in the Design of Simulators for Operator Training*. Stanford, Connecticut, Dunlap and Associates, Inc. (Technical Report No. NAVTRADEVCEN 1103-1), 1963.
73. Loubert, J. D.: *The Trans-Cultural Research and Training Institute (TCI)*. McLean, Virginia, Human Sciences Research, Inc., 1967.
74. Kersh, B. Y.: *Simulation with Controlled Feedback: a Technique for Teaching with the New Media*, op. cit.
75. Foster, R. J., and Danielian, J.: *An Analysis of Human Relations Training and its Implications for Overseas Performance*. Alexandria, Virginia, Human Resources Research Office, George Washington University, August, 1966.
76. Stewart, E. C.: 'The Simulation of Cultural Differences'. *Journal of Communications*, 16, 4, 1966.
77. Stewart, E. C.: *Simulation Exercises in Area Training*. Alexandria, Virginia, Human Resources Research Office, George Washington University, 1965.
78. Danielian, J.: 'Live Simulation of Affect-Laden Cultural Cognition'. *Journal of Conflict Resolution*, 11, 3, 1967.
79. Grace, G. L., and Hofland, N. A.: *Multi-Media Training for Cross-Cultural Interaction*. Santa Monica, California, System Development Corporation, 1967.

80. Gagne, R. M.: *The Conditions of Learning.* New York, Holt, Rinehart, and Winston, Inc., 1965.
81. Bugelski, B. R.: *The Psychology of Learning.* New York, Holt, 1965.
82. Gagne, R. M.: 'Simulators'. *Training Research and Education,* op. cit.
83. Cox, J. A., Wood, R. O., Jr., Boren, L. M., and Thorne, W. H.: *Functional and Appearance Fidelity of Training Devices for Fixed-Procedure Tasks.* Alexandria, Virginia, the George Washington University, Human Resources Research Office (Technical Report 65-4), 1965.
84. Gryde, S. K.: *Fidelity of Simulation and Training Effectiveness.* Los Angeles, California, University of Southern California (256436/1105, NROS 11-1), 1966.
85. Crawford, M. P.: 'Concepts of Training'. *Psychological Principles in System Development* (ed. R. M. Gagne), New York, Holt, Rinehart, and Winston, 1962.
86. Grimsley, D. L.: *Acquisition, Retention, and Retraining: Effects of High and Low Fidelity in Training Devices.* Alexandria, Virginia, Human Resources Research Office, 1968.
87. Smode, A. F., Gruber, A., and Ely, J. H.: *Human Factors Technology in the Design of Simulators for Operator Training,* op. cit.
88. Newton, J. M.: *Training Effectiveness as a Function of Simulator Complexity.* Port Washington, New York, U.S. Naval Training Device Center (Technical Report, NAVTRADEVCEN 458-1), 1959.
89. Smode, A. F., Gruber, A., and Ely, J. H.: *Human Factors Technology in the Design of Simulators for Operator Training,* op. cit.
90. Muckler, F. A., et al.: *Psychological Variables in the Design of Flight Simulators for Training.* Urbana, Illinois, Aviation Psychology Laboratory, University of Illinois (WADC Technical Report 56-369), 1959.
91. Miller, R. B.: *Handbook on Training and Training Equipment Design.* Wright Patterson Air Force Base, Ohio, the American Institute for Research, Wright Patterson Air Development Center, 1953.
92. Gagne, R. M.: *The Conditions of Learning,* op. cit.
93. Gryde, S. K.: *The Analysis of Three Transfer Theories that Affect Simulator Design.* Los Angeles, California, University of Southern California.
94. Twelker, P. A., Crawford, J., and Wallen, C. J.: *Of Men and Machines: Supplementary Guide.* Monmouth, Oregon, Teaching Research Division, Oregon State System of Higher Education, 1967. (Reproduced by permission.)
95. Smode, A. F., Gruber, A., and Ely, J. H.: *Human Factors Technology in the Design of Simulators for Operator Training,* op. cit.
96. Lumsdaine, A. A.: 'Design of Training Aids and Devices'. *Human Factors Methods for System Design* (ed. J. D. Folley, Jr.), Pittsburgh, Pennsylvania, American Institute for Research, 1960.
97. Smode, A. F., Gruber, A., and Ely, J. H.: *Human Factors Technology in the Design of Simulators for Operator Training,* op. cit.
98. Parker, J. F., Jr., and Downs, J. E.: *Selection of Training Media,* op. cit.
99. Solarz, A. K., Matheny, W. G., Dougherty, D. J., and Hasler, S. G.: *The Effect of Attitude Toward Link Training Upon Performance in the Aircraft.* University of Illinois, Aviation Psychology Laboratory, 1953.
100. Muckler, F. A., et. al.: *Psychological Variables in the Design of Flight Simulators for Training,* op. cit.

101. Braby, R.: *Basic Characteristics of Training Devices.* Orlando, Florida, Naval Systems Simulation Center, 1968.
102. Lee, R. H.: 'The Most Dangerous Game: an Experiment in Viewer-response Television'. *Audio-Visual Instruction,* 13, 1968.
103. Lee, R. H.: 'The Most Dangerous Game: an Experiment in Viewer-response Television Conducted in Cooperation with the Foreign Policy Association'. Boston, Massachusetts, Education Division, Lowell Institute Cooperative Broadcasting Council, 1967.
104. Centennial Schools: *Progress Report.* Warminister, Pennsylvania, Centennial Schools, 1967.
105. Silber, K. H., and Ewing, G.: 'Environmental Simulation'. *The Affective Domain of Learning: the Implications for Instructional Technology* (ed. J. Crawford), Monmouth, Oregon, Teaching Research Division, Oregon State System of Higher Education, 1969.
106. Morrow, H. E., and Dessel, N. F.: *Three-dimensional Holography.* San Diego, California, U.S. Naval Electronics Laboratory, 1966.
107. Rodemann, A. H.: 'The Application of Holography of Training Devices'. *Naval Research Reviews,* 21, 4, 1968.

8

Teacher education looks at simulation: a review of selected uses and research results

Donald R. Cruickshank

Professor Cruickshank is Chairman of the Faculty of Early and Middle Childhood Education in the Ohio State University's College of Education.

He was educated at the State University College at Buffalo, New York, and at the University of Rochester, and before joining the Ohio State faculty in 1969 had taught in schools and universities, acted as principal for two schools, directed an Educational Research Bureau, and from 1963–1966 was Professor of Education at the State University College at Brockport, New York. He has held many advisory positions on aspects of Educational Technology.

In the last few years Dr Cruickshank has had a developing interest in two broad areas: firstly, he has been interested in the application of simulation to preparation programmes, particularly in the training of teachers to work with the disadvantaged; and secondly, he is interested in the development of innovative professional curricula for teachers.

Some factors contributing to the general interest in use of simulation in teacher education

Little speculation is required to envision widespread utilization of simulation techniques in the future, pre- and in-service preparation of teachers and other professional education personnel. Three major factors, among others, assure that eventuality. At least as recently as the Conant Report,[1] teacher education has been undergoing rigorous examination, particularly with regard to the adequacy of laboratory experiences. Historically it has been assumed that the placing of a neophyte in the classroom as an observer, participant, or student-teacher was the very best preparation for teaching. In that context he would learn from the master teacher and practise teaching. Several unfavourable conditions make this assumption suspect. The most notable problem in the United States is that colleges and universities have never made real provision for any form of teacher training to occur in the public schools. Pre-service personnel are assigned to laboratory experiences and supervising teachers on almost a willy-nilly basis. The factors considered most often in such assignments are proximity of the public school and relationships with the school principal or superinten-dent. Many public schools look upon this service as a necessary evil and consequently seek the institution of a reward system for supervising teachers as a requisite for participation.

Teachers in service just do not consider teacher training to be among their functions. This condition is not surprising since at no time in the undergraduate and rarely in the graduate programme do they consider this eventuality, and consequently are unprepared and ill equipped for it. In many cases, thrust into the role of teacher trainer and left to their own devices, public school teachers attempt to superimpose their teaching philosophy and strategy upon the novice. All too often this results in dichotomous reactions: either the student succumbs and is moulded (the 'model the master' approach), or he experiences the phenomenon of role conflict. Spurious attempts by college personnel to provide training for supervising teachers usually can be characterized as too little, too late.

Even if adequate training could be provided for the supervising teachers, the number of pre-service teachers to be trained would require a relatively permanent and vast public school cadre of strategically located teacher trainers. The odds against overcoming either the training or retention contingencies are perilously high.

More promising alternatives to the problem include developing career ladders for teachers through differentiated staffing patterns and institut-ing the notion of the Portal School.[2]

Given the present system, the University of Maryland Teacher Education Center concept which accepts responsibility for training supervising teachers is perhaps the most responsive and responsible effort.[3]

Many argue for the institution of internships. However, changing the name of the game and only a few of the rules is not likely to result in a different kind of play or outcome.

Summarizing, resurrection of the laboratory system minimally would require acceptance of teacher training as a real function of the schools and the preparation of a thoroughly trained and relatively permanent cadre of supervising teachers.

Aside from disenchantment with present-day laboratory experiences, a second movement augers for the utilization of synthetic approaches.

This trend is supported in the AACTE publication *Teachers for the Real World*.[4] Therein Smith argues for the use and study of actual behavioural situations using 'protocol' materials and simulations. Stages leading to such study consist of identifying the most general categories of situations teachers face, organizing the situations according to the purposes of teacher preparation, and finally instructing the teacher in the theoretical knowledge needed to understand them. The final stage is done *in situ*, that is, the theoretical knowledge is given *in the context* of the teaching situation under scrutiny. Smith notes:

> It is then possible to hold and to study situations at length and to use concepts (from psychology, philosophy, sociology, etc.) to interpret them.[5]

> This theoretical content must be taught and learned in the context of systematically ordered protocol materials and simulated situations.[6]

> Furthermore from analyzing protocol materials, he will be aware of the great variety of ways of handling each teaching task and of the different ways teaching behaviours and situations may be interpreted. This greater range of insights should render the prospective teacher more flexible, deliberative and aware of a greater number of choices.[7]

A third factor worthy of mention, which contributes to the movement toward a more controlled and scholarly study of teaching and learning, is the development and utilization of educational technology. Use of newer media, particularly television, in the context of laboratory experience provides opportunity for self-study and self-appraisal not formerly available. It permits 'live' observation of classrooms and so forth. Unfortunately media do not tell you how to see what you see. A comprehensive report of the use of newer media in teacher education is found in *Teacher Education and the New Media*.[8]

Reviewing, several factors are contributing to the increased interest in the application of simulation to teacher education. First is a general disappointment with the shortcomings of student teaching and other forms of laboratory experiences. Second is the growing recognition that theory can be taught best in the context of reality from which the theory is generated. Finally, the advent of newer media permit a more systematic study of teaching as the teaching act and classroom behaviour can be 'held' in one's hand and examined.

A fourth, yet tremendously important, event favouring simulation is the recent stance taken by the National Council for Accreditation of Teacher Education (NCATE) in its draft of proposed new standards.

Each advanced program in education includes direct and/or simulated experiences . . . which relate specifically to the school position for which the candidate is being prepared.[9]

To the writer's knowledge, this is the first time the national accrediting agency has mentioned simulation as an alternative training method. In the context above it appears to be completely acceptable and is equated with laboratory work.

Advantages of simulation training

Although simulation by itself does not overcome the problems cited, it can diminish them somewhat. For example, simulation training can be conducted on the college campus, thus obviating the need to find student stations and trained classroom supervisors. For those who argue for direct contact (and they should), forms of microteaching can be utilized which provide this with much greater control and feedback than is possible in the usual laboratory experience. Effectively prepared, utilizing simulations and microclasses, the student could move into a much more independent teaching role initially than is possible at present.

Obviously, simulation is what Smith is suggesting when he talks about developing and utilizing protocol materials. Simulating a classroom situation permits it to be frozen and studied systematically, applying concepts available from the behavioural sciences. Smith notes that the moments of student teaching are fleeting, not to be recovered, and scarcely ever examined.

As simulation, or at least most of it, is media dependent, it capitalizes on the things media can do well. Particularly, media simulates reality 'but at a level closer to direct experience than an abstract symbolization'. . . .[10]

Proponents of the development and use of simulations in teacher education propose numerous additional advantages including the following:*

(a) Simulation establishes a setting wherein theory and practice can be joined. As LaGrone stated,

> The professional component of a program of teacher education for the last 25 or 30 years has taken for granted that the teacher education student will put together the talk about education and his teaching. The recent research in teaching and work in theory suggest that an assumption of this magnitude is more likely false than true.[11]

·* The text of this chapter focuses upon the use of media-ascendant, role simulations with background models.

Very often, in fact, teachers upon entering the classroom appear to operate at a visceral level, disregarding what they have been told about teaching and learning theory. Opportunities such as those suggested by Smith earlier, will serve to focus the student's attention on the intellectual dimensions of teaching performance and how concepts and knowledge may be utilized in classroom problem solving.[12]

(b) Simulations force students to take action and bear resultant consequences. Simulations generally require the participant to do something. Commonly, students read *about* and talk *about* but seldom engage *in*. In simulation:

> The student would find it necessary to make a personal decision based on his informed stand. . . . He would find himself bearing the responsibility for the consequences of his decisions and actions.[13]

(c) Simulations are relatively safe. The required decision is made and carried out without physical or psychological harm to children, parents or schools. Thus children, to a large degree, are saved the effects of practising upon them.

(d) Simulations are psychologically engaging. Once the student has made a decision based upon personal knowledge, experience and values, he can enter into dialogue with one or more problem solvers. The resultant interchange in a very real sense is sensitivity training as participants react to each other as teachers and human beings.

(e) Simulations permit control. Rather than putting students into laboratory settings such as student teaching and hoping they will have appropriate interchanges with children and teachers, students can be placed in carefully selected situations. In this manner a college can ensure that its graduates have had experience deemed to be critical. Too often student teaching assignments are sterile, routine and unrealistically safe.

(f) Simulations broaden the training horizon. It is possible to create simulations which will provide preliminary training for entering any educational setting. For example simulations are or could be available to prepare teachers to work in suburban schools, inner-city schools, nongraded programmes, team teaching settings, special education classes, and so forth. It is unlikely that colleges have access to the range of laboratories required to meet many of these needs.

(g) Simulations are relevant. Since simulations create models of reality and are based upon it, the attention of students constantly is focused upon the real world, the school as a social system, and the role of the teacher in society.

(h) Simulations enable the student to be himself. In a well conducted programme, students are not expected to identify a 'party line' and follow it. However, this often is the case during laboratory experiences. Too frequently students are told, 'When in Rome do as the Romans.' Consequently, it is entirely possible that a student can go through the usual laboratory experiences as an actor playing the role of understudy with little or no opportunity for expanding the dimension of the role or deviating from it.

(i) Simulation seems to work. Although simulations in teacher education are not abundant and are relatively untested, some evidence exists that they are worthy of further study and use. Cruickshank and Broadbent note:

> Simulation training when tested under the most stringent conditions was an unqualified success as a teaching device that motivates and involves students and that, although simulation was only partially successful in changing the student teachers' behavior, it was at least as effective as an equal amount of student teaching.[14]

How simulation is being used in teacher education

The initial work utilizing simulation in teacher education was done at the Teaching Research Laboratory of the Oregon System of Higher Education. The rationale and *modus operandi* are discussed by Kersh.

> Beginning teachers frequently have trouble in transferring into practice their knowledge of text book recipes and verbal descriptions of model teaching behaviour. One explanation for their difficulty is that there is relatively little opportunity for a student teacher to systematically practise his teaching skills under close supervision. . . .

> Many educational psychologists would agree that a more nearly ideal instructional program for student teachers should include something in addition to supervised experience in a real classroom. The supplementary experience should allow the student teacher to practice new behaviors without embarrassment or censure—to learn how it feels. . . .[15]

In order to provide opportunity for students to 'practise teaching under close supervision' without 'embarrassment or censure' and to 'learn how it feels', the Classroom Simulator, a replica of a sixth grade class-room, was developed employing motion picture forms and printed materials.

In the Classroom Simulator an experiment was conducted to deter-mine the need for 'realism' or fidelity in presenting classroom problems. The hypothesis was tenable, based upon Thorndike's identical elements theory of transfer. A two-factorial design was employed and forty subjects, comprising two intact college classes of juniors and seniors, were assigned to one of four treatment groups. The factors investigated were size of image (small *v*. large) and motion (moving *v*. still).

Following treatment assignments, subjects were oriented to a hypo-thetical school, community and classroom in which they would 'teach'. Each subject in addition was provided with a set of cumulative record cards for twenty-two children. From this point on, subjects all assumed the role of a student teacher in a sixth grade.

Content of study in the four groups was the same. The problems were merely presented differently. For example, subjects in the 'still' treatment groups were shown the problem using single frames from a continuous film viewed by subjects in the 'moving' treatment group. Of course, whatever was on the sound track of the film had to be read to the 'still' group.

As each classroom problem was presented on film (moving or still, large or small image), subjects were requested to act out a response. Depending upon the subject's response, an experimenter selected and projected one of two or three filmed feedback sequences. The choice of the feedback sequence presented was based upon standards developed by a jury of three master teachers.

The intention of the simulation was to shape the subject's behaviour, that is, to get him to react to classroom situations in ways judged to be optimal by the jury. Each problem sequence was repeated up to ten times until the subject demonstrated an acceptable response.

Results of the study provided mild support for small, still projection. More practice trials were required in order to shape subject behaviour when motion pictures were employed.[16]

In conclusion, Kersh suggested:

Practically speaking, if the relevant features of the classroom can be presented on a small screen using slides, the technique would be considerably more feasible for use in teacher education on a broad scale. Instead of the large screen and complex display facility used in the present experiment, a small portable and inexpensive display . . . could be employed.[17]

Additional data collected indicated that the more realistic mode of presentation produced greater feelings of tension, fear and frustration. It was reported that reactions to the classroom simulator on the whole were favourable.

Throughout the report several limitations or shortcomings are evident. Most of them are noted by the experimenter.

(a) For some problem situations presented to subjects, the experimenter had a minimum of feedback sequences to choose from. Obviously there are numerous responses a teacher might make to any classroom event. At the same time, there are countless ways in which a class or individual students can react to the teacher. The classroom simulator could provide only the 'most likely' feedback.

(b) All feedback was determined by a jury of three master teachers. Their determination of the appropriateness of teacher behaviour in problematic situations was the sole criterion of teacher effectiveness.

(c) The simulator attempted to shape behaviour. Subjects were expected to modify their teaching behaviour to a predetermined acceptable pattern. The acceptable pattern is questioned above. Another question worthy of thought is, 'Will what works for others work for me?'

(d) The experimental design failed to control for certain learning which Kersh says, 'Must have resulted from . . . experience shared by all subjects.'[18] Prior to the instructional phase all treatment groups were provided with orientation and testing using the more realistic large motion picture projection. Campbell and Stanley describe this kind of event as a reactive arrangement and note that it threatens the external validity of a study.[19] The possibility exists that the observed effects are due, in part, to the interaction of the pre-treatment condition (orientation using large motion picture projection) with the various treatment conditions. Thus, the observed effects could be applicable only in situations where subjects receive the same pre-treatment.

(e) The quality of the sound on the motion pictures may have had a deleterious effect on subjects in two of the treatment groups. Kersh notes, 'Despite many retakes and attempts to improve the quality of the film . . . the sound track is still very impoverished on many of the sequences.'[20]

(f) The Classroom Simulator required a special facility and utilized expensive equipment.

(g) Instruction was individualized, therefore permitting very few students to undertake simulation training without building additional simulators.

Taken as a whole, development and utilization of the Classroom Simulator was a giant step toward introducing an exciting and promising training technique to the field of teacher education. Subsequent events in the field all have been affected by this classic work.

An offshoot of the early work at Teaching Research was a study done by Vlcek.[21] The study investigated (a) the effect of Kersh's Classroom Simulator in providing teacher-trainees with experience in identifying and solving classroom problems prior to student teaching, (b) the transfer value of the experience, (c) the effect of the simulator on trainee self-confidence and ability to teach, and (d) trainee attitudes toward the simulation experience.

Procedures employed in the study seem identical with those used by Kersh.

Vlcek reported the following results of tests of the hypotheses.

(a) Awareness of classroom problems is not developed through classroom simulator experience. Teacher-trainees apparently possess this ability to identify problems prior to the simulator experience.

(b) Effective responses to classroom problems can be developed through classroom simulation experience prior to the teacher-trainee's student teaching assignment.

(c) Principles which can be used in solving classroom problems can be developed through classroom simulator experience prior to the teacher-trainee's student teaching assignment.

(d) Experience gained in responding to problems within the classroom simulator do not transfer to the teacher-trainee's student teaching experience. However, evidence does exist which supports the postulate that experience with more simulated classroom problems increases transfer.

(e) Principles developed for application in solving classroom problems do transfer to the teacher-trainee's student teaching experience.

(f) Teacher-trainee confidence in ability to teach is increased through classroom simulator experience.[22]

Before employing the Classroom Simulator generally, Vlcek poses the following questions for investigation:

Would individual discussion of the problem without the use of an elaborate simulator result in the same outcomes? What relationship exists between the number of problems encountered in the simulator and amount of transfer during student teaching? Are simulations depicting problems in one classroom superior to live recording of random real classroom episodes?[23]

Further studies at Teaching Research using the Classroom Simulator have been concerned with investigating mode of response, mode of feedback,[24] and prompting as an instructional variable.[25] According to Twelker:

Findings have suggested that realism in simulation, and prompting, are not important variables in enhancing transfer in comparison with instructor differences, and possible length of training.[26]

Most recently, and as a result of the earlier studies, the Low Cost Instructional Simulation Materials for Teacher Education Project was undertaken.[27] The project is described by Cruickshank and Broadbent:

Teaching Research's 'low cost' simulation is geared toward helping participants become more effective classroom managers and thus better teachers. The two phases of the simulation are intended to teach certain principles of classroom management and to exercise the application of the principles in the simulation. The simulation contains a variety of feedback. In Phase I, using an exercise book and a film-tape presentation on an Audascan projector, participants react to the way a teacher handles classroom management. Seeing two teaching episodes, the participant must choose which teacher behaviour is preferable and state why in the exercise book. The participant receives feedback as he compares his written response with one contained on the following page of the book. During the final part of Phase I, feedback a la Kersh is used; that is, participants see a film of how the class would respond according to the two teaching strategies employed. Phase II gives the participant . . . an opportunity to practice . . . application of principles (learned in Phase I). In this Phase participant responses to filmed incidents are compared with responses to the same incident made by 'expert teachers'. Finally a third section of the film depicts how children would probably respond to the 'expert teachers' behavior. Ultimately feedback is obtained as the participant compares his response with that of the expert.[28]

It is apparent that the greatest effort at Teaching Research has been directed toward investigating problems of developing and utilizing instructional communications systems. Less concern seems to have been given to measuring effects of the utilization of simulation on subsequent behaviour.

194

A second important project utilizing simulation, Project Insite, was carried on at the University of Indiana. Rice describes the project and how it utilized simulation.

We are testing a number of rather new facilities and techniques for teaching and learning, and we are working out practical use of such methods and techniques. These include all of the modern educational media such as films, television and other uses of graphic arts. We have been giving special attention to the potentialities of 'simulation' as a more realistic way of providing decision making experiences. . . .[29]

Simulation was employed in both elementary and secondary programmes during an 'acroclinical semester'.* During the secondary acroclinical semester, simulation training occurred during the last week. In the same vein as University Council on Educational Administration (UCEA) simulations,[30] students were oriented to a hypothetical setting in which they would work. First they were introduced to the community and then to the high school. Subsequently students took on roles of English, history or mathematics teachers and participated in experiences requiring decisions including the employment of new teachers, plagiarism by a student, and the classroom teacher's responsibility for guidance.

McQuigg summarizes the simulation experience for secondary majors noting:

The . . . experience takes the student out of his role as a *student teacher* and into one of a *beginning* teacher. In placing him in a realistic situation in which he reacts *as* the beginning teacher, his attitudes and philosophies concerning professional, instructional, student behavior and sponsorship of activities are exposed and analysed. The experience thus serves as both a *summary* of what he has been asked to learn through student teaching and methods earlier in the semester, and as a way of *formulating* what he has learned into a course of action. The experience operates at a level above the 'task to be done' and 'how to do it'—and reaches into the realm of *why* and a deeper consideration of alternatives and consequences.[31]

Apparently no discreet research was carried out on the effects of simulation training. Neither was form or mode of presentation manipulated as at Teaching Research. Considering the scope of Project Insite and its support, it is less well known than it should be, or needs to be.

In an attempt to increase realism in teacher preparation, Cruickshank and Broadbent undertook a study to (a) examine the methodology of simulation in order to judge its effectiveness in presenting teaching

* acro = terminal, clinical = practical [*Editor's Note*].

problems, and (b) determine whether or not exposure to simulated teaching problems had an observable effect on a trainee's subsequent behaviour.[32]

The initial phase of the investigation identified what the researchers termed 'critical teaching problems'. The problems were derived from statistical analysis of self-reports of 163 teachers of kindergarten through ninth grade.

The second phase of the study recreated each problem in a realistic school and classroom setting. Again, as with Kersh and others, the UCEA approach was employed. Fifth grade was selected as the class-room level and a 'media ascendent role simulation with a background model was developed'.[33] Using video tape, role plays or written incidents, each of the critical teaching problems was produced so that it occurred in the hypothetical fifth grade classroom.

The hypothesis to be tested was stated as consisting of five consequences.

If student teachers are given pre-student teaching opportunities to encounter, analyse, and attempt to solve critical teaching problems;

(C_1) *Then*, such problems will be less numerous.

(C_2) *Then*, general student teaching performance will be improved.

(C_3) *Then*, they will develop more positive feelings toward concepts related to such problems.

(C_4) *Then*, they will be more confident.

(C_5) *Then*, they will be able to assume full-time responsibility for student teaching sooner.[34]

To test the hypothesis with its five consequences, a randomized control group pre-test, post-test design was used and two field tests were conducted in which experimental subjects undertook two weeks of simulation training in lieu of the first two of nine weeks of student teaching.

In general the objectives of the two week simulator were to:

(a) have each subject assume the role of a beginning fifth grade teacher,

(b) provide each subject with professional (background) materials normally available to teachers,

(c) expose subjects to critical teaching problems,

(d) provide subjects with opportunities to analyse and solve the problems, and

(e) provide subjects with feedback regarding their problem solving behaviour through subject interaction.

After initial orientation to a hypothetical school district and school, via filmstrips and audio tapes, subjects were given sets of professional materials which included cumulative record cards for a fifth grade classroom, a curriculum guide, an audio visual manual, sociograms and so forth.

A carefully adhered to sequence of problem solving followed the presentation of each critical teaching problem. The general schedule involved working towards the solution of an average of four problems each day with approximately one and three-quarter hours devoted to each. Experimenters took no part in problem solving activities except to set the stage for presentation of each incident. In contrast to Kersh, all feedback resulted from subject interaction during group problem solving.

According to the researchers, results of the study indicated that the first purpose of the study, examining the methodology of simulation to judge its effectiveness in presenting classroom problems, was accomplished successfully. Data indicated that subjects became highly involved and stimulated.[35] The second purpose, to judge the effect of simulation training on subsequent behaviour, did not appear to have such a clearcut result. Of the five consequences tested, only the first—(C_1) that such problems will be less numerous—received any statistically significant results. The other tests, some of which had statistical support in the studies of Kersh and Vlcek, although all favouring the simulation groups, did not receive statistical support.

It is important to note that neither student teaching nor simulation and student teaching combined resulted in many significant changes as measured on the instruments used in this study. Either the lack of power in the instruments or the selection of consequences may be a possible cause for the lack of results. Another cause for the failure of S^s [subjects] to achieve significant results is the fact that simulation was based upon problems of beginning teachers rather than student teachers.[36]

The investigators suggest that two changes might increase the effectiveness and the results of use of such a simulator. First, the simulation should be divided so that both student teaching experience and simulation experience reinforce each other. Second, some way should be found to control the simulation experience more by providing additional input requested by a subject.

The researchers conclude,

It can be said that the simulation training when tested under the most stringent conditions was an unqualified success as a teaching device that motivates and involves students and that, although simulation was only partially successful in changing the student teachers' behavior, it was at least as effective as an equal amount of student teaching. Changes in the materials, placement [or the simulation] in the program and in the role of the instructor promise to increase the overall effectiveness of this set of simulation materials in future trials.[37]

When compared with the work of Kersh it is obvious that the Cruickshank–Broadbent approach differs in several ways. Most notably in the latter no attempt was made to shape behaviour in a predetermined way. Recall that the Classroom Simulator experimenter expected subjects eventually to demonstrate more acceptable classroom behaviour. In contrast, the latter study had developed no criteria or model for acceptable classroom behaviour. It is obvious that if criteria and models of effective teaching exist they should be employed. At the present time, although the Kersh approach is more consistent with the application of psychological principles, it applies reinforcement in too unsophisticated a fashion to the uncommonly complicated classroom setting. The generalizations that classroom simulator subjects gain need to be leavened with knowledge of other teacher behaviours which under certain conditions can be equally or more effective than the behaviours called for. On the other hand the Cruickshank–Broadbent work provides the subjects with no rules of the game. Rather, subjects are expected to suggest many alternative teaching strategies and to project consequent effects of each on students, parents, administrators and others. Thus, in this simulation, the problem solving activities and alternatives are all a function of the knowledge and experience of the group. Subjects using the simulation early in a preparation programme could be accused of resorting to 'pooled ignorance'. The developers do provide subjects with reading lists related to individual problems. Subsequently, revisions of the Cruickshank–Broadbent work give the instructor a more significant role in providing input and bringing special consultants into the problem solving sessions.[38] Cruickshank recognizes the superiority of the Kersh feedback technique could it be implemented with greater rigour or precision.

Developers of new simulation models also should strive to provide normative data regarding probable pupil reaction to a variety of teacher behaviors expressed under a variety of classroom conditions. Determination of such probabilities would enable simulation models to program consequences for a variety of teacher behaviors and to make simulation training highly individualistic. Such developments could portend using simulation either as a mode of operant conditioning or merely a mechanism by which learners could see the probability of occurrence of pupil behavior.[39]

Gaffga used one of the field trials conducted by Cruickshank and Broadbent to investigate three questions: Was subject behaviour in the simulation consistent with later behaviour during student teaching? Does the simulation change subject behaviour? And, is evaluation of a subject in simulation a better predictor of student teaching performance than ratings typically supplied by college professors?[40]

The first question received statistical support, that is, there was sufficient similarity between ratings given subjects during simulation and later during student teaching to accept the null hypotheses. Subjects in the simulation performed in ways which seemed to be consistent with their student teaching behaviour. Since transfer is among the most significant issues posed for investigation by developers of simulations, this is a significant finding.

Question two also was supported. Statistically significant differences were reported between experimental and control groups on 'averaged scores [ratings] by the college supervisors and [supervising] teachers'.[41] The finding differs from conclusions reached in the Cruickshank–Broadbent report. Since it is not entirely clear when Gaffga obtained his observations and since he apparently employed a somewhat different methodology this question requires further scrutiny.

Results of the investigation of question three support that ratings given to subjects during simulation when compared with ratings made by college professors more closely approximated ratings given during student teaching. Gaffga concludes,

This indicates that the observation of behavior in the simulated setting by the observers is more effective [as a predictor of performance during student teaching] than the observations of behavior by college professors in the classroom setting.[42]

Venditti closely paralleled techniques and format of the *Teaching Problems Laboratory* as he developed a media-ascendent role simulation with a background model intended to prepare teachers to work in desegregated schools.[43] Participants in the simulation assumed the role of a fifth grade teacher and, following orientation to the community and school, engaged in solving problems faced by teachers in schools which recently have been integrated. The simulation was intended to cause faculties of such schools to address basic racial problems.[44] According to Venditti, the simulation 'has proved itself to be a flexible and effective inservice education tool throughout a large geographic region and in a wide variety of inservice education situations'.[45] As a result of use in fourteen inservice programmes, he concludes:

. . . participants tend to become highly involved with the problems of the Valleybrook School, to interact more and more honestly and sensitively with each other, and to engage in progressively more insightful and constructive problem solving.[46]

Simulations, known less well by the writer, have been developed for the preparation of teachers by Lehman[47] and Urbach[48] (science), Utsey, Wallen, and Beldin[49] (reading), and Tansey and Unwin[50] (secondary education).

Theoretical considerations related to the development and use of simulations in preparing school personnel for diverse roles are set forth and discussed by Cruickshank and Broadbent.[51] For persons relatively unfamiliar with the notion of simulation this document and its citations should be standard references.

Few simulations for teacher preparation are available commercially. *The Teaching Problems Laboratory*[52] and more recently the *Inner-City Simulation Laboratory*[53] dominate. At last count, over 300 universities and public school districts are utilizing the former in either pre-service or in-service education.

Summarizing, this chapter attempts to do two things. First, reasons for increased interest in simulation techniques are discussed and selected advantages are enumerated. Second, the use of simulation in teacher education is surveyed and, where available, research results are reported.

Clearly simulation is one powerful method of training which can contribute significantly to teacher preparation. It can be assumed that vastly superior, more sophisticated simulations can be developed as computer availability for training purposes increases. The greatest drawback to use of simulations is fitting them into the course structure of colleges and universities or employing them in 'hit or miss' after school in-service programmes.

Teacher educators will continue to develop and use simulations and other methodologies which permit real scrutiny of teaching and learning and the setting in which it occurs. This kind of investigation will result in the generation of theory and research which have all too often been absent from the thoughts of both college professors and their students. Such study and subsequent activity should prove to be far more intellectually and psychologically challenging to students and should be more productive of teacher-scholars who can operate from a real conceptual base.

REFERENCES

1. Conant, J. B.: *The Education of American Teachers.* McGraw-Hill Book Company, 1964.

2. Vogel, F. S.: *A Model for the Preparation of Elementary School Teachers.* Final Report, Vol. 1, Grant No. Vogel OECO-8-089021-3308(010), U.S. Department of Health, Education and Welfare, 1968, p. 118.
3. American Association of Colleges for Teacher Education: *Excellence in Teacher Education.* The Association, 1968, p. 1.
4. Smith, B. O., Cohen, S. B., and Pearl, A.: *Teachers for the Real World.* American Association of Colleges for Teacher Education, 1969.
5. Ibid., p. 52. (Footnotes 5, 6, and 7 are reproduced by permission of the AACTE, and of B. O. Smith.)
6. Ibid., p. 64.
7. Ibid., p. 56.
8. Schueler, H., and Lesser, G. S.: *Teacher Education and the New Media.* American Association for Colleges of Teacher Education, 1967.
9. American Association of Colleges for Teacher Education: *Standards and Evaluative Criteria.* The Association, 1967, p. 25. (Reproduced by permission of the AACTE.)
10. Schueler and Lesser, op. cit., p. 20.
11. LaGrone, H. F.: *A Proposal for the Revision of the Pre-Service Professional Component of a Program of Teacher Education.* The American Association of Colleges for Teacher Education, 1964, p. 63. (Reproduced with the permission of the author.)
12. Smith, op. cit., pp. 41–65.
13. Rogers, C. R.: 'The Facilitation of Significant Learning'. *Instruction: Some Contemporary Viewpoints* (ed. L. Siegel), Chandler Publishing Company, 1967, p. 49. (Reproduced with the permission of the author.)
14. Cruickshank, D. R., and Broadbent, F. W.: *The Simulation and Analysis of Problems of Beginning Teachers. Final Report*, Project No. 5-0798, U.S. Department of Health, Education and Welfare, 1968, p. 110. (Reproduced with the permission of F. W. Broadbent.)
15. Kersh, B. Y.: 'Simulation in Teacher Education'. Paper read at the American Psychological Association annual convention in St Louis, 1962, p. 2. (Material referred to in notes 15 and 17 and is reproduced with the permission of the author.)
16. Kersh, B. Y.: *Classroom Simulation: A New Dimension in Teacher Education, Final Report*, Title VII, Project Number 886, National Defense Education Act of 1958, Grant No. 7-47-0000-164. U.S. Department of Health, Education and Welfare, 1963, p. 8.
17. Ibid., p. 9.
18. Ibid.
19. Campbell, D. T., and Stanley, J. C.: *Experimental and Quasi-Experimental Designs for Research.* Rand McNally and Company, 1967, pp. 20–22.
20. Kersh, B. Y.: *Classroom Simulation*, op cit., p. 26.
21. Vlcek, C. W.: 'Assessing the Effect and Transfer Value of a Classroom Simulator Technique'. Unpublished doctoral dissertation, Michigan State University, 1965. (Material referred to in notes 21, 22, and 23 is reproduced with the permission of the author.)
22. Ibid., Abstract, pp. 2–3.
23. Vlcek, C. W.: 'Classroom Simulation in Teacher Education'. *Audiovisual Instruction*, 11 (2), 1966, p. 90. (Reproduced with the permission of *Audiovisual Instruction*.)

24. Kersh, B. Y.: *Classroom Simulation: Further Studies on Dimensions of Realism*. Final Report Title VII Project 5-0848, National Defense Education Act of 1958, Department of Health, Education and Welfare, 1965.

25. Twelker, P. A.: 'Prompting as an Instructional Variable in Classroom Simulation'. Paper read at the American Educational Research Association annual convention in Chicago, 1966.

26. Ibid., p. 6. (Reproduced with the permission of the author.)

27. Teaching Research: *Low Cost Instructional Simulation Materials for Teacher Education*. Oregon State System of Higher Education, 1968.

28. Cruickshank, D. R., and Broadbent, F. W.: *Simulation in Preparing Educational Personnel*. ERIC Center for Teacher Education, 1969, pp. 29–30. (Reproduced with the permission of F. W. Broadbent.)

29. Rice, A. H., and Jaffe, J.: *Four Years of Insite*. School of Education, Indiana University, not dated, p. 1. (Reproduced with the permission of the author.)

30. University Council on Educational Administration, 29 West Woodruff Avenue, Columbus, Ohio.

31. McQuigg, R. B.: 'The Capstone Experience: a Week of Simulation for the Secondary Acroclinical Student'. School of Education, Indiana University, not dated, mimeo, p. 3. (Reproduced with permission of the author.)

32. Cruickshank, D. R., and Broadbent, F. W.: *The Simulation and Analysis of Problems of Beginning Teachers*, loc. cit.

33. Cruickshank, D. R., and Broadbent, F. W.: *Simulation in Preparing Educational Personnel*, op. cit., pp. 10–17.

34. Cruickshank, D. R., and Broadbent, F. W.: *The Simulation and Analysis of Problems of Beginning Teachers*, op. cit., p. 9.

35. Ibid., pp. 77–86.

36. Cruickshank, D. R., and Broadbent, F. W.: 'An Investigation to Determine Effects of Simulation Training on Student Teaching'. Paper read at the American Educational Research Association annual convention in Los Angeles, 1969, p. 7. (Notes 36 and 37 are reproduced with the permission of F. W. Broadbent.)

37. Cruickshank, D. R., and Broadbent, F. W.: *The Simulation and Analysis of Problems of Beginning Teachers*, op. cit., p. 110.

38. Cruickshank, D. R., Broadbent, F. W., and Bubb, R. L.: *Teaching Problems Laboratory*. Science Research Associates, 1967.

39. Cruickshank, D. R.: 'The Use of Simulation in Teacher Education: a Developing Phenomenon'. *Journal of Teacher Education*, 20 (1), 1969, p. 26. (Reproduced with permission.)

40. Gaffga, R. M.: 'Simulation: a Method for Observing Student Teacher Behavior'. Unpublished doctoral dissertation, the University of Tennessee, 1967, p. 9.

41. Ibid., p. 71.

42. Ibid., p. 87. (Reproduced with the permission of the author.)

43. Venditti, F. P.: *Handbook for Teaching in Valleybrook Elementary School: a Simulation Game Focusing Upon Problems of the Racially Desegregated School*. College of Education, the University of Tennessee, 1969.

44. Ibid., p. 6.

45. Ibid., p. 45.

46. Ibid. (Reproduced with the permission of the author.)

47. Lehman, D. L.: 'Simulation in Science: a Preliminary Report on the Use and

Evaluation of Role Playing in the Preparation of Secondary School Student Teachers of Science'. Paper read at the AAAS Meeting in Washington, D.C., 1966.

48. Urbach, F. Personal correspondence with F. W. Broadbent cited in Cruickshank and Broadbent: *Simulation in Preparing Educational Personnel*, op. cit., p. 20.

49. Utsey, J., Wallen, C., and Beldin, H. O.: 'Simulation: a Breakthrough in the Education of Reading Teachers'. *Phi Delta Kappan*, 47, 10, 1966.

50. Tansey, P. J., Bulmershe College of Education, Berks, England, by personal correspondence.

51. Cruickshank, D. R., and Broadbent, F. W.: *Simulation in Preparing Educational Personnel*, op. cit.

52. Cruickshank, D. R., Broadbent, F. W., and Bubb, R. L.: *Teaching Problems Laboratory*, op. cit.

53. Cruickshank, D. R.: *Inner City Simulation Laboratory*. Science Research Associates, 1969.

9
Simulation: a catalogue of judgements, findings, and hunches

Dale M. Garvey

Dale M. Garvey is an Associate Professor of Political Science at Kansas State Teachers College. His experience in simulation stems from a desire to provide more interesting instructional situations both in pre-college and college instruction. His research into the effectiveness of simulation as an instructional technique was one of the earliest projects directed at assessing simulation. He has utilized simulation and gaming experimentally in all grades from the seventh grade through college undergraduate courses, as well as in courses at the graduate level. Currently, his efforts are concentrated on developing the abilities of students to construct simulations of selected social processes in an endeavour to acquire greater understanding of the complexities of political activities and behaviour.

The assigned purpose of this chapter was to evaluate simulation as a teaching technique. That objective is much more difficult to accomplish, however, than would appear at first glance. Evaluation is the act of determining the value, or of ascertaining some means of stating the value, of an unknown in terms of that which is known. Precision of measurement is difficult at best, and frequently impossible in education. At times, the difficulties of measurement are the result of using instruments which are not precise. At other times, the difficulties lie in the fact that there are no satisfactory instruments with which to measure.

This essay, then, is concerned with presenting what is known and what is believed of the value of simulation as a teaching technique. Some of the judgements are the result of thorough investigation in experimental studies. Others are the results of observations made by persons who have had considerable experience in the use of simulation as one technique in achieving educational objectives. The statistical data upon which some of the judgements are based are not reproduced here, as this chapter is intended for the teacher who may care to use simulation in the classroom, not the researcher who desires to measure precisely the effects of different variables.

It is apparent, then, that to state that the intent of this chapter is to evaluate simulation as a teaching technique is not precisely accurate in the sense of establishing the value of an unknown in terms of that which is known. Rather, it is an attempt to answer questions such as one frequently asked by both in-service and pre-service teachers, 'How does one evaluate simulation?' This writer customarily replies that a teacher does not evaluate simulation as a technique any more than he evaluates lectures, or group discussions, or any other technique used by him. Such a reply is true, but not quite accurate, because it evades the basic question. The question implied by requests concerning the evaluation of simulation actually asks, 'Is the learning achieved by students worth the extra effort which is demanded of the teacher who utilizes simulation as a technique?' It is to questions such as this that this chapter is directed.

Some assessment of simulation as a technique must be undertaken, if for no other reason, because as a technique it has become to some proponents a universally useful tool for teaching. No assumption could be further from the truth. And yet, as a technique, some judgements concerning simulation must be made to permit teachers to determine whether it would be a useful tool for them to develop for their own use. Such an approach dictates that simulation be measured with reference to its effectiveness as a means to achieve one or a combination of several different objectives. It need not be assessed in comparison with other techniques only with reference to their relative effectiveness in enabling students to learn conceptual and factual substantive knowledge or to acquire mechanical and social skills. It is the contention of this essay that simulation should be evaluated only as one tool which a teacher may employ to achieve specified educational objectives.

To attempt a more precise statement of the thesis, simulation should not be evaluated only by measuring the amount of substantive material which a student acquires as the result of his experiences in simulated exercises. That type of evaluation is properly an evaluation of the *student*, NOT of the *technique*. The evaluation of the technique, then, should be directed toward assessing how it may be used by teachers to achieve their teaching objectives. The evaluation of simulation must be essentially a subjective judgement of the technique as a motivational device, because there is almost no useful empirical evidence to support one teaching technique as being more effective than another with reference to the rapidity of learning or the amount of information which students acquire as a result of the use of various techniques. To facilitate the evaluation here, the several purposes for which it may be employed should be considered.

Simulation as an educational tool may be employed to achieve any one of or a combination of several different objectives. The various objectives include, but are not limited to:

(a) Providing a vehicle by which participants (students) may acquire conceptual or factual information, or may integrate information, contributing to the comprehension of the 'structure' of knowledge.

(b) Providing a laboratory experience in which participants may acquire and/or improve skills in social processes. The skills may be those which the participant may be preparing to utilize in real life situations, or they may be those in which it will be useful for the participant to gain some familiarity in order to appreciate the utility, the complexity, or the situation and attitudes of other individuals who perform those skills in real life.

(c) Providing the participants with an opportunity to experience, acquire or alter attitudes relating to real life roles which the participant may portray, but which he may not normally have an opportunity to experience in reality.

(d) Developing theory concerning a social process.

(e) Testing theory concerning a social process.

Objectives (a), (b), and (c) are directly concerned with the instruction of students. Objectives (d) and (e) are almost entirely research tools except in a limited number of situations with advanced students. Therefore, this chapter is concerned with an exploration of the first three objectives and an evaluation of the manner in which simulation can effectively be used in their accomplishment.

To this point, the term 'simulation' has been used without specifying its precise meaning. To avoid misunderstandings, it is appropriate to define each of several terms as they are used throughout this chapter.

Simulation

Simulation is the all-inclusive term which contains those activities which produce artificial environments or which provide artificial experiences for the participants in the activity. A simulated situation provides an opportunity for one person, a few, or several persons to perform a selected portion of a process. The present interest is solely in those social processes which are replicas of processes observable in the real world. The replicas may be greatly simplified in comparison with the original.

Simulations may be operations which require their performance by humans (a so-called manual, or all-man simulation); operations performed entirely by technological means (such as a computer); or any mixture of the two extremes. Simulation embraces three types of activities, (a) role playing, (b) sociodrama, and (c) gaming.

Role playing Role playing is the simplest of the activities included in the all-embracing term 'simulation'. It is essentially one of either of two types of activities. It is

(a) the act of 'being someone else', or
(b) the act of acquiring experience in a set of activities in which the actor seeks to acquire or to increase his competence.

The role assumed in role playing is one in which the actor portrays either a fictitious role or an actual role, but performs that role in an artificial environment. By definition, the role portrayed may be one with which the actor has little or no familiarity at the start of the simulated situation. This is the use of role playing to enable the participant to acquire understanding of a situation or of relationships among real life participants of a social process, or the role playing may be used to assist the participant to gain some perception of the actions, attitudes, and/or situation of another person.

A six-year-old child playing the part of a school crossing guard is engaged in role playing to encourage him to appreciate some of the problems encountered in the process of controlling young children in crossing a busy traffic artery. Perhaps the youngster has been one who was slow to obey the instructions of the crossing guard. Requiring the child to play the part of the crossing guard and to control the actions of other children in a simulated situation may enable the young actor to appreciate the situation of the real life crossing guard and to revise his behaviour pattern in his relationship with 'the crossing guard.

The role portrayed by the participant may also be one in which the actor desires to acquire competence, or one in which the actor has previously acquired some familiarity, but desires to improve his level of competence. The use of driver-training simulators and flight simulators are examples of this type of role playing. In the social processes with which this essay is concerned, role playing may be utilized, for example, to familiarize students with parliamentary procedure, or to improve the student's ability to utilize parliamentary procedure in preparation for later participation in a real world situation.

Sociodrama Sociodrama is the use of role playing as a means of enabling the role players to seek a solution to a social problem which is posed for them. The problem may be one extracted from the real world, or it may be one designed to present a selected situation for solution. Regardless of the type of situation employed, the role players (or actors) are required to devise an acceptable solution to the situation presented.

Sociodrama differs from role playing only in the objective which is sought. Role playing seeks to provide competence or understanding in a particular role for the person playing that role. Sociodrama, on the other hand, seeks to utilize role playing as a means of devising a solution to a problem situation which is prescribed for the role players. The problem may be fictional or it may be an abstraction from real life.

Gaming   Gaming is the addition to the technique of sociodrama of an element which demands the development and choice of strategies (or decision making), and some type of pay-off—rewards or deprivations dictated either by chance or by the choice of strategies. 'The decisions and the rewards are subject to the strictures of rules known to all players. By definition, the situations employed involve outcomes which are affected by decisions made by one or more decision makers. The game may be designed in a manner which enables chance to affect the outcome, or chance may be prohibited.*

The decision makers in a game may be competing for nondivisible objectives or their preferences may be such that they seek essentially the same objectives, but place the objectives in different rank order of priorities. Thus gaming involves the making of decisions in situations which depict conflict. Conflict is a normal part of any social process, and gaming is, therefore, a useful tool for providing situations in which participants may learn of the real world in a manner which is relatively inexpensive in terms of time, personnel, facilities, and frayed nerves. Errors of judgement may be punished in a non-fatal manner, or the fictitious world may be 'wiped out', and the players may begin again as if no error had occurred.†

---

* As used here, the term 'game' departs from that used by Anatol Rapoport in *Two-Person Game Theory* (University of Michigan Press, 1966). Rapoport states that there must be a minimum of *two* players, neither of whom may be *chance*, as *chance* cannot be the recipient of a pay-off. The term here is considered to include one-person games in which chance may or may not have a part.

† Under the definition employed here, a game includes a simulated situation. There are educational games which do not do so, and their use is not considered in this chapter. It should be noted that all simulation games include both the game element and the simulated situation. However, not all educational games include simulated situations, just as not all simulated situations require the inclusion of a game.

The uses of simulation

To evaluate simulation as an instructional technique requires that it be categorized in some manner. For the purposes of this essay it is more useful to evaluate the technique by an examination of the uses to which it may be put.

There are several uses for which simulation is an effective technique. This chapter will limit the examination of the effectiveness of simulation to the following situations:

(a) The use of simulation as a device for motivating students.
(b) The effectiveness of simulation as a means of altering the attitudes held by students.
(c) The effectiveness of simulation as a means of enabling students to acquire factual and conceptual knowledge and to retain the knowledge acquired.
(d) The effectiveness of simulation as a means of enabling students to acquire and to improve social skills, and to gain confidence in their ability to employ those skills.
(e) The use of simulation as a social laboratory to provide for students an opportunity to exercise the social skills acquired, to utilize in an artificial environment knowledge previously acquired, and/or to gain some comprehension of the complexities of selected social processes.

Obviously, the above uses are not mutually exclusive. It is impossible to design a simulation to achieve one of the objectives and to avoid including others. It is equally obvious that the uses listed above are not the only ones for which simulation can be employed. For the purposes of this chapter, however, these are the uses which will be examined. It should be borne in mind that although the various uses are examined individually, they are in practice frequently inseparable.

Summation of research findings and hunches

There is little empirical evidence to indicate that simulation is more effective or less effective than other teaching techniques. There are some indications which are not conclusive. Consequently, although of interest, such evidence leaves something to be desired in a serious attempt at evaluation. There is no dearth, however, of subjective judgements made by persons who have used simulation extensively.

There should be no hesitation to examine subjective judgements when they are the best judgements which are available. In all honesty, one must admit that one rarely makes decisions on the basis of objective evidence, but one makes purchases, chooses a wife (or husband) and friends, and makes innumerable other equally important decisions upon the basis of subjective evaluations. There is no apology, therefore, for employing subjective judgements in the evaluations which are a part of this chapter. The assessments of the uses indicated above are offered here individually in reference to each use. When empirical evidence is available to support an evaluation, the source of the evidence is indicated. If the judgement is subjective, some indication is usually provided concerning the basis for the judgement.

As a device for motivating students Perhaps the most important of the uses to which simulation may be put is that of motivating students. No student learns unless he is sufficiently motivated. Simulation provides the teacher with a means by which the student is placed in a situation calling for maximum performance by the student. The teacher is removed from the traditional position of director of the class. Consequently, a student with a need to express disagreement with the teacher as a symbol of authority, for example, does not have the usual authority figure available, and his need to be liked by his fellow students may provide adequate motivation for optimal performance. Peer pressure usually requires the student to carry his share of the burden of adequate group performance.

Repeatedly, both in high school and in college undergraduate classes, the author has observed students perform at a level of excellence above that which was normal for the same students under more conventional classroom situations. Many students who have previously been hesitant to participate in class discussions, for example, frequently will begin to voice their opinions when a simulated situation places demands upon them. Good students also find stimulation in simulated situations and continue to perform well.

In other instances, students who have been placed in a role to which considerable prestige is attached, as that of the President of the United States or of a judge, have attended class dressed in a manner which they apparently felt befitted the role they were enacting, and have comported themselves in a manner in keeping with the dignity of the real life role. Immediately after the termination of the simulated situation, they would return to the next session of the class in the dress which they normally wore and return to their usual classroom behaviour. It appears to be a tenable assumption that such a student is motivated to acquire and to demonstrate both visible and invisible characteristics of the assumed role. Such behaviour demonstrates, at least, that simulated situations motivate the participant to adopt changed behaviour patterns, even if for only a short period of time. And changes in behaviour are the goals of education.

Based on the amount of time devoted by a student in preparation for a class, there is additional support for the belief that simulation provides positive motivation for students. In one high school class in which the technique was employed, questioning of the students indicated that they spent approximately twice as much time in preparation for the unit of instruction in which simulation was used as compared with the amount of preparation time spent in the course prior to the beginning of the use of simulation.

During the conduct of one experiment, the high school students became so intensely involved in research needed to enable them to function more effectively in a simulation, that they began to use the library facilities of a nearby university in addition to the high school library. The demands thus placed upon the university library in terms of services and space was sufficiently burdening for the university to prohibit further student use of the university library. The assumption is that any technique which can motivate students to alter normal study patterns to the degree noted here as the result of voluntary action, must possess a high motivational capability.

Such observations are not conclusive, of course, of any contention that simulation is universally useful in providing positive motivation for students. In the judgement of this writer, however, they afford powerful support for contentions that, in comparison with lectures and other less student-oriented techniques, simulation offers a teacher an excellent tool for motivation.

Assumptions concerning the effectiveness of simulation as a motivational device receive strong support from an evaluation conducted by Hall T. Sprague and R. Garry Shirts[1] under the auspices of the Western Behavioral Sciences Institute of La Jolla, California. This experiment was designed to test the feasibility of simulation as a teaching technique. The project involved forty simulation runs in seventeen schools, and included thirty teachers and 2,500 students. There was a statistically significant percentage of the students who reacted favourably to simulation as a technique. Of the junior high school students, 93 per cent rated simulations favourably. Although the senior high school percentage was lower (75 per cent), it was still a three-to-one favourite of students. The response of the teachers was also predominantly one of high enthusiasm.

Students do not usually display enthusiasm for classroom learning situations. To do so would frequently subject them to expressions of disapproval by their peers. And yet in the above experiment, as well as many others, there has been overwhelming approval indicated by the participants for a technique which they stated was enjoyable. It is realized that enjoyment and learning are not the same dimensions, and thus cannot be measured by identical yardsticks. There is, however, a strong correlation between the two. If students find a learning situation enjoyable, it is reasonable to expect that they will learn more than if they are compelled to take part in an unenjoyable situation. That performance improves in pleasant surroundings compared with usual performance in less pleasant surroundings is widely accepted.

The simulated situation is the natural learning environment for children. It replaces the childhood game (which is not an activity without object). If the role to be performed in the simulated situation is that of an adult in the referent situation, the student participant is able to portray that role more nearly as an adult would do. For example, the student is not required to continue to play the role of a child or of an individual subservient to the teacher, a symbol of authority. Coleman[2] states that in games and simulations, the participant learns in much the same fashion that he would learn in childhood games. That is, the participant does not view the goal of the game as being to learn, but the goal is to achieve a designated objective.

Findings such as those reported above lead to speculation that simulation might be useful in the education of children experiencing mental, emotional, or physical handicaps or social deprivations. Some evidence is available that simulation games are beneficial when used with students who are under-achievers. Farran[3] reports that simulation games were used in an effort to improve the academic performance of eighth grade pupils who had average or above average intellectual ability but were low achievers in comparison with their assumed ability. The pupils were categorized as having behaviour problems, motivational problems, remedial problems, or all three. Possessing a history of failure and an experience that identified learning as, at least, uninteresting, the experimental group was considered to have benefited from the competitive elements which games introduced.

Competition is a useful device for generating motivation. Either as an individual competing against another individual, or an individual competing with a team against another team, competition tends to elicit greater intensity of effort and application than is usual in non-competitive situations.[4] Simulation games offer the teacher a relatively easy opportunity to introduce into the learning situation the competitive element.

An additional benefit resulting from simulations, including games, is the increased attention span which the young appear capable of sustaining. Observations suggest that young children are limited in the amount of time during which they are able to concentrate in conventional learning situations. There is evidence to suggest that educational games enable four-year-olds to play highly cognitive games for more than thirty minutes without loss of attentiveness.[5] Observations of older students offer support for a similar conclusion. This writer cannot recall an instance in which a college undergraduate has fallen asleep during a simulation—an observation that cannot be duplicated in lectures and other conventional learning situations.

Reactions of students when asked to evaluate a course in which simulation games or simulated situations have been used are usually favourable, although not unanimous. Samplings of opinions of students ranging from grade nine through grade twelve provide support for the assumption that the students devoted more effort to that portion of the course in which simulation was employed, and that they were generally more intensely involved in the course work than when the technique was not used. Many of the students volunteered the information that the simulation experience was, from the standpoint of their own interest, the culminating event of the course.[6]

Some of the students who found simulation especially enjoyable were students who did not usually perform well academically, and who did not generally display evidence of interest in a learning situation. There are data which support a tentative conclusion that the students as a group found their social studies to be less interesting than the other courses in which they were enrolled. The evidence for this is based upon the grade point averages of the group, comparing the average grade for the group as scored in the social studies course with the average for all other courses in which they were enrolled. Based on a scale on which 4·00 equals 'A', the class at the end of the first nine-week grading period had an average grade 0·39 points lower than the average for all other courses. However, for each of the succeeding three nine-week grading periods, during each of which simulation was employed, the average grade increased for the social studies class, compared with a decline in the average for all other courses during the second and third grading periods, and an increase during the fourth, although not as high as the grade for the social studies course. The comparable grades for the social studies course for each of the nine-week grading periods, using the average of all other courses as a base, was minus 0·39, plus 0·04, plus 0·02, and plus 0·11. Although not conclusive evidence, the data suggest that simulation provides a strong motivational potential.[7]

As a means for affecting student attitudes This is an especially difficult assessment to undertake. It involves, among other things, assumptions concerning what constitute attitudes, and which attitudes are to be considered. For the purpose of this chapter, an attitude is considered to be the expression of an internal value (like–dislike; good–bad) toward an external object or objective. The attitudes for which change can be detected as the result of the use of simulation are those attitudes concerned with

(a) the students' view of their own abilities to affect the operation of a given system;
(b) the students' assessment of games and simulated situations, in reference to the utility of simulations;
(c) the assessment of demonstrated student reactions to situations in terms of their attitudes expressing more (or less) realism (as contrasted to idealism).

The students' view of their own abilities   This writer has been impressed with the apparent surprise which some students have displayed after participating in a simulated situation. Frequently, some student has indicated his surprise that he has been able to manipulate the elements of the simulated situation to produce what he apparently considered to be a desirable outcome.

The underlying assumption here is, of course, that the simulated situations reflected in a reasonably isomorphic manner a social process in which the student might be expected to participate either currently or at some time in the future. Granting this assumption, participation in simulations probably can be useful in enabling students to gain a new perspective of themselves in relation to their environment and their ability to manipulate that environment. When they observe the results of their own successful operation in the simulation, and experience the pleasure resulting therefrom, it is safe to assume that their attitudes about themselves and their abilities are favourably influenced, even though there is no hard evidence to support the assumption.

The students' assessment of simulation   This portion of the assessment is a combination of two views. In part, it considers the motivational aspect of simulations, and in part the students' assessment of simulated situations. We have already established the value of simulation and games as means of motivating students, but it is worth a brief examination to view the students as they see themselves, and in doing so, the attitudes they display toward the educational process.

Students frequently do not find learning enjoyable. They employ words like 'dull' and 'boring' to describe their opinion of the customary learning situation. Experience has demonstrated, however, that the use of simulation and games in a classroom apparently alters the attitudes of a majority of the students toward the educational objectives. Descriptive words change to indicate pleasure with the classroom, and frequently the students demonstrate an eagerness to engage in the class work, even that portion which does not directly include the use of simulation.

Although no hard conclusion can be drawn that being 'fun' and being 'useful' are the same, it is reasonable to assume that the inclusion of activities which elicit favourable student reaction is beneficial to the entire classroom atmosphere. It is common for students to volunteer remarks which indicate their enjoyment of the classroom and their activities within it. The demonstration of such attitudes by students who have not usually demonstrated their enjoyment of classroom activities is strongly suggestive of a change in attitude.

The students' attitudes towards simulated situations   In this part of the assessment, we undertake to examine two aspects of attitudes. First, we shall examine experimental evidence concerning an hypothesized ability of simulation to change the attitudes in the direction of realism in reference to world situations, as contrasted to an attitude of idealism. The second aspect will deal with the recognition of reality as evidenced by an awareness of complexity, as contrasted with an unsophisticated attitude.

In an experiment conducted in two high schools with a control group and an experimental group in each school, it was hypothesized that the experimental group (employing simulation) would demonstrate a change of attitude in the direction of realism with reference to an appraisal of foreign affairs, and that the control group (without simulation), if change occurred, would not change as greatly. A total of 351 students was involved in the attitude tests.[8]

The results of the experiment were inconclusive. Statistically significant differences were obtained on twenty of thirty-one statements included on a test to determine attitudes of the student sample and the direction in which those attitudes moved between pre-test and post-test. On the basis of z-score values, the null hypothesis that there existed no difference between experimental and control groups should be rejected seventeen times. The null hypothesis that there was no difference between the two schools should be rejected fifteen times. (Some of the data indicated both hypotheses should be rejected, accounting for a total of thirty-two rejections on only twenty statements.)

The statements used on the test were assertions made concerning the conduct of American foreign policy. The student was asked to mark his answer-sheet to indicate 'strong agreement', 'agreement', 'undecided', 'disagreement', or 'strong disagreement'. The test was administered again at the termination of the experimental period. The direction of movement was that change of a group or of a student towards agreement or dis-agreement, using the position indicated on the pre-test as a reference point.

Although no statistically significant results were obtained in examin-ing the use of simulation as a means of enabling students to comprehend the reality of real world situations, the data suggest that the group which experienced simulation was somewhat more aware of reality than was the comparison group, although the data are tenuous.[9] The recognition of reality included the comprehension that complex relationships produce complex problems which require complex solutions. An educational experience which elicits a recognition of the complexity of real world relationships is particularly useful in a world which apparent-ly is growing ever more complex.

It has been remarked that today's student is a product of the age of television, a medium in which virtue always triumphs. Problems are simple, bifurcated situations in which justice and morality are concen-trated on one side of the issue, with the opposing side capable of claiming only injustice and evil as its allies. Simple solutions to the simple prob-lems are obtainable in a single half-hour show, or at most in one hour of viewing time (with time out for commercials).

Whether the allegations concerning television are entirely correct is not particularly pertinent. Experience with both adults and children supports the observation that people tend to over-simplify problems and to seek overly simple solutions to them. In simulated experiences of realistic design, however, participants gain a realistic view of the com-plexities of the referent situation, in spite of the fact that a simulation does not reproduce all of the complex relationships which exist in the real world situation. After participation in a simulation, participants frequently remark, 'Now I know why it takes Congress so long to act', or 'Now I understand why the President can't make Congress do just what he wants them to do', or similar remarks indicative of some com-prehension of the complexity of the real world.

It is important to emphasize that the simulated situation must be realistic if the complexities of real life situations are to be recognized. The model upon which the simulation is based need not be a replication of the total complexity of the referent situation, but it must incorporate the essential structure of the situation and the principles (or theories) which illustrate the relationships which connect the parts of the real system. If principles cannot be demonstrated in the course of the simula-tion, the participants can learn no more from the simulation than they would from a completely spontaneous *scenario* in which each actor portrays only his personal values.

Conversely, the rules of play in a simulation may be too complex for educational value to be realized by the participants. If the play is too highly complicated, or if report forms are too difficult for the participants to complete, the simulation may encourage the participants to seek to learn how to defeat the rules imposed, rather than to achieve the designed objective of the simulation. Permitting such results to occur defeats the objective of a simulation, which should be that of enabling the participants to engage in activities which possess a realistic relationship to a real life situation, and should encourage the participants to develop the attitude that they are capable of operating effectively in the situation being modelled. The hope is, of course, that the participants will acquire an attitude of personal efficacy in reference to the simulated system and that the attitude will transfer to the referent situation. If a young participant acquires a belief in his ability to make the system respond to his efforts to influence it, there is foundation for hope that he will likewise acquire a degree of confidence in his ability to influence the operation of the referent system or situation.

As a means for facilitating the acquisition and retention of knowledge   To be utterly candid, there is no evidence known to support an hypothesis that simulation is more effective than any other teaching technique in enabling a student to acquire knowledge. But most proponents of simulation contend that the technique is effective in achieving educational objectives in what Bloom and Krathwohl term the cognitive domain and the affective domain.[10]

At the upper or more complex end of the taxonomy of cognitive educational objectives, Bloom and Krathwohl include those objectives which illustrate the structure of concepts, theories, principles, and relationships of an educational discipline. It is in the realm of demonstrating structure or of requiring a student to develop structure that simulation is believed to be particularly useful. The burden of successful performance in a simulation is placed squarely upon the student, not the teacher. Yet successful performance cannot be achieved by mere rote recall of bits of knowledge acquired as unrelated pieces of information. In a well-designed simulation, the student is compelled to develop some recognition of relationship among the component elements of knowledge which are included in the situation. By careful prodding and explication, the teacher can at first demonstrate the structure of knowledge which is reflected within the simulated system. Later, as the student acquires experience, the teacher can encourage the student through discreet questions to develop his own recognition of the structure of knowledge displayed in the situation. It is probably safe to state, however, that a participant in a simulation is never capable of obtaining the full measure of usefulness from a simulated situation unless an observer (teacher) is available to direct the attention of the participant for the same reason that expert golfers take lessons to improve their play. It is impossible for a participant (or a golfer) to be aware of all he is doing and of the complete relationship of his actions.

Two experiments have provided some empirical evidence which indicates that simulations facilitate the acquisition of what is variously termed 'principles', or 'concepts', or 'structure'. Robinson et al.[11] determined that those students who preferred simulation seemed to do better at learning principles rather than fact-mastery. In the comparison group, which preferred case studies, better performance was noted on fact-mastery. Garvey and Seiler[12] found similar results, in that the students who did not participate in simulation during a controlled experiment performed better in the acquisition of knowledge which was termed factual. The experimental group, which participated in an internation simulation, demonstrated a superiority in answering questions which were designed to test conceptual knowledge.

The latter experiment also provided some support for a contention that simulation facilitates the retention of knowledge by its participants. The experimental group began the experiment with an overall grade point average 0·03 points lower than that of the control group. On the basis of grades, it is evident that the control group possessed a very small, and probably relatively unimportant, advantage over the experimental group, which engaged in simulation. Although the measurements indicated by grade point average and by the content examination are not the same dimensions, it would seem reasonable that the group with the higher grade point average should perform as well or better than the one with the lower average, and that the group with the higher average should probably retain the acquired information at least as well as the other group. In actuality, the control group, which did not experience simulation, indicated that it acquired more factual knowledge and the experimental group using simulation indicated it retained more conceptual knowledge. Thus, the group with the lower grade point average (the experimental group) indicated slightly greater retention of conceptual knowledge than did the one with the higher grade point average (the control group).[13]

In all honesty, it is necessary to suggest that the results noted for the participants of simulations probably receive considerable reinforcement because of the intensity of application and concentration which is characteristic of a majority of simulation participants. Participants frequently engage in conversation long after the termination of a class period in which simulation has been used. They will continue to bargain or to discuss strategies with their classmates. Such activites are likely to affect the measurements which have been attempted concerning the retention of knowledge. However, even if the resultant retention is more attributable to the motivational aspects of simulation than to its ability to enable participants to retain knowledge, the end result appears to be the same, and a desirable one.

As a means for developing social skills   It is a truism that the peoples of the world are becoming increasingly interdependent. Yet the 'conventional' classroom encourages students to sit quietly, read quietly, and recite when called upon. Such conventional classroom behaviour places the teacher and the student in a one-for-one relationship and fails to capitalize upon the benefits which accrue from peer interactions. Simulation is not the only technique by which a teacher may place students in a position in which they do much more than merely soak up knowledge like a sponge. It is, however, a technique which places the student in the position of performing required actions in situations in which successful outcomes are usually dependent not only upon his own actions and choices of strategies, but also upon the actions and choices of his peers. He is compelled to recognize the fact of interdependence, and in so doing he develops social skills which are easily transferred to the real world.

As used in this chapter, skill is interpreted to mean a generalized technique or ability to deal with other persons in an interpersonal situation. It includes, but is not limited to, the abilities to bargain, to persuade, to collect and to categorize information in a manner which facilitates decision making, to compete, to co-operate, to command, to accept commands; in short, to do all those things which are embraced in the terms 'to lead' and 'to follow', i.e., manipulative skills and responsive skills. Such skills are essential in a world composed of interdependent persons and groups.

In a simulated setting, a participant may be placed in a situation in which he is required to make decisions. He does much more than merely read about what decisions could have been made. He experiences some of the agonies of indecision during the decision making process, and once he has committed his resources, he then undergoes the experience of determining if his decision was acceptable in the given conditions. If the simulation run is of sufficient length, he will be afforded an opportunity to visualize the results of his decision, be they 'good' or 'bad'. The capability of compressing time in a simulated situation provides adequate opportunity for the development of feedback, allowing the participant to observe the actual results of his decision and to compare them with anticipated results. And the decisions are made in a setting in which no lasting harm derives from an incorrect decision. Rather, if an error occurs, it is quite simple to 'wipe the world clean', and to begin a new situation to which the participant can respond.

From observation, it appears that one useful result of such experience in decision making is that participants discover that they are compelled to make a selection among competing values. For example, as the head of government of a developing nation-state, a participant may desire to develop the industrial capacity of his country and to invest all available capital in the quest of that objective. However, the population growth rate in his country is sufficiently great that a strain is placed on the economy merely to maintain the current standard of living. If the standard of living declines, irresistable pressures may generate which would call for the overthrow of the head of government. He may then see his only salvation to lie in seeking assistance from another nation-state, a course of action which may be distasteful to his pride. Such experiences tend to develop an awareness that most complex decisions are not susceptible to simple 'yes' or 'no', 'good' or 'bad', 'right' or 'wrong' judgements. Complex problems demand the development of complex solutions which are complicated by the necessity to consider competing values. It is the belief of this writer that the acquisition of such awareness is an important and necessary part of the education of people who are going to live in an increasingly interdependent world, and that simulation is the most realistic and least expensive means by which students can acquire the requisite experiences.

One of the benefits of experience in decision making is the confrontation by the participant with the necessity to define the problem situation and to develop a strategy for attacking it. It is always more difficult to bake a cake than to read about baking a cake. More variables are encountered than are conceived when reading about the problem. Experiencing the necessity to make life-like decisions in an environment which is non-punitive, enables participants to develop their skill at making decisions, and simultaneously develops their confidence in their ability to make sound decisions.

During the course of many types of simulations the participants encounter situations which require them to bargain with their competitors, or to persuade those with whom they are maintaining relationships. The manipulative and the responsive skills are not the native properties of only a small number of fortunate individuals. All reasonably capable persons can learn to increase their competence at manipulating others and of responding to the manipulations of others in the process of solving problems. (As used here manipulation carries no undesirable connotation.)

Burgess and Robinson[14] suggest that during the next half-century there will develop an increasing need for people skilled at problem-solving—that is, people capable of working on political, social, or business problems of great complexity. They foresee that such people will require problem-solving skills for the purpose of making decisions based upon a great volume of specialized knowledge available on a variety of issues. Problem-solvers will not be restricted to one area of competence, but will be able to transfer their skills from one type of issue to another with comparative ease. If such views of the future are realistic, simulations afford a means by which future problem-solvers can acquire and sharpen their skills. The capacity of simulations to compress time, to differentiate roles, and to introduce a large variety and volume of information *in anticipation* of the occurrence of the situation in the real world provides educators with an opportunity to have available at the appropriate time people who possess the appropriate skills.

As a means of providing laboratory experiences Some of the benefits indicated in the discussion concerning the enhancement of skills are also apparent in any consideration of laboratory experiences which may be obtained by participation in simulation exercises. Simulations provide opportunities for students of the social sciences to investigate social processes in a manner similar to the laboratory investigations which are performed by students in the life and the physical sciences. The student experiences the results of his actions and observes reactions of other persons in a controlled or a semi-controlled environment. Pay-offs are in terms of satisfaction or dissatisfaction, not in the permanent results which are the usual pay-off of the real world. Errors of judgement do not result in unchangeable or fatal consequences.

Laboratory experiences include the following types of activities in which participants may engage:

(a) Simulations provide a means of utilizing or applying in a realistic setting information which has been acquired during a course of study, and of testing principles, theories, and concepts of social relationships.

(b) Simulations enable a participant to experiment in a situation which is relatively simple, compared with the real world, and thus isolated from extraneous but complicating factors which would be present in the real world.

(c) Simulations permit a participant to perform roles
   (i) to acquire or to increase his competence in role-related tasks;
   (ii) to experience the pressures, demands, and/or satisfactions of roles which the participant otherwise would have no opportunity to encounter.

Each of the above activities will be examined in more detail below.

Simulation is useful as an introductory, a developmental, or a culminating activity in a course of study. The choice is dependent upon the objectives to be achieved. As an introductory activity, students may be exposed to situations which demand knowledge beyond that currently held by them. In such circumstances, it is common for students to undertake independent and self-directed study to acquire the required information. When employed as a developmental or a culminating activity, it is usually presumed that the requisite knowledge has been acquired by the student, and now must be put to use. In either aspect, the simulated activity is a vehicle designed by the teacher to place the students in a situation which demonstrates what they do not know and demands that they acquire knowledge which they can apply in the situation, or the simulation provides a ready opportunity to apply knowledge already acquired.

As an example of an introductory activity, this writer introduced a class of seventh and eighth grade students to a simulated American government system. The students had had only limited instruction in American government and were provided with only minimal directions concerning the operation of the simulation prior to the beginning of the exercise. The student portraying the role of the Vice-President of the United States was informed that he was the presiding officer of the Senate when it convened, and that it was his function to ensure the Senate was organized properly and that a president *pro tempore* of the Senate was chosen. This seemed to the student to be a task easily accomplished, and he immediately went about the business of organizing the Senate. The procedure was accomplished with relative ease until all tasks for which he had been given instructions were achieved. There then developed an embarrassing silence which became deeper as it lengthened.

It was readily apparent to the students in the simulation that they were not fully prepared to operate a 'government', even one that was greatly simplified. As the result of questions directed to the students by the teacher they developed for themselves an awareness that governments function only in response to expressed demands from sources within the system. They also recognized that such sources of demands were not yet present within their simulated system. In addition, they recognized that there existed no means of presenting to the decision making bodies within the simulated government the demands of interest groups once they developed. It is submitted that these concepts are extremely sophisticated for students of the age of thirteen to fourteen years. As a result of engaging in the simulated activity, however, the students were able to recognize some of the concepts involved and to undertake research, within their abilities, directed towards overcoming their recognized deficiencies of knowledge.

When the research had been completed to a point that was adequate for operation of the simulation to recommence, the system was again activated. During this run of the simulation, it was readily evident that the students had acquired information and comprehension of relationships that enabled them to operate the model of American government. They were, indeed, applying knowledge of facts and principles applicable to the model.

The second type of activity indicated above (experimentation in a relatively simple universe) is also demonstrated by the simple simulation described. The students were well aware that the model of American government they were operating was far from the complicated structure of reality. The simplified model provided them with the opportunity to view many of the fundamental operations of a modern government, but it was stripped of elements which complicate and obscure the operation of the real world model. The students were enabled to experiment in the security of the classroom by devising solutions to selected issues of their own choice or with issues current in the real world. The solutions developed did not require the assessment of permanent deprivations or distribution of rewards. Once the simulated situation ended, the participants were materially unaffected by their decisions. The only residual effects can be presumed to be improved understanding of the relationships among the parts of the replicated system, and an improved ability to utilize the social skills which were employed in the simulation.

The simulation described also depicts the third type of activity which simulation can provide as a laboratory experience, the opportunity for students to perform roles in which they desire to acquire or enhance their competence, or to perform roles which they otherwise would normally have no opportunity to experience. Both types of roles were utilized in the simulation. The acquisition and the improvement of useful social skills is demonstrated by several instances in the simulation. For example, several students played the roles of United States Senators. In doing so, they were required to learn something of the elements of parliamentary procedure. They were also keenly aware of the difficulty of stating their thoughts and ideas to their colleagues and to their constituents. The difficulty of communicating ideas was frequently demonstrated, and was the subject of comment by the students. Both parliamentary procedure and the articulation and communication of ideas are social skills which are prime requisites in an increasingly interdependent world.

The other type of role is demonstrated in the experience of the students participating in the role of President of the United States, the Vice-President, Senators, and members of the President's Cabinet. Obviously, few people ever have the opportunity to engage in the actual conduct of the positions portrayed. To engage in simulated activities of those roles provided the participants with an occasion to sample the pressures, the demands, and even some of the prestige which attaches to those public offices.

Repeatedly in simulated situations, participants have demonstrated an increasing cognizance of the necessity to make simulated public policy decisions on the basis of conflicting, and at times even contradictory, values. Medial solutions are frequently recognized as more desirable than those which seek to maximize or to minimize the results to be obtained when developing a solution to the simulated conflict situation.

No hard evidence can be offered to support the beliefs reported above. These observations have repeatedly been corroborated by other observers, however. Alger presents a concise statement of numerous users of simulation as an educational tool when he reports that students found simulation to be 'fun', and that their interest and motivation was heightened; that there was greater understanding by the students of the manner in which the world is usually viewed by real world decision makers; that most simulations produce a miniature world that is easier for participants to understand than the real institutions which are replicated; and that there are numerous claims that simulation provides an opportunity not only for applying and testing knowledge, but that there are some suggestions that simulation also leads to integration of information.[15] Such conclusions provide strong support for the assumption that the use of simulation affords a highly useful laboratory experience for participants.

Summary

The evaluation of simulation is a complex undertaking. There does not appear to be any hard evidence to support any contention that simulation is more, or less, effective as a teaching technique than any other technique. Present instruments for measuring achievement by students are constructed to measure their performance after exposure to conventional instructional methods. Such measurements probably do not assess all types of changes which may occur as a result of participation in simulated situations. Effective evaluation of simulation as a technique would require the design of measuring instruments which assess the students' acquisition of skills, their change of attitudes and behaviour, as well as the amount of knowledge gained.

As a device for motivating students, simulation is exceptionally effective. Numerous observations by many investigators support the conclusion that an overwhelming majority of students find simulation enjoyable and that students frequently devote more time to class preparation than is customary when more conventional techniques are employed. Students who do not normally participate actively in more conventional classroom activities frequently become active participants in simulated situations.

Simulation also affords an opportunity for students to acquire a measure of comprehension concerning their ability to operate effectively within the social system replicated within the simulated environment. There is some support for the conclusion that simulation contributes to desirable changes of student attitude in reference to

(a) The ability of the student to operate successfully within a simulated social process.
(b) Change in students' attitudes toward the educational setting and thus, hopefully, to be more receptive to other aspects of the classroom.
(c) The recognition by students of the complexity of social processes, of the interdependence of social groups, and of attitudes of realism in reference to real world situations, as contrasted with idealistic attitudes.

There is no hard evidence that simulation is more effective than any other technique for the acquisition and retention of factual or conceptual knowledge. Some authorities have drawn tentative conclusions that there is some tendency for simulation to contribute to the development of a coherent structure of knowledge and understanding of conceptual knowledge, as contrasted with factual knowledge. One experiment produced a tentative indication that students who participated in simulation were more effective in retaining knowledge they obtained in a unit of instruction which employed simulation as a supplement to other techniques. Those students who engaged in simulation indicated slightly more retention than the group of students who did not participate in the technique.

Simulation is an unusually effective means for placing students in a situation in which they must perform in settings which require them to react with other persons, thus enabling them to develop both manipulative and responsive social skills employed in such interactions. Participants may be placed in positions in which they are required to make decisions which approximate those made by real world decision makers, and time compression possible in simulated situations permits them to view the results which such decisions produce. Decisions are made and skills are exercised in situations in which no permanent penalties are assessed, i.e., 'wars' do not result in irreparable damage; casualties and deaths are revocable. Although the area of skill development does not appear to be one in which there has been scientific investigation, observations by this writer are convincing that participation in simulation produces an increase in demonstrated competence of the skills employed.

As a laboratory experience, simulations enable participants to apply in a relatively simple, uncluttered situation, that information which they possess or acquire in a course of instruction, and to acquire or increase their competence in role-related tasks. They may also engage in the performance of roles which they otherwise would have no opportunity to experience, such as enacting the role of the chief-of-state or head-of-government. Observation of students participating in such exercises has included students in the seventh through the twelfth grades, in undergraduate classes, and in graduate courses. In experience at all of those levels of instruction, students were carefully observed. Although there is no means known by which the effectiveness of simulation can be assessed in this regard in comparison with other techniques, this writer is convinced of the efficacy of simulation as a means of supplying vicarious experience, and his views are supported by the observations of many others who have used simulation as an educational technique.

Although the judgements, findings, and hunches catalogued here are not always supported by empirical evidence, there is no room for doubt that simulation possesses some solid advantages for use in education. That it is always successful is obviously not supportable. It is equally obvious, however, that simulation affords some advantages which cannot be duplicated by other instructional techniques. There can be no doubt that it is a highly useful technique when employed by teachers with adequate substantive preparation and when carefully incorporated into units of instruction for use in conjunction with other techniques.

REFERENCES

1. Sprague, H. T., and Shirts, R. G.: 'Exploring Classroom Uses of Simulation'. Project SIMILE, Western Behavioral Sciences Institute, 1966, mimeo, pp. 6–7.
2. Coleman, J. S.: 'Simulation and Games'. Johns Hopkins University, mimeo, p. 9.
3. Farran, D. C.: 'Competition and Learning for Underachievers'. *Simulation*

Games in Learning, eds. S. S. Boocock and E. O. Schild, Sage Publications, Inc., 1968, pp. 191–203.

4. Braddock, Clayton: 'Project 100,000'. *Phi Delta Kappan*, XLVIII, 426, 1967.
5. Crawford, Jack, and Twelker, Paul: 'Affect Through Simulation: the Games-man Technologist'. Teaching Research, Oregon State System of Higher Education, mimeo, p. 17.
6. The information contained here was obtained from Professor Merle Loewen, School of Education, Kansas State Teachers College. The information was generated during the process of student-and-teacher course-end evaluations in May 1969 at Roosevelt High School, the laboratory secondary school at the College.
7. Ibid.
8. Garvey, D. M., and Seiler, W. H.: 'A Study of Effectiveness of Different Methods of Teaching International Relations to High School Students'. Final Report, Co-operative Research Project S-270, Kansas State Teachers College, 1966, mimeo, pp. 65–93.
9. Ibid. See also Alger, C. F.: 'Inter-Nation Simulation in Undergraduate Teaching'. *Simulation in International Relations: Developments for Research and Teaching*, Prentice-Hall, Inc., pp. 152–154.
10. Bloom, B. S., and Krathwohl, D. R.: *Taxonomy of Educational Objectives; Handbook I, the Cognitive Domain*, and *Handbook II, the Affective Domain*. David McKay Company, Inc.
11. Robinson, J. A., *et al.*: 'Teaching With Inter-Nation Simulation and Case Studies'. *The American Political Science Review*, LX, 65, 1966.
12. Garvey and Seiler, op. cit.
13. Ibid.
14. Burgess, P. M., and Robinson, J. A.: 'Political Science Games and the Problem-Solver State'. *Simulation Games in Learning*, eds. S. S. Boocock and E. O. Schild, Sage Publications, Inc., pp. 243–248.
15. Alger, C. F.: 'Inter-Nation Simulation in Undergraduate Teaching'. *Simulation in International Relations: Developments for Research and Teaching*, Prentice-Hall, Inc., pp. 152–154.

10
Crisis decision making and simulation

Robert Boardman and C. R. Mitchell

Robert Boardman is currently researching into functionalism and problems of international organization. He graduated in economics and has a doctorate in International Relations from London University. As a Lecturer in Political Theory and International Relations at the University of Surrey, he helped to direct diplomatic and crisis games for senior high school students in Manchester. He is the author of several articles on the use of simulation techniques for teaching international relations, and of a forthcoming study of Britain's China policy since 1949.

C. R. Mitchell lectures in International Relations at University College, London, and is a research associate at the Centre for the Analysis of Conflict, where he is currently working on a comparative study of armed intervention. Prior to this, he taught for one year in a primary school, and then was an Assistant Master for six years in a secondary modern school, where he taught history. He has had experience of simulation both as a teaching method in undergraduate courses and schools, and also as a research technique in a simulation programme run by his Centre. He has also helped to organize diplomatic simulations for BBC sound and television broadcasts.

Mention 'war games' to a British audience, and you may well conjure up visions of enthusiasts in elaborate formal dress uniform poring over tin soldiers and mock battle scenes, or else Dr Strangelove figures gleefully contemplating the macabre consequences of various types of nuclear apocalypse. To add that children in schools are being encouraged to take part is to risk anything from mockery or gracious condescension to righteous indignation. We hope in this chapter[1] to dispel some of the more popular misconceptions about these exercises, and to show that the political and diplomatic game can perform a valuable educational function within the array of techniques already at the disposal of the current affairs or social studies teacher.

Simulation may be described as an attempt to involve the student, to encourage his participation, in an environment artificially constructed, but analogous in structure to the situation or set of relationships to be studied. Ideally the participant should be able to gain, through the extension of his range of unmediated experience, insights not obtainable by other teaching methods.

Whether this aim is fulfilled will be examined in later sections. But first we must look more closely at games themselves. The discussion focuses on three: MANEX[2] and ISRAEL,[3] two crisis games on the Vietnam and Middle East conflicts respectively, several runs of each of which were played over 1968–1969 in Manchester Central High School, and SINTRACC,[4] a problem-solving game on external involvement in communal conflict, at Kent College, Canterbury, and Merchant Taylors' School. The players in each case were sixth-form pupils (sixteen to eighteen years) of the schools concerned.

Description of international games

The most noticeable difference between these games was that the first two were designed for 'real' countries—Egypt, China, and so on—whereas the latter utilized primarily imaginary ones. The SINTRACC exercises took place in a fictitious environment in South-west Asia in the mid-1960s, and centred around two countries, Arcania and Dakotar, which had recently achieved independence from colonial rule. As can be seen (Fig. 10.1), siting them in the Bay of Bengal required some ingenious adaptation of southern Asian geography. But although the overall framework was hypothetical, it was also realistic in the sense of

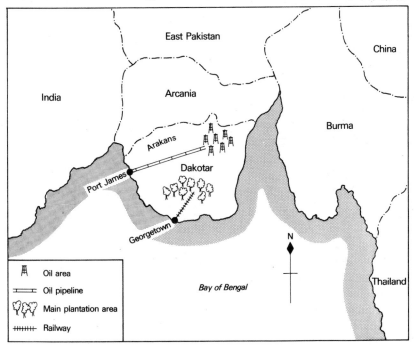

Fig. 10.1   Map used in the SINTRACC games (simplified)

229

containing a mixture of problems typical of many states in the Third World. Many features of the *scenario* were in fact taken from actual situations that have developed during the 1950s and 1960s in the Middle East and Asia.

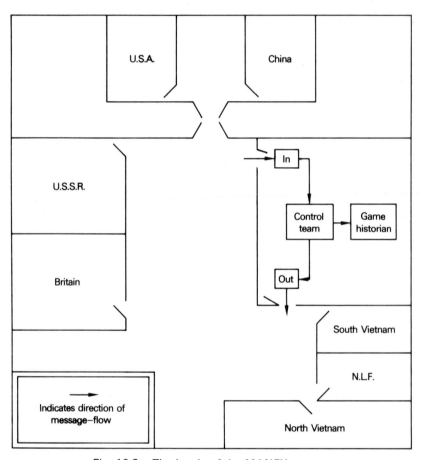

Fig. 10.2   The locale of the MANEX games

Participants in all games played in teams located in separate rooms (Fig. 10.2). While discussion *within* team rooms was verbal—not to say abusive on occasions—communication *between* teams was solely by messages written on specially-duplicated forms and transmitted through the Control team. With two important exceptions, all other means of contact were forbidden. So was spying: to quote from the MANEX *scenario*, 'although the real world may have its James Bonds, players are

MANEX (April 1968)

U.S.A.
President Johnson
Secretary of Defense
General Westmoreland
Dean Rusk
Senator Fulbright

South Vietnam
President Thieu
Marshal Ky
A Buddhist politician
A civilian non-Buddhist politician

North Vietnam
Ho Chi Minh
General Vo Nguyen Giap
Pham Van Dong
Le Duan

N.L.F.
Nguyen Huu Tho
Nguyen Van Hieu

Chinese People's Republic
Mao Tse-tung
Mme Mao
Chou En-lai
Lin Piao
Chen Yi

U.S.S.R.
Mr Brezhnev
Mr Kosygin
Mr Gromyko
Mr Suslov

Britain
Mr Wilson
Mr Brown
Mr Jenkins

ISRAEL

Israel
Prime Minister
Foreign Minister
Defence Minister

Egypt
President Nasser
Vice President
Foreign Minister

Jordan
King Hussein
Opposition politician

Syria
Prime Minister: Ba'ath Party
Pro-Nasser politician

Iraq
Prime Minister
Defence Minister

Saudi Arabia
King Faisal
Foreign Minister

Lebanon

Algeria

Tunisia

Morocco

Guerrilla forces
El Fateh
Pro-Nasser group

U.S.A.
President
Secretary of State
Secretary of Defense

NATO powers
Britain
France
Canada

U.S.S.R.
Mr Kosygin
Mr Brezhnev
Mr Grechko

U.N.O.
Secretary-General
Special Representative

Fig. 10.3   Teams and roles

231

Teams and roles (continued)

SINTRACC

Pre-Game	Main Game Player becomes:
Dakotar	
Leader of Dakotar Liberation Front	Prime Minister
Director of Operations	Home Affairs Minister
Left-wing extremist	Foreign Minister
Leader in Oil Area	Head of National Oil Company
Deputy Director of Operations	Minister of Defence
Leader in urban areas	Minister of Labour
Guerrilla leader	Minister for Economic Affairs
Orthodox Religious leader	(same)
Smallholders' representative	Minister of Agriculture

Representative of Dakotar
  People's Democratic
  Party
	Leader of D.P.D.P. Opposition

Plantation owners	(same)
Arakan minority	(all players remain in same roles)
Leader of Arakan People's Party	
Deputy leader	
Religious leader	
Arakan Oil Workers Union	
Arakan Plantation Workers' Association	
Urban ghetto dwellers representative	
Arakan peasants representative	
Arcanian Government	(all players remain in same roles)
President	
Foreign Minister	
Defence Minister	
Religious Primate	
Economic Affairs Minister	
Leader of Opposition Party	

on their honour not to use morning breaks for espionage activity, or to spend whole move periods with their ears glued to thin walls.' Teams and roles are summarized in Fig. 10.3.

The Vietnam and Middle East games speak for themselves; the actual number of teams in each was chosen by the designers, who tried to balance the conflicting demands of realism and practicability. In the SINTRACC exercises, the Arakans were a minority community in Dakotar, the majority community of which, the Dakotas, controlled the government and large sectors of the economy; the neighbouring country, Arcania, had ethnic affiliations with this minority.

The exceptions to the general rule of communication through Control by written messages were two. First, direct face-to-face meetings could be arranged between members of different teams, provided that permission was granted by Control. These international exchanges took place in the presence of a member of Control who recorded the main points brought up by each side, and any agreements made. The second problem also arose from the imperative of plausibility. Thus the N.L.F., in the Vietnam game, was allowed separate facilities for policy discussions, but in a room affording easy access to North Vietnam, and further, as an experiment half-way through the first run, one member of the N.L.F. was granted permission to communicate at will with left-wing and dissident Buddhist elements in the South. Similar arrangements were made for the Arab teams in ISRAEL, and also in the SINTRACC games to allow freer discussion of issues by the majority and minority communities of Dakotar.

Distributed beforehand to players, the *scenarios* summarized the rules and introduced the settings of the games. Pupils in the Vietnam and Middle East games whose knowledge was a little shaky thus obtained a convenient means of brushing up on the facts; and in addition, the scene was set for an artificially contrived, but plausible, crisis point which was to start the game going. *Scenarios* included all necessary background information—for the crisis games, such things as maps, a history of the conflict, positions of the parties with regard to a negotiated settlement, and types and strengths of armed forces. To give an added air of realism to the MANEX games, the Vietnam situation was described by means of press reports—some real, but mostly imaginary ones invented by the designers.

But something more was required than merely giving the players a description of the game's structure. Firstly, since the essence of the simulation concept lies in pupils learning by *acting*—in both senses of the term—they had to be helped in the difficult task of so identifying with their roles and teams that this would come virtually spontaneously.

One MANEX device was to incorporate in the *scenario* a discussion of the situation entirely in 'we' terms, just as it might have been written by an official of the government concerned. This excerpt, for example, is taken from the American document: 'It has been argued by many that there are independent elements in the N.L.F. . . . If so, we could do business with them. But the history of coalition governments with Communist participation shows that these are most likely to fall to the Communists in the long run; and South Vietnam would be no exception to this rule. However, our eyes are of course always open for signs of real independence of the N.L.F. from Hanoi.'[5]

Secondly, students were of course not only 'Americans' or 'Dakotans': they played specific roles within their teams. In SINTRACC, therefore, players whose interests would normally be expected to be at variance with other members' concerns—the Arakan oil workers for example— were individually briefed before the games to act as an opposition group within their teams. It was one purpose of the game 'to try to develop a sense of competing role demands in certain key players, and also to create in the game . . . an atmosphere of competing and clashing interests within the formally structured teams'. Such devices, however, met with only limited success, as these players tended to find themselves isolated and ostracized, and to conform after a short period of time to team norms and policies.

Reference has already been made to the Control team. Its role is 'to receive the teams' moves, mesh them, add other elements of the situation, and confront the teams with a re-structured situation reflecting the implications of their strategies . . . it acts as an omniscient "God and Nature", determining the outcomes of particular actions ordered by teams; it simulates the military and civil departments and staffs reporting to each team; and it simulates all governments not already represented by actual playing teams. Control does not function primarily as an "umpire". . . . It does, however, have the power to rule out egregious moves on the grounds of implausibility.'[6]

One of these assumed a particular significance in the SINTRACC exercises. As there were only three actual teams, and the game was described as taking place in a 'South-west Asian environment', Control had to provide such an environment—create the surrounding world of Asia, the declining cold war, withdrawal of colonial powers, and so on. This was a heavy task, and a completely self-contained section of Control, known as 'News and Noise', was kept hard at work writing and dispatching messages to individual players and teams, supposedly from, for example, the Soviet Union, the Australian External Affairs Minister, or the U.N. Secretary-General. Further, if any player requested a meeting with U Thant or Chou En-lai, or someone else not actually represented in the game, this role had to be filled plausibly by a Control member. The SINTRACC Control team thus had to be large, flexible, well-organized and to have a thorough understanding of the game situation.

The distinguishing characteristic of a crisis game[7] such as MANEX, is its use of countries interacting over a very short period of time of high tension. In contrast, SINTRACC, like Inter-Nation Simulation (INS)[8] exercises, postulated no necessary or built-in crisis situation: behaviour was envisaged as being based upon the calm deliberation of policy reactions and alternative options. The situation could equally well deteriorate into inter-communal hostility, violence, and external intervention, or have its problems solved by agreements for trade, aid, or for the integration of the minority into Dakotan political life.

This raises a crucial point. It is the players *themselves* who decide the actions of their teams. Policy outcomes are not pre-determined. Within the bounds of the *scenario* and of plausibility, there are no 'right' or 'wrong' decisions, nor is there any goal, such as the negotiated settlement of a crisis, towards which teachers are expecting pupils to move, perhaps to provide some sort of neat 'finish' to the game. The emphasis throughout the *scenarios* was on choices, dilemmas, and possibilities for alternative courses of action, even in the more restricted framework of the crisis game.

However, a major difficulty with crisis games using 'real' countries is that participants will in fact be initially predisposed in favour of a unique outcome—the way things actually developed or are developing in real life. To minimize such effects, the Vietnam and Middle East situations were played out *in the future*, the difference between game date and the actual date being anything from two months to a year. For example, in the first ISRAEL run, played at the end of 1968, the *scenario* made extrapolations to the autumn of 1969—occasional artillery duels across the Suez Canal, guerrilla raids, problems of arms supplies, and so on. No suggestion was made that this was the state of affairs as the designers thought it would actually be at that date: all that was required was a plausible situation that would produce a stimulating game.

Finally, in SINTRACC, a preparatory period—the 'Pre-Game'—gave players an additional means of familiarizing themselves with the rules and the situation. This was supposed to be taking place several years before the game proper when Arcania had recently achieved independence after the withdrawal of the French. Apart from this, all games were played continuously in move periods lasting over two to three days, and culminated in a de-briefing in which players met together with Control to survey the game as a whole.

Educational value

Learning through experience   It may seem surprising in future retrospect that earlier use was not made of simulation for teaching about society and politics. Any brief summary of some of the many points of contact with other fields may spark a shock of recognition: the emphasis on participation in small group studies, and on the deleterious consequences for learning and personality-development of its thwarting, the use of role playing in T-group theory, psychotherapy and group therapy, the wider use of improvisation for training and performance in theatre and music, individual psychology studies of experimentation in human behaviour, the link between action and thought brought out in the older Asian and more recent French philosophical traditions, to mention but a few. In education, one might point to the role in learning of unstructured discussions with peers, the need, suggested by Coleman, Sherif, and others, to harness inter-group, as opposed to inter-personal, competitive spirit to academic learning, stress on discovery and exploration in Nuffield science and the new mathematics, involvement of pupils in historical reconstructions and child-centred approaches in educational research in general; and finally of course the learning function of play in small children investigated by Piaget, and its characteristic features of intense involvement and of the transcending of conventional Western adult distinctions between performer and spectator, enjoyment and gravity, thought and action, work and play, and spontaneity and obligation. Simulation may perhaps be regarded as an ambitious attempt to hone such observations and intuitions into an efficient teaching instrument. If Koestler's remark is valid, that the creative act is generated when two diverse strands of thought impinge on each other, then it would appear that the users of simulation techniques are on to a good thing.

The air of excitement and involvement was indeed the most apparent aspect of the games. There were many indications. For example, it was common for players at the end of exercises to request more time—even out of school hours if necessary—to continue with 'just one more' game period which they had convinced themselves was all that was necessary for them to 'win'. Identification with roles spilled over into rest periods as 'Arab brothers' or 'fellow Americans' conversed heatedly about future strategy or other countries' motivations. The wandering observer was frequently regarded with hostility as a possible spy ready to whisper state secrets to the next room. Involvement was equally apparent in the ability of players, even the more reticent, completely to ignore outsiders, such as note-taking Control members in ambassadorial meetings. There was general agreement among players at the close—often to their genuine surprise!—that they had just gone through a thoroughly enjoyable, interesting and stimulating experience. The grounds for believing that such arousal is closely related to learning remain untested in the present case, but seem not implausible.

It was clear from their remarks, moreover, that the participants had benefited from direct and immediate, if vicarious, experience of foreign policy decision making. This is clearly something afforded only to a few in real life, and then only from the vantage point of one country. Particularly in international relations, a great deal of human behaviour appears, from the outside, as inexplicable, wicked, or downright silly. The use of simulation derives from recent emphasis in international studies on investigation *from the inside*—of trying to see the world as it looks to governments or Foreign Offices, and not to 'detached' or 'objective' external observers.

The uniqueness of simulation is its ability to allow pupils to *discover* facts and notions for themselves. Often the discovery was disguised: players complained to Control that the game was 'going wrong', and this proved to be an especially valuable means of demonstrating by example the lessons to be learned. For example, there were protests that there was not enough time to shape policies as messages from other teams came flooding in, and that this hectic situation was alternating with periods in which nothing seemed to be happening. It could be suggested to players that perhaps this might correspond to what actually happens in policy making circles. Players similarly complained that Control was not correcting their misbeliefs when they made a succession of decisions based on information later found to be erroneous. The Control team was accused in such cases of tampering with the flow of messages, whereas in fact intervention was only occasional and insignificant. (So great, in fact, were resentments at the malicious machinations of Control that in one Vietnam game, a national team began circulating clandestine messages with bribed messengers calling for united action by all teams to end the 'tyranny' of the Control team!) In games modelling actual situations, complaints also revealed possible insights discovered by accident into real life perceptions and behaviour. The British, for example, who were generally ignored as ineffective, argued that they 'could not understand' the Russians, who, they said, seemed to be following two quite inconsistent lines of policy. There were murmurings of discontent from the Chinese that 'nobody is writing to us' and that 'we don't know what's going on'. Sections of moderate Arab opinion demanded that Control 'correct' the attitude of the Syrian team, who were being 'completely unrealistic' in their attitude to Israel, the 'deviation' being blamed both on Control's refusal to allow crucial messages through and on the behaviour of irresponsible pupils in that team who were refusing to play according to the rules.

Learning about society and politics   The present discussion is intuitive and impressionistic; research in the British context lags behind quantitative evaluatory work in American schools, though this is now going ahead. Before moving on, some clarifying remarks may be helpful. Firstly, some arguments for simulation have suffered, in our view, from a vagueness of purpose. It would be useful to distinguish emphasis on the factor of discovery, enjoyment and participation as, on the one hand, a variable functionally related to learning about a specific topic, which constitutes a powerful generating source of hypotheses, and on the other as being desirable *per se* in terms of the child's individual and social personality development, a cluster of value judgements either not testable, or suggestive of tangential or very different avenues of research.

Secondly, at least part of the motivation of the authors has stemmed from an awareness of the inadequacies of social studies teaching in British schools.[9] Even in the United States, where the situation is in many respects better, an educationalist could recently find it pertinent to complain that 'every child realizes that what he studies in school has almost no relation to the world in which he lives'.[10] The objective has been, in other words, not so much to improve existing teaching about society and politics, as to help promote such subjects in the curriculum in the first place. Thirdly, it would of course be presumptuous too readily to assume that pupils are in fact learning about a topic or situation; even the most careful safeguards could not prevent that which is studied being the teacher's or Control's view of it.

International games indicate that simulation is of value as an approach to the study of systems of human behaviour of great complexity. Instead of beginning with a baffling multitude of discrete 'facts'—dates, personalities, events—the pupil is first presented with a framework with which to view them, this initial pattern being relatively complete and realistic according to the student's grasp of the situation. Games fulfil an illustrative function by providing many concrete instances of ideas which may be introduced to participants beforehand, or raised—with the 'evidence'— after the exercise. Both types are rich in practice with examples of the role of uncertainty in decision making, misperception, pressures of time, events, and lack of information, problems of accommodating demands from allies and key groups at home, the burden of past policies and the imperatives of prestige, and much more. From talking to players it appeared also that the exercises had performed a valuable integrative function—a way of bringing together the many facets of a situation and of incorporating previous material gleaned from talks and reading. The simulations also seemed to lend greater predictive power to the views of players, the Jordan team in one ISRAEL run being delighted when King Hussein appeared on television one evening and made a statement about negotiation with Israel in very much the same terms as the game's own 'Hussein' had done that same afternoon.

Complexity in social and political life manifests itself in other ways. To grasp the *fact* of the existence of widely diverse outlooks even within the same culture—let alone in international relations—is an intellectual task of some magnitude. International games introduce pupils to the experience of being not only Czechoslovakian or 'Arakan', but also Prime Ministers, Foreign Secretaries, or members of ethnic minorities. We would probably dispute the view that international simulations of the sort described are useful for generating empathy; though a degree of empathic involvement is an essential precursor to the critical understanding of international relations at the cognitive level, foreign policy decision making, particularly in crises, seems to be influenced less by cultural factors than by the exigencies of the situation. Affective learning might call for differently structured inter-cultural games than those we have been dealing with.[11]

These considerations inevitably raise the thorny question of the teaching of history, where too often the impression is left on the child—if, indeed, any interest can be stimulated in the first instance—that he is being taught about men and women no different from those of his own time, apart from the fancy dress. Historians who combine intellectual with empathic understanding of previous ages, such as Mattingley, Plumb, or Wedgwood, or historical novelists like Duggan or Prescott, are rare, and may be instructive only to pupils of certain ages and abilities. It is here that simulation may be appropriate, though difficulties arise which will be touched on later.

Secondary learning If, as Henry[12] has suggested, the 'noise', in information theory terms, of the classroom situation ought properly to be regarded as constituting its essential message, what is the 'noise' of the simulation environment? Without prejudging unsettled issues in learning for transfer, it is possible that players were utilizing skills—through scrutinizing incoming information, assessing the situation, discussing alternative policies, devising relevant strategies, deciding, judging the outcomes of actions, adjusting accordingly—of much wider relevance than learning about the making of foreign policy (assuming of course that not all will proceed into careers in the diplomatic service!).

Moreover, certain aspects of the structuring of simulation games may be found to be of significance in the longer run. We are thinking, for example, of the greater involvement of the child himself in the learning process, the co-operative pursuit of knowledge, the opportunity provided for initiative and exploration being encouraged instead of penalized, continuity of interest in a single subject for a period of up to three days, responsiveness of peers and teachers to the pupil as a person of significance, substitution of the connotations of learning, of boredom, and drudgery, by those of exhilaration and interest, and emphasis on the pupil as actor and moulder of events.

Problem areas

Small group reality   The dynamics of the game situation must to some extent operate autonomously of the structuring of relationships in the *scenario*. Thus it was possible to observe players falling into set patterns of participation noted by small-group researchers—making suggestions, seeking orientation or approval, initiating, deciding, and so on. Since learning in simulation is dependent upon a congruence between pupils' perceptions of the game structure and the reality of the Arab–Israeli conflict or communal strife, these inevitable processes were detrimental to learning. Working in the opposite direction, however, discussion about role performance was common, at least in the earlier stages; and an indignant or triumphant flourish of the *scenario*—'Hey, you're not supposed to be acting like that!'—often sufficed to minimize role deviance.

The overlapping of *scenario* relationships by friendship groups was a related source of difficulty in ensuring persistence of individual roles against contrary pressures within teams. It also gave rise to some unexpected inter-team relationships: friendly corridor discussions between President Johnson and Mme Mao Tse-tung had to be nipped in the bud in one MANEX game. But even worse in such cases was the withdrawal into boredom or depression of pupils alienated by intra-team processes, or through game inexperience, shyness, or their being placed in an impotent or ignored team. On occasion, the physical isolation of teams did seem somewhat counterproductive, especially if a country's role was regarded by others as being of minimal importance. These points, it must quickly be emphasized, are not arguments against the use of simulation. Most are remediable by such means as the careful choice of players and roles, the special individual briefings before the SINTRACC games, maintaining a close watch on what is going on in the exercise, and making sure that all teams are kept reasonably busy.

At the other extreme, the exuberance of players—which, after all, is one of the merits of simulation—sometimes merged into their treating the game solely as a source of amusement, or as being comparable to MONOPOLY or chess. Comparisons with such games can be made, but not pushed too far. On the whole though, role taking ability, at the cognitive, affective, and decision making levels, appeared to be excellent. Hardly any players showed signs of difficulty in absorbing themselves in their allotted roles. It has even been possible in some research exercises using such countries as 'Livonia' or 'Ruritania' to measure the growth of a sense of national pride among participants.[13]

Uses of simulation One of the main differences between using simulation in university departments of politics and in schools is the very much wider range of ability, knowledge, academic interests, and the like, in the latter. A prime need of its successful use in schools is therefore flexibility on the part of designers and organizers. As is amply demonstrated in the other contributions to this volume, simulation has already proved itself an immensely flexible tool, being utilized for research, training, recruitment, and policy planning in such fields as industrial relations, local government, foreign policy, and business. It may become of increasing value in teacher and youth leader training,[14] and has been put to practical use in some American high schools in, for example, the reduction of anxiety before a job interview[15] and the prevention of drug addiction.[16] One could imagine a variety of possible extensions, the use of simulation as an assessment method, for example, or in the study of literature through improvizations with characters and scenes from novels or plays. Games may prove to be a convenient means of introducing scientific specialists to the humanities; and their potential has been suggested for securing the fuller participation in class activities of children of lesser academic abilities.[17]

The use of 'real' countries—France or China—demonstrably sparks off in the student his own pet images and prejudices, a fact which may diminish the educational efficacy of the crisis game. Similarly, the danger of using 'real' persons is that the pupil playing, say, 'President Nixon' may interpose a mental picture of the actual President between receiving messages and acting: ask himself, that is, what Mr Nixon might do if faced with this situation, rather than acting *himself* on his own knowledge of it. On the other hand, games on the Middle East and other concrete situations may benefit from the reservoir of knowledge in most pupils, their interest in learning about the situation itself, and the more obvious connection with the real world. A game such as SINTRACC allows players much greater latitude for creative and imaginative strategies, and the use of fictitious countries in no way reduces interest or capacity for involvement in roles. Non-crisis games are extremely valuable for

241

demonstrating the operation of longer-term factors—the impact on foreign policy of declining support for a government, changes in living standards, or the growth of military power—parameters which in the crisis game must be taken as 'givens'.

One-room simulations within the confines of the normal school time table and classroom obviously diminish the administrative load on the teacher, and may avoid some of the problems of isolation of multi-room games. At the most simple level, the teacher might ask pupils to imagine themselves as, say, the Tsar and his advisers in February 1917, or trade union leaders facing an unofficial strike when committed to an incomes policy, and call for suggestions about how 'we' are to deal with this situation. More technically complex, some games have focused completely on the individual student making decisions at his own computer terminals,[18] a development of some potential for international relations teaching.

Design and administration   There seem to be at least four prerequisites for a topic to be the basis for a successful simulation in social studies teaching. First, the structure: clearly identifiable *groups* or *parties* which it would not be unrealistic to separate physically in the game; second, distinguishable *attitudes, perceptions, motivations* and *goals* on the part of each of the teams; third, *interrelations* between the groups in real life—preferably, for a stimulating game, including some relations of a conflictual nature; and fourth, some specific concrete *issue* or *problem* for the teams to tackle, though as an alternative the simulation may, as in some INS exercises, develop its own problems and issues as the players interact. It can readily be seen that international games fit the bill on each of these counts. But many other sources of possible games spring to mind from contemporary British society: local government and town planning, race relations, industrial relations, communication between generations, Scottish and Welsh nationalism, the working of Parliament, changing moral values—the list is endless.

Control plays a vital role both in and before the exercises. Administrative constraints have to be considered—the availability of rooms, paper, pupils, and so on—and a suitable *scenario* designed (though some are marketed commercially). It may be preferable that a player be asked to occupy a position antipathetic to his own political leanings, but equally games may be more enjoyable, and therefore that more conducive to learning, if participants have some sympathetic predisposition towards their roles. Probably the Control team is doomed to be pilloried and accused of a variety of crimes; perhaps the most we can hope for is that awareness of the need to avoid heavy-handedness may prevent excessive complaints, though it has to be added that the expression of discontent with Control has been shown to be of value for learning. Frivolity, a predominance of colourful propaganda in messages, diversion of team resources into imaginative espionage activities, and the like, are perhaps also unavoidable. A major role of Control is therefore emphasis throughout on the seriousness of the enterprise, for example by insistence on such things as formal mode of address—'Mr President'. Finally, the de-briefing is an integral part of the whole: often it is the most interesting part of the exercise; the pent-up frustrations of players, accumulating for two days, need some outlet; it enables participants to see the game as a whole through the eyes of the Game Historian—no one team will know everything that has gone on—and to question other teams on specific points; it is a means by which Control can check with players about the organization of the game and possible improvements; and later de-briefings can be used to sum up by concrete example what has been learned or demonstrated in the exercise.

It would be impossible even to mention all possible variations of design: the use of advisers for teams, reward systems for good individual or team role playing, computers to work out consequences of decisions, design of *scenarios* by students themselves, or 'false' finishes before the official one to avoid the more outrageous all-or-nothing moves which crop up at the end of games (one ISRAEL game closed with a joint U.S.–Soviet nuclear attack on Damascus). It would be as well, however, to mention some problems in history teaching. Games can most satisfactorily be used here to study the possibilities inherent in a situation— what *might have* happened rather than what actually did.[19] The danger is of a straightforward reconstruction by pupils with the advantage of hindsight. One device used for research into the First World War at Northwestern University has been to disguise the situation by using fictitious teams instead of 'Germany' or 'Britain', but keeping the essentials the same.[20] A similar tactic is adopted in the Foreign Policy Association's high school game DANGEROUS PARALLEL, for the study of the Korean War. The precaution is not, however, essential, and the 1909 Bosnian crisis and the 1967 Arab–Israeli June war have been studied at Lancaster and Essex Universities using the 'real' teams.

Integration   It was said recently that the Dainton Report arrived 'when it needed only one more loudish voice to establish the fact that we are now all in favour of reforming the sixth form curriculum and examinations'.[21] It is in general studies, in which is usually included social studies, that innovation and experiment have the least damaging effects in terms of careers.[22] Now would therefore seem to be an especially apt point in time to suggest the value of simulation for teaching about problems of modern society.

The problem of integration becomes relevant if we are to assume that games are viable in more than an 'end-of-term' sense—as an enjoyable and possibly instructive means of occupying minds in the gap between examinations and holidays—or as a stimulant of interest so that pupils may go away and do the 'real work' by reading books. There are two aspects. Firstly, as life does not divide itself neatly into the compartments of university faculties or G.C.E. examination syllabuses, simulation may be used to integrate teaching about several 'subjects'. An international game brings in ideas conventionally taught also in economics, geography, history and government. One of the problems of the MANEX games was that some players had insufficient grounding in economics to tackle international monetary difficulties facing their governments.

Secondly, games should of course be evaluated in the context of other teaching methods. No one would suggest that they make redundant all other techniques: the problem is in what ways games can be most efficiently combined with them. In general terms, their value must be assessed against cost in terms of time, administrative complexity, and so on, and against what could have been learned using other media. For international relations, we would argue specific advantages. The use of simulation would be a considerable improvement on 'United Nations forums' or biased historical textbook treatments of, say, Anglo–French relations; and debate—asking 'who is *right*?' in the Arab–Israeli or Nigeria–Biafra conflicts—is a particularly unconstructive approach to international problems. Background reading is clearly essential with regard to concrete situations, and the MANEX and ISRAEL games were held during school terms in which a substantial portion of current affairs periods were taken up with discussion of these situations. Integration of several approaches has been used in American high schools for study of Vietnam,[23] and one simulation in Britain has been organized in conjunction with improvization by drama students and films.[24] The teaching of American foreign policy at Northwestern University combines simulation and case studies.[25] Similar investigations are being made in the Schools Council Projects at the Universities of York and Keele. It may be the case that a 'law of diminishing returns' operates with successive runs by a pupil.[26] Certainly the 'sense of occasion' surrounding games at present may give a false impression of their value; if we get to a point where novelty has worn off, and pupils are complaining, 'Oh, no, not *another* simulation!', then we may have to think again.

There is, finally, the wider context. Other factors within the school will have a bearing on the impact of simulations, such as the teacher's attitude to games, institutional theories of learning and implicit models of child development processes, and teacher–pupil relationships outside the game environment. Research has suggested that the teacher is in a relatively weak position in the process of political socialization as against extra-school influences.[27] Must we infer that teaching about society and politics is just not worth the effort? Probably not; the teaching itself might however be made more relevant to the wider social environment of the school, and it might achieve this, the discussion here would conclude, through the wider use of simulation games.

REFERENCES

1. Parts of this chapter have been adapted from sections in previous articles by R. Boardman. See 'Simulation and the Teaching of International Relations'. *Higher Education Journal*, 16, 6, autumn, 1968, pp. 3–6; 'Simulated Conflicts and International Crisis Games: a Report on the MANEX Project'. *The World and the School*, 14, October 1968, pp. 53–68; 'The Theory and Practice of Educational Simulation'. *Educational Research*, 11 (3), June 1969, pp. 179–184.
2. Boardman, R., Podmore, W., and Lewis, B.: *MANEX: a Vietnam Crisis Game*. Manchester Central High School, 1968.
3. Boardman, R., Podmore, W., and Lewis, B.: *ISRAEL: a Crisis Game on the Middle East Conflict*. Manchester Central High School, 1968.
4. Bayley, J. C. R., and Mitchell, C. R.: *SINTRACC: an Interim Report*. Centre for the Analysis of Conflict, University College, London, 1968.
5. Boardman, R.: 'Simulated Conflicts and International Crisis Games: a Report on the MANEX Project'. *The World and School*, 14, October 1968, pp. 53–68. (Reprinted with the permission of Dr Otto Pick.)
6. Groom, A. J. R., and Banks, M. H.: *CONEX I: a Simulation of a Middle Eastern Conflict Situation: Operations Plan*. Conflict Research Society, London, 1966, p. 1. (Reprinted with the permission of A. J. R. Groom.)
7. See, for example, Giffin, S. F.: *The Crisis Game: Simulating International Conflict*. New York, Doubleday, 1965; Bloomfield, L. P., and Padelford, N. J.: 'Three Experiments in Political Gaming'. *American Political Science Review*, LIII, 1959, pp. 1105–1115.
8. See, for example, Guetzkow, H., et al.: *Simulation in International Relations: Developments for Research and Teaching*. Prentice-Hall, 1963; Robinson, J. A., et al.: 'Teaching with Inter-Nation Simulation and Case Studies'. *American Political Science Review*, LX, 1966, pp. 53–66.
9. Boardman, R.: 'The Theory and Practice of Educational Simulation'. *Educational Research*, 11 (3), June 1969, p. 182.
10. C. Jencks, of the Harvard Graduate School of Education, quoted in *The New York Review of Books*, XII, 9, 8 May 1969, p. 26. (Reprinted by permission of the New York Times Company.)
11. There are a number of social-psychological studies in this area. See, for example, Culbertson, F.: 'Modification of an Emotionally Held Attitude through Role-playing', *Journal of Abnormal and Social Psychology*, 54, 1957, pp. 230–233; King, B. T., and Janis, I. L.: 'Comparison of the Effectiveness of Improvised

Versus Non-improvised Role-playing in Producing Opinion Changes'. *Human Relations*, 9, 1956, pp. 177–186.

12. Henry, J.: *Culture Against Man*. London, Tavistock, 1966.

13. Druckman, D.: 'Ethnocentrism in the Inter-Nation Simulation'. *Journal of Conflict Resolution*, XII (1), March 1968, pp. 45–68.

14. Tansey, P. J., and Unwin, D.: 'Simulation and Academic Gaming: Highly Motivational Teaching Techniques'. In *Aspects of Educational Technology* (eds. W. R. Dunn and C. Holroyd), London, Methuen, 1969, Vol. II, pp. 171–178.

15. Lindgren, H. C.: *Educational Psychology in the Classroom*. New York, Wiley, 1962, p. 393.

16. Shelley Z. Green, Vassar College, personal communication.

17. *New Dimensions: Simulation Games for the Social Studies Classroom*. New York, Foreign Policy Association, 1966, pp. 35–36.

18. See, for example, Wing, R. L.: 'Two Computer Based Games for Sixth Graders'. *American Behavioral Scientist*, X (3), November 1966, pp. 31–33.

19. For a recent discussion of some of the philosophical issues, see Leontief, W.: 'When Should History be Written Backwards?' *Economic History Review*, 16, 1963, pp. 1–8.

20. Hermann, C. F., and Hermann, M.: *On the Possible Use of Historical Data for Validation Study of Inter-Nation Simulation*. Evanston, Illinois, North-western University, 1962.

21. Editorial, *Universities Quarterly*, 22 (3), June 1968, p. 251.

22. Irvine-Smith, R.: *General Education after Fifteen: Outline of Schools Council Curriculum Project at the University of York, 1968–71*. University of York, Department of Education, 1968, p. 1.

23. *Vietnam Curriculum*. Boston Area Teaching Project, Inc., 1969.

24. Bolam, R.: *Adventure in Learning 1967: Report on the Vietnam Crisis Simulation Workshop*. Bingley College of Education, 1968, p. 3.

25. Anderson, L. F.: *Combining Simulation and Case Studies in the Teaching of American Foreign Policy*. Evanston, Illinois, Northwestern University, 1964.

26. Bloomfield, L. P., and Padelford, N. J.: 'Three Experiments in Political Gaming'. *American Political Science Review*, LIII, 1959, p. 1114.

27. Langton, K. P.: 'Peer Group and School in the Political Socialization Process'. *American Political Science Review*, LXI, 1967, pp. 751–758.

11
Simulations and games: descriptions and sources

Derick Unwin

Derick Unwin is Senior Lecturer in New Media at the Education Centre, New University of Ulster, Northern Ireland. Trained as a physicist, he became interested in educational technology while teaching in a secondary school, and moved to Loughborough University to carry out research into programmed learning. Mr Unwin has published a variety of books and papers on several aspects of educational communication and is currently engaged in the production of an encyclopaedia of educational media and technology.

A great number of simulations and academic games have been devised, particularly in the United States, but there is increasing activity in the United Kingdom and elsewhere. The list given in this chapter includes nearly one hundred items with one common feature only: they have all been fairly widely reported. Undoubtedly there are several omissions, and it may well be that some of the inclusions are now obsolete.

The list of simulations is followed by addresses likely to prove useful in obtaining details of simulations. Again, there will be omissions due to the very fragmented nature of information dissemination in this field. Finally, there follow two bibliographic sections, the first citing papers, etc., devoted largely to descriptions of specific games and simulations in action, the second giving some general sources of further reading and information.

Games and simulations which have been fairly widely publicized

Some of these are available commercially, in the case of others it may be possible to obtain full details from their designers. In each instance, the name of the simulation is followed by the institution from which further details may be obtained, and in most cases a brief description is given.

A MAYOR FOR MOUNT VAN BUREN
Chicago Public School System (John D. Gearon)
Simulated local politics.

ADMINISTRATORSHIP
Solidarity House Inc.
A business game.

ADVENTURING
Abt Associates Inc.
Sociology game which focuses on three generations of yeomen, gentry and merchants at the time of the Civil War in England. It illustrates how status could be raised, and the effect of this process on the politics of the period.

ALLEGIANCE
Western Behavioral Sciences Institute
Politics game.

BMG
Western Behavioral Sciences Institute
Designed to demonstrate function of competition in a big corporation. The student assumes role of businessman selling bulldozers in competition with two other corporations; he wins the game if he raises the sales, profits and total assets of his corporation above those of his competitors.

CABINETS IN CRISIS
Foreign Policy Association
A simulation involving international decisions, based on the 1950 rejection by Yugoslavia of Soviet domination. The game was originally played in America over a period of a month from 25 April to 23 May 1968. Television was used as the medium, with various teams located on a regional basis. It was designed to allow participation by many schools in each area.

CAPSTONE
Insite Project, Indiana University
This experiment takes place in the final week of the final teaching practice term. Each student assumes the role of teacher in an actual community to which he is introduced by colour slides and written material. He forms opinions as to the socio-economic levels of the town, tours the school and expresses reactions. The objective is to present the

248

student with the situation of being a new teacher at this school, taking him out of his 'under training' role, and helping him to analyse the implications for a teacher following the various preceding teaching techniques.

CARIBOU-HUNTING
Education Development Center
Upper elementary level: a board game simulating the difficulties Eskimos encounter in eking out an adequate food supply from a harsh environment. Students learn the advantages of a co-operative approach. (*See also* SEAL-HUNTING.)

CARNEGIE TECH MANAGEMENT GAME
Carnegie Institute of Technology (Graduate School of Industrial Administration)
Probably the first fully developed management game, introduced in 1957 and now highly sophisticated. Computer controlled.

CLUG-CORNELL LAND USE GAME
Cornell University
Geography game.

CONFIGURATIONS
Wff'n Proof Inc.
This series, devised by Professor Harold Dorwait, consists of mathematical and geometric puzzles for all ages.

CONSUMER
Johns Hopkins University (Gerald Zaltman)
A game which can be adapted to economics courses; it is designed to teach adolescents about buying by instalments. Background sheets, checklists and rules for the game are provided. It is played in groups of sixteen of whom thirteen are consumers and three are credit and loan managers. The game can be played more than once, with additional learning taking place on each play.

CRISIS
Western Behavioral Sciences Institute
In this simulation of international conflict, students form teams to manage the affairs of six fictional nations. The nations vary in military strength, and are faced with the problem of resolving a tense situation in a mining area of immense importance to the world. The players

learn the consequences of each of their decisions, but are given almost complete freedom within the game.

CRISISCOM
Massachusetts Institute of Technology
An all-computer simulation of information-processing by individuals in an international context.

CROSS NUMBER PUZZLES
Science Research Associates Ltd
A mathematics games kit designed to make practice and drill in whole numbers, decimals and percentages, and fractions more palatable. (There is no element of simulation in this kit. It is concerned with abstraction in the same way as the Layman E. Allen games are.)

DANGEROUS ·PARALLEL
Foreign Policy Association
Simulation of a historical crisis which turns on the question of whether to cross the 38th parallel in the Korean War. Objective is to teach students about decision making and analysis of the possible actions of other nations. The intention is not a 'recapitulation of history' but rather to teach an analytic approach to international affairs. It is a programmed, limited choice game which is part of a larger education programme called 'Analysis and Judgement Making in Foreign Affairs'.

D-DAY
Avalon Hill Co. Inc.
War game tracing the Second World War from the Normandy landings onwards. Each team has an accurate representation of the forces available and the various problems confronting them.

DEMOCRACY
Johns Hopkins University (James S. Coleman)
Eight games on the legislative process of which the best known is the 'Great Game of Legislature'. Can be purchased from the National 4-H Foundation.

DIPLOMACY
Intellectual Diversions Ltd
Concerned with the European great powers, 1900–1914. Each player takes the part of a power and seeks to control Europe. He may make and break alliances, spread rumours, threaten, cheat, etc. 'In Diplomacy nothing is sacred; deciding who to trust is part of the game.'

[This latter statement is true also of DEMOCRACY. It causes me a measure of concern because it is designed as an educational game whereas DIPLOMACY, like MONOPOLY, is basically an entertainment. Are we correct to say to children that we are right to lie and cheat because that is the way the world goes? Ed.]

DISASTER (COMMUNITY RESPONSE)
Johns Hopkins University

Simulates citizens' roles under disaster conditions, and encourages players to organize co-operative effort and plans for the future. They are allotted roles and a limited amount of 'energy' to protect their family and carry out their social responsibilities.

DISUNIA
El Capitan High School

Junior to Senior High School level; players face problems of disunity encountered in the United States in 1781–1789 on a new planet, year 2076.

ECONOMIC DECISION GAMES
Science Research Associates Ltd (Erwin Rausch)

These are 'pencil and paper' economic games for upper high school and undergraduate levels. In a series of eight booklets, they cover a variety of subjects from The Firm to International Trade. Each booklet is sufficient for six students to use and re-use.

ECONOMIC SYSTEM GAME
Johns Hopkins University (James S. Coleman and J. Robert Harris)

Simulation of the interrelationship of various elements in the economic system, e.g., manufacturers, farmers, who are trying to advance their own position. Designed for high school classes.

ECONOMY
Abt Associates Inc. for University of Chicago (Industrial Relations Center)

Objective is better understanding of the circular flow of goods and services within the economic system. Designed as part of a sixth grade curriculum in association with MARKET (*q.v.*).

EDUCATIONAL SYSTEM PLANNING GAME
Abt Associates Inc.

Two teams of educators, students, etc., interact to produce an educational policy which provides the greatest educational results. Aim is to facilitate education and innovative planning.

(A number of education systems analysis and planning games have been developed by Abt Associates for such groups as the Harvard Graduate School of Education, Office of Economic Opportunity, and the Office of Education.)

EL SOMBRERO CAFÉ
Berkshire College of Education

Social studies simulation involving teenage behaviour in a café, including drug pushing, etc. The simulation was prepared as a project by college students, and used in workshop sessions with school pupils.

EMPIRE
Education Development Center

A trading game modelled on the economic factors involved in British subjects becoming Americans in the eighteenth century. Published as part of a unit 'From Subject to Citizen'. 'Slave Trade' is an interlude in the game. The players are all slaves, and the object of the game is to survive. It shows the kinds of misery suffered by Negroes when they were transported as slaves.

EQUATIONS
Wff'n Proof Inc. (Layman E. Allen)

A five-game kit for use at all levels at home and at school. It provides practice in elementary arithmetic procedures, and in a variety of numeral bases—decimal, binary, etc., as well as in the use of fractions, decimals, powers (exponentials) and roots of numbers. The object of the game is to form equations.

FARMING
High School Geography Project

An agricultural investment game for senior high school classes staged in three different periods of United States history.

GALAPAGOS
Abt Associates Inc.

A science simulation in which three or four teams watch the simulated evolution of finches. They then predict the survival, and structural formation of the species. The game allows students to exercise scientific observation, evaluation, prediction and theory formation at senior high school level.

GITHAKA
C.B.S. Learning Center, Princeton, N.J.
In this game the children simulate the Kikuyu system of land use, assuming the roles of tribesmen. Available as part of unit on Kikuyus.

GREAT GAME OF LEGISLATURE
Johns Hopkins University
 See DEMOCRACY.

HIGH SCHOOL
Johns Hopkins University
 A simulation of the guidance type.

INSIDE THE CITY
High School Geography Project
 Unit number 2 of 'Geography in an Urban Age'.

INSITE
Indiana University (School of Education)
 INSITE stands for Instructional Systems in Teacher Education. The project uses simulation in preparing student teachers and makes use of slides and audiovisual media. It is basically concerned with decision making in the classroom situation.

INTER-NATION SIMULATION
Northwestern University
 Simulation of international relations, *see* Science Research Associates' INTER-NATION SIMULATION. Also World Affairs Council of Philadelphia, Pa., has a simplified simulation involving some of the elements of I-NS.

INTER-NATION SIMULATION
Science Research Associates Ltd
 Simulation of international relations, including the inter-relationship of domestic and foreign policy. This is a school (or college) version of the original Northwestern University INTER-NATION SIMULATION.

INTERNATIONAL RELATIONS SIMULATION
Michigan State University
 Simulation of international politics.

INTOP
University of Chicago, Graduate School of Business (Hans B. Thorelli and Robert L. Graves)
A business simulation, computer based in Fortran II and Fortran IV versions, it has been used by about thirty groups in eight countries. It is focussed on the problems of international operations and foreign competition.

JEFFERSON TOWNSHIP
University Council for Educational Administration
A simulation for training educational administrators, it was the first simulation designed for this purpose and has subsequently been considerably modified.

LABOR vs MANAGEMENT
Chicago Public School System (John D. Gearon)
The participants assume roles of citizens of a town of 36,000 people, one sixth of whom are union members employed at the factory. A strike occurs and the players form four groups, employers, labour, chamber of commerce, and mayor and councillors. Aim is to give insight into labour/management relations and clarify labour history. (See *Social Education*, 30, pp. 421–422, October 1966.)

LIFE CAREER GAME
Johns Hopkins University (Sarane S. Boocock)
Simulation in which players work with a fictitious person, and allot his time between school, a job, family, leisure, studying.

LONGACRE SCHOOL
Science Research Associates Ltd (D. R. Cruickshank, F. W. Broadbent, and R. I. Bubb)
See TEACHING PROBLEMS LABORATORY.

MANCHESTER
Abt Associates Inc. for Education Development Center
Part of a unit designed for high school students on the Industrial Revolution in England. It focuses on the migration to the towns and the economic forces which gave rise to the movement.

MANEX
University of Surrey (Robert Boardman)

Simulation of an international crisis. This is a modification of an earlier game, in the manner of those developed at Northwestern University and the Peace Research Centre.

MANUFACTURING
High School Geography Project
A unit in the same series as FARMING, INSIDE THE CITY, and METFAB.

MARKET
Abt Associates for University of Chicago (Industrial Relations Center)
Part of a unit on 'Exchange' designed for eleven to twelve year olds. It is designed to show students how prices are determined, and the relationship of price levels to supply and demand.

MARKET GAME
Holt, Rinehart and Winston Ltd
Simulates some features of the free market process. Part of 'Comparative Economic Systems'.

METFAB
High School Geography Project
Simulates some of the factors involved in the location of a factory.

METROPOLIS
Michigan State University
A simulation of politics.

NAPOLI
Western Behavioral Sciences Institute
NAPOLI (NAtional POLItics) is a simulation in which players serve as members of a legislature, representing one of two political parties and one of eight geographical regions. It illustrates the nature of democracy by combining aspects of both houses of the United States Congress.

NEGOTIATION
Massachusetts Institute of Technology
Re-creates events of the East–West disarmament negotiations of the mid-1950s. Players are given information about preceding events and then, assuming the roles of negotiators from the United States, Soviet Union and United Kingdom, they resolve their differences over disarmament.

NEIGHBORHOOD GAME

Abt Associates Inc. (Curriculum Development Center)

Teaches the economics of land development in a simulation based on the settlement and growth of Boston's North End. Illustrates political decisions on public transport, taxation, education, public services, etc.

NONSUCH YOUTH CLUB

Wiltshire Training Agency (Andrew A. Aldrich)

Simulation used in the training of part-time youth workers in a rural area of the United Kingdom. Combines elements of sociodrama and 'in-basket' simulation.

ON-SETS

Wff'n Proof Inc. (Layman E. Allen)

A kit of thirty games which introduces the fundamental concepts of the 'new' mathematics. Instructs the six year old in elementary set theory concepts: difference of sets, set-identity, union of sets, etc.

ORWELL SCHOOL

Berkshire College of Education

A documentary simulation used in teacher-training. A single pupil's records are fully documented, and problems are based on this single case. The records are introduced in three phases representing superficial, incomplete and complete information and decisions are made at each stage.

PACIFIC EXPRESS

University of Michigan

Students simulate the construction of the transcontinental railway as they think it should have been done, and compare their results with what actually happened. (A similar type of game has been developed and used widely in this country by Rex Walford, see chapter 3.)

PARENT–CHILD GAME

Johns Hopkins University (E. O. Schild and Sarane S. Boocock)

Simulates the relationship between parent and child as they argue over what can be regarded as permissible behaviour, while each tries to gain maximum satisfaction. The game takes up to an hour and can be played by four to ten players.

PLANS

Western Behavioral Sciences Institute

Players are each members of one of six interest groups which use their influence to change American Society—Military, Civil Rights, Nationalists, Internationalists, Business and Labour. The students become involved in the process of bargaining, exerting pressure, and see the consequences of their decisions on the American economy.

POLITICAL PARTY NOMINATING GAME
Horton Watkins High School
A party political simulation.

POLLUTION
Abt Associates Inc. (Curriculum Development Center)
Simulates the discussions between leaders of various industries over the use of pollution prevention and elimination equipment.

PORTSVILLE
Rutgers University (Urban Studies Center)
Players simulate the development of an undeveloped area into a busy industrial city called 'Portsville'.

PROPAGANDA
Nova Academic Games Project
'Students simulate the techniques professionals use to mould public opinion—e.g., quotation out of context, rationalization, technical jargon, faulty analogy.'

REAL NUMBERS
Wff'n Proof Inc. (Layman E. Allen)
A kit of five games which prepares beginners for playing EQUATIONS, also published by Wff'n Proof. The kit comes clipped to a ball-point pen, and is handy for play when a few minutes only are available.

SEAL-HUNTING
Education Development Center
A board game which simulates some of the difficulties Eskimos have in securing adequate food, and demonstrates the need for sharing in order that the tribe can survive. (*See also* CARIBOU-HUNTING.) These games are intended to be used as part of a unified fifth grade social studies unit 'Man: a Course of Study'

SECTION
High School Geography Project

A senior high school level simulation designed to provide students with understanding of the conflicting interests of sections of a political territory as expressed in the political process. Players identify needs, priorities, and must negotiate to attain them.

SIERRA LEONE
Westchester Board of Co-operative Educational Services

Designed to teach aspects of national economic development to eleven to twelve year olds. A board game version has been originated as a manual analogue to a computed game played by students of the same age. It is designed to give students an awareness of the problems of African countries which have recently become independent and an understanding of economic principles as they relate to under-developed countries.

SIMILE
Western Behavioral Sciences Institute

Project SIMILE (Simulation in Instruction) has produced a number of separate simulations, including CRISIS, NAPOLI and PLANS (*q.v.*).

SIMSOC
University of Michigan (W. A. Gamson)

A sociology simulation.

SIMULATION OF AMERICAN GOVERNMENT
Kansas State Teachers College

A simulation of the political type.

STRUCTURAL LINGUISTICS
Nova High School

An English Language simulation.

SUMERIAN GAME
Westchester Board of Co-operative Educational Services

A computer-based game in which a player assumes the role of ruler of Sumeria (an agricultural economy) and must improve the lot of his people by his decisions.

TAC-TICKLE
Wff'n Proof Inc.

A kit of eight problem solving games like chess, draughts, etc.,

Tac-Tickle compares in complexity with tic-tac-toe about the same as chess compares with draughts.

TEACHING PROBLEMS LABORATORY
Science Research Associates Ltd
 A simulated class-room, it makes use of various media and techniques. Thirty-one problems are presented, using film, role plays and documentation.

TEMPER
University of Pennsylvania
 TEMPER (*T*echnological, *E*conomic, *M*ilitary, *P*olitical, *E*valuation *R*outines) is a computer operated model representing a general simulation structure designed to handle different theories rather than a single body of international relations theory.

VENTURE
Proctor & Gamble Ltd
 A business simulation in which the participants make the decisions necessary for operating their companies in a competitive economy.

VIETNAM CRISIS SIMULATION
Bingley College of Education
 A crisis simulation, one of the few in use in the United Kingdom.

VOTES
El Capitan High School
 A political simulation.

WAR OR PEACE
Chicago Public School System (John D. Gearon)
 A simple international relations game for fifteen year olds in world history classes. Players form groups representing seven nations of varying strengths and the game starts with a crisis, war between two nations. Aims to help students understand terms such as 'balance of power'. (See *Social Education*, 30, pp. 521–522, November 1966.)

WFF (THE BEGINNER'S GAME OF MODERN LOGIC)
Wff 'n Proof Inc. (Layman E. Allen)
 A two-game kit for beginners. Provides practice in constructing and recognizing WFFs (Well-Formed Formulas), expressions that are in mathematical logic as sentences are in English.

WFF 'N PROOF (THE GAME OF MODERN LOGIC)
Wff'n Proof Inc. (Layman E. Allen)

A kit of twenty-one games which vary from those that can be mastered by six year olds to some that can challenge intelligent adults. Provides practice in abstract thinking and an opportunity to learn some mathematical logic.

YOUTH LEADER SELECTION SIMULATION
Berkshire College of Education

Gives older school pupils some idea of the problems of interviewing and assessing. Designed by students.

Addresses of organizations marketing games and simulations and of centres of research and development

ABT ASSOCIATES INC.,
14 Concord Lane, Cambridge, Massachusetts, U.S.A.
BERKSHIRE COLLEGE OF EDUCATION,
Woodley, Reading, Berkshire, England.
BINGLEY COLLEGE OF EDUCATION,
Bingley, Yorkshire, England.
CARNEGIE INSTITUTE OF TECHNOLOGY,
Schenley Park, Pittsburgh, Pennsylvania 15213, U.S.A.
C.B.S. LEARNING CENTER,
Social Studies Unit, Princeton, New Jersey, U.S.A.
CHICAGO PUBLIC SCHOOL SYSTEM,
(John D. Gearon, Social Studies Consultant), Chicago, Illinois, U.S.A.
CORNELL UNIVERSITY,
Ithaca, N.Y., U.S.A.
CURRICULUM DEVELOPMENT CENTER,
Wellesley School System, Seawood Road, Wellesley Hills, Massachusetts 02181, U.S.A.
EDUCATION DEVELOPMENT CENTER,
15 Mifflin Place, Cambridge, Massachusetts, U.S.A.
EDUCATIONAL SERVICES INC.,
15 Mifflin Place, Cambridge, Massachusetts, U.S.A.
EL CAPITAN HIGH SCHOOL,
Lakeside, California, U.S.A.
ELEMENTARY GAMES PROJECT,
Industrial Relations Center, University of Chicago, 1225 East 60th Street, Chicago, Illinois 60637, U.S.A.
EUROPEAN RESEARCH GROUP ON MANAGEMENT (ERGOM),
53 rue de la Concorde, Brussels 5, Belgium.

FOREIGN POLICY ASSOCIATION,
345 East 46th Street, New York, N.Y. 10017, U.S.A.
HIGH SCHOOL GEOGRAPHY PROJECT,
P.O. Box 1095, Boulder, Colorado 80302, U.S.A.
HOLT, RINEHART AND WINSTON LTD,
116 Golden Lane, London E.C.1, England.
INDIANA UNIVERSITY,
Bloomington, Indiana, U.S.A.
INSTITUTE OF WORLD AFFAIRS,
668 Bolton Hall, University of Wisconsin, Milwaukee, Wisconsin
53211, U.S.A.
INTELLECTUAL DIVERSION LTD,
products available from:
Hamleys Ltd, Regent Street, London W.1, England.
JOHNS HOPKINS UNIVERSITY,
Baltimore, Maryland 21218, U.S.A.
KANSAS STATE TEACHERS COLLEGE,
Emporia, Kansas, U.S.A.
LEARNING CENTER, THE,
Social Studies Department, Princeton, New Jersey, U.S.A.
MARCT COMPANY,
1111 Maple Avenue, Turtle Creek, Pennsylvania, U.S.A.
MARIA GREY COLLEGE OF EDUCATION,
Twickenham, Middlesex, England.
MASSACHUSETTS INSTITUTE OF TECHNOLOGY,
Cambridge, Massachusetts, U.S.A.
MERRILL, CHARLES E., INC.,
1300 Alum Creek Drive, Columbus, Ohio 43216, U.S.A.
MICHIGAN STATE UNIVERSITY,
East Lancing, Michigan, U.S.A.
NATIONAL 4-H CENTER,
7100 Connecticut Avenue, Washington D.C. 20015, U.S.A.
NEW UNIVERSITY OF ULSTER,
Coleraine, Northern Ireland.
NORTHWESTERN UNIVERSITY,
1834 Sheridan Road, Evanston, Illinois 60201, U.S.A.
NOVA HIGH SCHOOL,
Fort Lauderdale, Florida 33314, U.S.A.
PEACE RESEARCH CENTRE,
58 Parkway, London N.W.1, England.
PROCTOR AND GAMBLE LTD,
St Nicholas Avenue, Newcastle-upon-Tyne 3, England.

RUTGERS UNIVERSITY,
New Brunswick, New Jersey, U.S.A.
SCIENCE RESEARCH ASSOCIATES LTD,
Henley, Oxfordshire, England.
SIMULMATICS CORPORATION INC.,
16 East 41st Street, New York 17, N.Y., U.S.A.
SOCIAL STUDIES CURRICULUM STUDY CENTER,
1809 Chicago Avenue, Evanston, Illinois 60201, U.S.A.
UNIVERSITY COUNCIL FOR EDUCATIONAL
ADMINISTRATION,
65 South Oval Drive, Columbus, Ohio, U.S.A.
UNIVERSITY OF CHICAGO,
Chicago, Illinois, U.S.A.
UNIVERSITY OF MICHIGAN,
Ann Arbor, Michigan, U.S.A.
UNIVERSITY OF PENNSYLVANIA,
Philadelphia, Pennsylvania, U.S.A.
WESTCHESTER BOARD OF CO-OPERATIVE EDUCATIONAL
SERVICES,
Yorktown Heights, N.Y. 10598, U.S.A.
WESTERN BEHAVIORAL SCIENCES INSTITUTE,
1150 Silverado, La Jolla, California 92037, U.S.A.
WFF'N PROOF INC.,,
Box 71, New Haven, Conn., U.S.A.
WILTSHIRE TRAINING AGENCY,
County Hall, Trowbridge, Wiltshire, England.

SELECT BIBLIOGRAPHY

The citations given below are mostly concerned with accounts of the use of specific games and simulations. The final section lists a number of bibliographies which will be of assistance to the reader seeking a wider coverage of the field.

ABT, CLARK C.
Heuristic Games for Secondary Schools.
Cambridge, Mass., Abt Associates Inc., 1965. (mimeo)
ABT ASSOCIATES INC.
Game Learning and Disadvantaged Groups.
Cambridge, Mass., Abt Associates Inc., 1965. (mimeo)
(A summary of Abt's experience in this area.)
ALLEN, L. E., ALLEN, R. W., and MILLER, J. C.
Programmed games and the Learning of Problem-Solving Skills: the WFF'N PROOF Example.
Journal of Educational Research, 60, pp. 22–26, September 1966.
(Claims increase in I.Q. after playing WFF'N PROOF. See Chapter 4.)

ATTEG, JOHN C.
The Use of Games as a Teaching Technique.
Social Studies, 58, pp. 25–29, January 1967.
(Games to give students an idea of decision making problems facing national leaders.)
BARRINGER, R. E., and WHALEY, B.
The MIT Political-Military Gaming Experience.
Orbits, 9, pp. 437–458, summer 1965.
BLAXALL, JOHN
Manchester.
Cambridge, Mass., U.S.A., Abt Associates Inc., 1965. (mimeo)
BOARDMAN, R.
Simulation and the Teaching of International Relations.
Higher Education Journal, 16, pp. 3–6, autumn 1968.
(Simulations in this field are highly motivating and encourage critical thinking.)
BOARDMAN, R.
Simulated Conflicts and International Crisis Games: a Report on the Manex Project.
The World and the School, 14, pp. 53–68, October 1968.
(Describes advantages and difficulties of games as a classroom technique.)
BOOCOCK, SARANE S.
An Experimental Study of the Learning Effects of Two Games with Simulated Environments.
American Behavioral Scientist, 10, pp. 8–16, October 1966.
(Deals with DEMOCRACY and the CAREER GAME.)
BOOCOCK, SARANE S.
Changing the Structure of Secondary Education with Simulated Environments.
Educational Technology, 8, pp. 3–6, 15 February 1968.
(Lists defects of U.S. education which can be countered by simulation.)
BOOCOCK, SARANE S.
Effects of an Election Campaign Game in Four High School Classes. Report No. 1, Johns Hopkins University, Baltimore, U.S.A. (Department of Social Relations), 1963. (mimeo)
(Attitudes of students became more realistic towards politics and politicians.)
BOOCOCK, SARANE S.
Life Career Game.
Personnel and Guidance Journal, 46, pp. 328–334, December 1967.
BOOCOCK, SARANE S., and COLEMAN, J. S.
Games with Simulated Environments in Learning.
Sociology of Education, 39, pp. 215–236, summer 1966.
(Useful paper covering a wide field.)
CHERRYHOLMES, C. H.
Development of Simulation of International Relations in High School Teaching.
Phi Delta Kappan, 46, pp. 227–231, January 1965.
(A six-week simulation in action.)
CHERRYHOLMES, C. H.
Some Current Research on Effectiveness of Educational Simulations: Implications for Alternative Strategies.
American Behavioral Scientist, 10, pp. 4–7, October 1966.

(Gives various hypotheses and suggests alternative strategies.)
CHRISTINE, C., and CHRISTINE, D.
Four Simulation Games that Teach.
Grade Teacher, 85, pp. 109–110+, 1967.
(Games concentrate on trading.)
COHEN, BERNARD C.
Political Gaming in the Classroom.
Journal of Politics, 24, pp. 367–381, May 1962.
COHEN, K. J., *et al.*
The Carnegie Management Game: an Experiment in Business Education.
Homewood, Illinois, Irwin, 1964.
CRUICKSHANK, D. R.
The Longacre School: a Simulated Laboratory for the Study of Teaching.
Mimeo for AACTE Workshop in Teacher Education, 1967.
(Simulation as a bridge between theory and practice for teacher training.)
CRUICKSHANK, D. R.
21 Questions about the Teaching Problems Laboratory.
University of Tennessee (mimeo), undated.
DAVIDSON, W. P.
A Public Opinion Game.
Public Opinion Quarterly, 25, pp. 210–220, 1961.
DILL, W. R., JACKSON, J. R., and SWEENEY, J. W.
Proceedings of the Conference on Business Games as Teaching Devices.
New Orleans, Tulane University, 1961.
(Discusses whole rationale of business games as teaching strategies.)
DUKE, RICHARD
Gaming Urban Systems.
Institute for Community Development, Michigan State University, East
Lancing, Michigan, U.S.A., 1966.
GAMSON, W. A.
SIMSOC, a Manual for Participants.
Ann Arbor, Michigan, Campus Publishers, 1966.
(A simulation concerned with economic and social factors.)
GARVEY, DALE M., and SEILER, WILLIAM H.
A Study of Effectiveness of Different Methods of Teaching Inter-Nation
Relations to High School Students.
Emporia, Kansas State Teachers College 1966.
(Compares simulation with lecture-discussion.)
GIFFIN, S. F.
The Crisis Game: Simulating International Conflict.
N.Y., Doubleday, 1965.
HAMMERTON, M., and TICKNER, A. H.
Visual Factors Affecting Transfer of Training from a Simulated to a Real
Control Situation.
Journal of Applied Psychology, 51, 1, pp. 46–49.
(Simulation training of a practical skill.)
HERMAN, C. F., and HERMAN, M. G.
An Attempt to Simulate the Outbreak of World War I.
American Political Science Review, 61, pp. 400–416, June 1967.
(Gives tabulated comparisons between simulation and real life situation.)

HONESS, C. B.
Management Games for Fun and Profit.
Business & Economic Review, Bureau of Business & Economic Research,
University of South Carolina, Columbia, S. Carolina, June 1967.
INBAR, M.
The Differential Impact of a Game: Simulating a Community Disaster.
American Behavioral Scientist, 10, pp. 18–27, October 1966.
(Statistical approach using the game DISASTER.)
INGRAHAM, LEONARD W.
Teachers, Computers and Games: Innovations in the Social Studies.
Social Education, 31, pp. 51–53, January 1967.
(Basic description of computerized gaming.)
JOSEPH, M. L.
Role Playing in Teaching Economics.
American Economic Review, pp. 556–565, May 1965.
(Price determination and labour management.)
KERSH, BERT Y.
The Classroom Simulator.
Journal of Teacher Education, 13, pp. 109–110, March 1962.
(Audiovisual simulation of a classroom.)
KIBBEE, J. M., CRAFT, CLIFFORD J., and NANUS, B.
Management Games: a New Technique for Executive Development.
New York, V. Reinhold Publishing Corporation Inc., 1961.
LUND, V. E.
Evaluation of Simulation Techniques to Teach Dental Office Emergencies.
Monmouth, U.S.A., Oregon State System of Higher Education, Final Report,
Contracted Project No. PH 108-65-23, 30 June 1966.
(Makes use of film.)
MacRAE, J., and SMOKER, P.
A Vietnam Simulation.
In P.R.C. Research Papers, Peace Research Centre, Lancaster, England, pp.
1-25, 1967.
(Full description of the simulation and relevant factors.)
McQUIGG, R. B.
The Capstone Experience, a Week of Simulation for the Secondary Acro-
clinical Student.
Insite Project, School of Education, Indiana University, undated.
(Faces the trainee teacher with various school conditions.)
ROBINSON, J. A., ANDERSON, L. F., HERMANN, M. G., and SNYDER, R. C.
Teaching with Inter-Nation Simulation and Case Studies.
American Political Science Review, 60, pp. 53–66, 1966.
ROSENBLOOM, PAUL C.
Review of WFF'N PROOF.
Mathematics Teacher, 57, pp. 346–347, 1964.
SHOUKSMITH, G.
Simulation and Industrial Selection.
Manpower and Applied Psychology, 1, pp. 143–147, 1968.
(Good description of simulation as an agent of selection.)
SMITH, G. A., and COLE, J. P.
Bulletin of Quantitative Data for Geographers. No. 7, Geographic Games.

Derick Unwin

Department of Geography, Nottingham University, England, March 1967.
(Describes the setting up of geographical games for sixth-formers and
students.)
THORELLI, H. B., and GRAVES, R. C.
International Operations Simulation.
New York, Free Press, 1964.
TWELKER, PAUL A.
Classroom Simulation and Teacher Preparation.
School Review, 75, pp. 197–204, summer 1967.
(Gives accounts of several simulations.)
UTSEY, J., WALLEN, C., and BELDIN, H. O.
Simulation: a Breakthrough in the Education of Reading Teachers.
Phi Delta Kappan, 47, pp. 572–574, June 1966.
(Film and printed material to teach administration of a reading inventory.)
VERBA, S.
Simulation, Reality, and Theory in International Relations.
World Politics, 16, pp. 490–519, 1964.
(Reviews several projects.)
WALLEN, C.
Low Cost Instructional Simulation Materials for Teacher Education.
Interim Report, Project No. 5–0916 U.S. Department of Health, Education
and Welfare, Oregon State System of Higher Education, Monmouth, Oregon,
January 1968. (mimeo)
WILKINS, C. L., and KLOPFENSTEIN, C. E.
Simulation of NMR Spectra: Computers as Teaching Devices.
Journal of Chemical Education, 43, pp. 10–13, January 1966.
WING, RICHARD L.
Computer Controlled Economic Games for the Elementary School.
Audiovisual Instruction, 9, pp. 681–682, December 1964.
(SUMERIA and SIERRA LEONE games are described.)

REFERENCE SOURCES

This list comprises books devoted entirely to simulation together with papers of a
bibliographic nature.
BOOCOCK, SARANE S., and SCHILD, E. O.
Simulation Games in Learning
Beverley Hills, California, Sage Publishers Inc., 1968.
CHERRYHOLMES, C. H.
Some Current Research on Effectiveness of Educational Simulations:
Implications for Alternative Strategies.
American Behavioral Scientist, 10, pp. 4–7, October 1966.
DUKE, RICHARD D., and SCHMIDT, ALLEN H.
Operational Gaming and Simulation in Urban Research: an Annotated
Bibliography.
Bibliography No. 14, Institute for Community Development, Michigan State
University, January 1965.
FABRI, DAVID A.
A Selected Bibliography of Simulations of International Relations.
Publication IV-6, Peace Research Centre, Lancaster, England, May 1967.

266

GARVEY, DALE M.
Simulation, Role-Playing and Sociodrama in the Social Studies.
(With an annotated bibliography by Sancha K. Garvey.)
Emporia State Research Studies, 26, 2, December 1967.
HARTMAN, JOHN
Annotated Bibliography of Simulation in the Social Sciences.
Iowa State University, 1966.
HOGAN, A. J.
Simulation: an Annotated Bibliography.
Social Education, 32, pp. 242–244, March 1968.
JOINT COUNCIL ON ECONOMIC EDUCATION
Bibliography of Games-Simulations for Teaching Economics and Related
Subjects.
N.Y., J.C.E.E., January 1968.
MALCOLM, D. G.
Bibliography on the Use of Simulation in Management Analysis.
Operations Research, 8, pp. 169–177, March–April 1960.
SHUBIK, MARTIN
Bibliography on Simulation, Gaming, Artificial Intelligence, and Allied
Topics.
Journal of the American Statistical Association, 55, pp. 736–751, December
1960.
SIMMONS, P. L., and SIMMONS, R. F.
The Simulation of Cognitive Processes, II: an Annotated Bibliography.
Institute of Radio Engineers Transactions, EC 11, pp. 535–552, August 1962.
TANSEY, P. J., and UNWIN, DERICK
Simulation and Gaming in Education.
London, Methuen, 1969.
TANSEY, P. J., and UNWIN, DERICK
Simulation and Gaming in Education, Training and Business: a Bibliography.
Coleraine, N. Ireland, New University of Ulster, 1969.
TANSEY, P. J., and UNWIN, DERICK
Sources in Simulation and Academic Gaming: an Annotated Bibliography.
British Journal of Educational Studies, 17, pp. 193–208, June 1969.
UNWIN, DERICK, and ATKINSON, FRANK
The Computer in Education.
U.K. Library Association, London, 1968.

Index of names

Index of names

Index of names

Shouksmith, G., 265
Shubick, Martin, 3, 18, 267
Silber, K. H., 176–7, 184
Simmons, H., 156, 181
Simmons, P. L., 267
Simmons, R. F., 267
Simon, H. A., 61
Simulmatics Corporation Inc., 262
Skinner, B. F., 66, 90
Smith, B. O., 187, 189, 201
Smith, G. A., 265
Smoker, Paul, ix, 1, 8, 18, 19, 24, 129, 130, 265
Snyder, R. C., 129, 265
Social Studies Curriculum Study Center, 262
Solarz, A. K., 169, 183
Sprague, Hall T., 211, 226
Stamp, L. D., 61
Standish, J. T., 180
Stanley, J. C., 201
Stewart, E. C., 164, 182
Stoll, Charise S., vii
Sweeney, J. W., 264

Tansey, P. J., ix, 1, 17, 18, 19, 20, 24, 200, 203, 246, 267
Tansey, M. R., 18, 20–24
Taylor, E. G. R., 40, 61
Taylor, G., 42, 61
Taylor, J. L., 52, 62
Teaching Research, Oregon, 143, 150
Thomas, C. J., 133, 178
Thorelli, H., 24, 129, 266
Thorndike, R. L., 157, 182, 191
Thorne, W. H., 183
Townsend, J. C., 160, 182
Tickner, A. H., 264
Twelker, Paul A., ix, 1, 7, 12, 13, 17, 19, 20, 179, 180, 182, 183, 194, 202, 227, 266

United States Naval Training Device Center, 134–5, 179
University College, London, 1

University Council for Educational Administration, 262
University of Chicago, 262
University of Michigan, 262
University of Pennsylvania, 262
Unstead, J. F., 61
Unwin, Derick, ix, 1, 17, 18, 19, 20, 200, 246, 267
Urbach, F., 200, 203
Utsey, J., 151, 180, 200, 203, 266

Van Valkenburgh, Nooger and Neville Inc., 138, 179
Venditti, F. P., 199, 202
Verba, S., 266
Vlcek, C. W., 193, 197, 201
Vogel, F. S., 201

Walford, Rex, viii, 52, 62
Wallen, C. J., 151, 180, 183, 200, 203, 266
Ward, T. W., 147
Waskaw, A., 130
Watkins, R. W., 181
Weislogel, R. L., 157, 182
Westchester Board of Co-operative Educational Services, 262
Western Behavioral Sciences Institute, 1, 8, 11, 179, 211, 262
Whaley, B., 129, 263
WFF 'N PROOF, Inc., 262
Wilkins, C. L., 266
Wiltshire Training Agency, 262
Wing, R. L., 18, 180, 246, 266
Woolley, F. L., 179
Woulff, J. J., 12, 19
Wrigley, E. H., 40, 61

Yount, David, 19, 24

Zaltman, G., 179

General index

Accroclinical semester, 195
Advantages of simulation, 133–4, 170–72, 186–7, 188–90
Affective outcomes, 160–64
American Association for Colleges of Teacher Education, 187
Attention span, 212
Attitudes:
  defined, 213–14
  effects of simulation on, 213–17
Auto-instructional simulator, 137, 142

Behaviour shaping, 191
Boundaries of simulation, 2

Case studies, 4
Classroom simulation:
  limitations of, 191–2, 197–8
  primary, 91–111
Classroom simulator, 190–93
Cognitive outcomes of simulation, 158–9
Competition, 212
Computer simulation, 91–111, 112–20, 153–4
Critical teaching problems, 195, 196
Cue identification, 159

Decision making skills, 159, 219–21
Dental emergencies simulation, 149–50
Determinism in geography, 41–3
Direct teaching, 26–7
Disadvantages of simulation, 116–17, 172–3
Discovery methods, 28–9
Distribution of towns, 54–6
Drama, 3, 36

Education, moral, 6
Environmental simulation, 175–7

Foreign language training, 139–41
Forest service training simulator, 150–51

Game theory, 3, 54–6
Games:
  as learning devices, 83–6
  Cabinets in Crisis, 134, 174
  Classroom, 70–76
  Consumer, 134

Democracy, 83
Equations, 31–2, 35, 63, 70, 71, 72, 74, 82, 83, 85, 87, 88, 90
International:
  Israel, 231, 233, 235, 244
  Manex, 230–35, 244
  Sintracc, 229–35
land use:
  CLUG, 51, 62
  LUGS, 51–2, 62
  Metropolis, 50, 62
  Micropolis, 49–50
  POGE, 50, 62
Manchester, 3, 134
Micropolis, 49–50
Monopoly, 3, 51
On-Sets, 63, 70, 72, 74, 82, 83, 87, 88, 90
Package, 163
philosophy of, 26–31
place in simulation, 3
Pocket Blinker, 138
Policy Negotiations Game, 34–5
programmed, non-simulation, 63–90
Queries 'N Theories, 63, 89
Sierra Leone Development Project, 153
Special Education Administration Task Game, 152
Sumerian Game, 153
The Most Dangerous Game, 173–5
urban interaction:
  Commuting, 53
  Shopping, 52–3
War, 228
WFF 'N PROOF, 3, 63, 64, 67–88, 90
winning at, 36
Gaming, definition of, 208
Geographic Education, components of, 38–9
Geography:
  determinism in, 41–3
  models in, 44–6
  regional, development of, 39–41
  simulation in, 45–62
  systems analysis in, 43–5
  teaching, new developments in, 43–6

General index

PRINTED AND BOUND IN ENGLAND BY
HAZELL WATSON AND VINEY LTD
AYLESBURY, BUCKS